Extending and Customizing Unreal Engine Editor

This book provides a broad overview of editor extensions and modifications that can be made to speed up your workflow in the Unreal Engine. It covers tips for both initial content creation as well as debugging already existing content.

The book explains how several editor systems work, with a focus on how you can extend and modify them to suit your own workflow. Chapters cover how to create your own editor modes with several different kinds of tools in them, covering tools for artists and for gameplay scripting, giving you the foundation to build further tools and personalize your workflow. It also covers how to personalize toolbars and editor windows and create custom variable visualization and Blueprint nodes.

Whether you are making a small indie game or an AAA game, this book will help you and your team in creating the tools needed to improve your workflow.

Roger Mattsson has worked as a gameplay programmer and a game designer for over 20 years at several AAA studios and small indie studios. He is currently working at Neon Giant as a Principal Programmer, a studio focused on making big ambitious games with few people.

Extending and Customizing Unreal Engine Editor

Methods for Improving Workflow and More Robust Scripting

Roger Mattsson

CRC Press is an imprint of the
Taylor & Francis Group, an **informa** business

Designed cover image: Shutterstock

First edition published 2026
by CRC Press
2385 NW Executive Center Drive, Suite 320, Boca Raton FL 33431

and by CRC Press
4 Park Square, Milton Park, Abingdon, Oxon, OX14 4RN

CRC Press is an imprint of Taylor & Francis Group, LLC

ISBN: 978-1-032-84216-5 (hbk)
ISBN: 978-1-032-84040-6 (pbk)
ISBN: 978-1-003-51174-8 (ebk)

DOI: 10.1201/9781003511748

Typeset in Times
by SPi Technologies India Pvt Ltd (Straive)

Dedication

For Johana, Viento and Abigail.

Contents

Introduction

Throughout my years in the game industry (20 years and counting), on every game, every company, every game engine I have worked with, the majority of the bugs have been the same. Game after game, it's the same bugs popping up again and again. Even worse, a lot of the bugs show their ugly heads at the end of the project (usually because the patterns leading to these bugs are ignored in the beginning of the project) when we really want to spend time polishing the game and improving it, not repairing it and patching it up.

This is obviously a really hard problem to solve, one might even say impossible. After all, part of the process of making a game is figuring out the game as you develop it. You never start with a perfect plan but with a direction to go in. But that doesn't mean we cannot improve our work. So why does this happen? Some of it is just from bad practices, from bad development patterns (and this is its own subject deserving its own book). Some of it is just the nature of making a game, of iterating on our work and changing it over time until we are happy with it. The idea we had for the system from the beginning will morph with time so our initial design of the system might not be ideal any longer and not what we would do if we were to recreate it, but every game development is its own journey.

But some of it comes from bad tools. If the tools we work with don't allow us to easily debug our work, to easily get an overview of it, mistake happens more frequently. But there's also another cost to it, and that is the iteration that never happens. If a workflow is cumbersome, error prone, and just a nuisance to work with, you will get fewer iterations done in the same amount of time, or people will choose to work on other parts, where the work process is more enjoyable. This hidden cost can be very hard to quantify, but personally I'm convinced it is big and worth the effort to address.

The different ways of extending the Unreal Editor I will be presenting in this book will be focused on this last problem. The primary focus will be on making things easier and faster to work with. Sometimes this will mean a completely new tool, other times it will mean presenting data in a better way. Whether I succeed with this or not is up to you to determine at the end of the book. But all the concepts I will go through will come with real, practical examples and from my personal experience as a professional game developer. Not just an abstract explanation of the various systems, but I will show real tools. So sometimes there will be a lot of code, feel free to skip it if the tool itself doesn't interest you, but I think using real examples makes it easier to see how the different systems can be useful and will give you more ideas on what is possible.

Now I will be making some assumptions about you dear readers. I assume you already know how to code, that you already are familiar with Unreal Engine and have a project already set up.

DOI: 10.1201/9781003511748-1

CODE STANDARD

The purpose with a code standard is, in my opinion, to make the code easier to read, not easier to write. It's a subtle but important difference. It is easier to write code than it is to read code. When you come back to some of your (or someone else's) code and edit it, it's very important that the code is easy to read. Otherwise, it's very easy to create new bugs due to small misunderstandings about the code you are editing. Thus, it's important that the code standard you are using helps with readability, not writability for this reason.

The code standard I will be using throughout this book is mostly based on Epic's code standard, but with a few differences.

Prefix

All classes, structs, enums will have a project prefix. I will be using Mars as a project name in this book.

The reason for this is so that it's always easy to see if something is coming straight from Unreal Engine, or if it's your own. Sometimes you will end up with very similar (or the same) name, so this will help differentiate them. It will make it easier to pick the right base class when creating a blueprint since you can clearly see the difference.

Variable Naming

Variable name format and capitalization will also be different.

- Member Variables: Always start with an upper-case letter.
- Local Variables: Always start with a lower-case letter.
- Function parameters: Always start with an underscore and lower-case letter.

This means you can always clearly see what scope a variable is in, even if they have similar names.

Engine Modifications

This will not be different from Epic's recommendations, but worth re-iterating. While it's always a good idea to avoid making engine modifications, if possible, sometimes we have to. There will be a couple of (optional) engine edits shown in this book. When we do it's very important that we mark our changes so that when we upgrade to a new version of the engine, we will have an easier job or merging in the changes.

So, every engine change will be marked up like this.

```
//ENGINE MOD START - The reason for the change.
//The old unmodified code should be commented out
Here the new modified code will go
//ENGINE MOD END
```

We keep the old unchanged code as a comment to make the merging easier.

CREATING OUR PLUGIN

We will be creating a new plugin where we will place all our tools. While Unreal has templates for creating a plugin containing an *Editor Mode*, an *Editor Standalone Window*, or an *Editor Toolbar Button*, we will be using the *Blank* template. We will be adding all those things, but step by step so we get a better understanding of everything.

So, let us start up the editor, then go to Edit -> Plugins, click Add in the plugins window. Select *Blank* and enter your plugin name, I will go with *MarsEditor*. Mars since that's my project name, and Editor since we will be placing editor-specific stuff in here. Filling in the Author/Description field is only important if you are planning on publishing your plugin, you can safely ignore them if you want. Now click *Create Plugin*. Now we have an empty plugin. Shutdown the editor and let us take a look at what we have.

In the solution explorer you will now see a new Plugins folder, with our plugin *MarsEditor* placed under it. We also have an icon in a resource folder, this is the icon that is visible in the Plugins window in the editor, so it's not terribly important.

UPLUGIN

Then we have a file called MarsEditor.uplugin, this file is very important and contains information about what type of plugin we have and when we want it to be loaded. It also has some meta information about the plugin (author, URLs).

Let us open this file and take a look at it.

```
{
  "FileVersion": 3,
  "Version": 1,
  "VersionName": "1.0",
  "FriendlyName": "MarsEditor",
  "Description": "",
  "Category": "Other",
  "CreatedBy": "Roger Mattsson",
  "CreatedByURL": "",
  "DocsURL": "",
  "MarketplaceURL": "",
  "SupportURL": "",
  "CanContainContent": true,
  "IsBetaVersion": false,
  "IsExperimentalVersion": false,
  "Installed": false,
  "Modules": [
        {
              "Name": "MarsEditor",
              "Type": "Runtime",
              "LoadingPhase": "Default"
        }
    ]
}
```

These are just some of the settings, however, there are more of them, and you can find them all with comments on what they do here:

\Engine\Source\Programs\UnrealBuildTool\System\PluginDescriptor.cs

Most of these are not important for us right now and we can ignore them. But there are a few worth mentioning.

CanContainContent – We will not be adding any content into our plugin, so we can change this to false.

Modules – Currently we only have one module in our plugin, but we can have several different modules here (and we will add more later in this book). This can be useful if we want some parts of our plugin to be accessible in runtime, while other only need to be in editor. It also allows us to have different dependencies on different modules, which can be handy in some cases.

Again, while we only have three visible fields for each module, there are actually more, and you can find them here:

\Engine\Source\Runtime\Projects\Public\ModuleDescriptor.h

For our use we can ignore those settings, they let you control on what platforms, configurations and target types the plugin can be used. Not something we need to worry about for our editor plugin.

But we do need to change the *Type* field from *Runtime* to *Editor*. We only want our plugin in the editor, not when running the game.

LoadingPhase allows us to control when our plugin is loaded, default is good enough for us right now, but we will also be changing this later when needed.

Plugins – This section is not visible by default, but here is where we add any other plugins that we require. For example, if we need to use the GameplayTagsEditor in our plugin we would need to add it like this

```
"Plugins": [
	{
		"Name": "GameplayTagsEditor",
		"Enabled": true
	}
]
```

Build.cs

Then we have a file called MarsEditor.Build.cs. This file controls all rules and dependencies for our module. As we go, we will be adding more modules as dependencies here.

This file also has a lot more options than what is visibly by default, you can find them all in

```
\Engine\Source\Programs\UnrealBuildTool\Configuration\
ModuleRules.cs
```

But for now, we don't need to edit anything in here.

MarsEditor.h/cpp

Finally, we have our two source code files where we will start building our tools. At this stage they are both fairly empty, just containing the bare minimum needed to set up our module.

That is everything we need to get started, we now have our module and from here we will register our editor modes, our standalone windows, and toolbars. We will also hook up our new entries to right-click menus and our own slate widgets to change how we show certain data types. This is our entry into extending the editor and the start point for most of the tools we will be creating in this book.

1 Editor Modes

The first area we will cover is editor modes. The Unreal Editor comes with several editor modes already, like the Landscape Mode or the Brush Editing Mode. An editor mode can be a big complex tool, but we can also use it to gather several small useful tools. This way we can gather several tools that are useful for one discipline in one place without having it interfere with other people. In this chapter we will be making one editor mode, but I recommend you make several of these in your own project (depending on the project size of course): having one mode for artists, with tools focusing on placing and manipulating assets, and another mode for designers that focuses more on showing more information about various gameplay actors and faster setup of the gameplay. And maybe you will have a mode for handling something that is completely unique to your project.

In our example editor mode we will be creating, we will make three different tools. One tool for quickly copying a material from the actor we click on and then being able to paste it on the actor we click on. Then a tool to re-import the static mesh asset on our selected actor. And finally, we will make a tool to handle a gameplay actor, in our case a hypothetical spawner actor, we will make placement of it easier, add functionality to mass edit them and to find spawners matching our settings. But before we start with that, we must first create our editor mode and register it.

There's not a lot we need to do to create a new, empty editor mode. We need a new class that inherits from `FEdMode` and we need an identifier name. We will also set up an icon for our mode and give it a priority to control where in the list of editor mode it shows up.

In /Plugins/MarsEditor/Source/MarsEditor/Public/EditorMode/ create MarsEditorMode.h and enter this code.

```
#pragma once

#include "CoreMinimal.h"
#include "EdMode.h"

class FMarsEditorMode : public FEdMode
{
public:
  const static FEditorModeID EM_MarsEditorMode;

  virtual void Enter() override;
  virtual void Exit() override;
  virtual bool UsesPropertyWidgets() const override { return
true; }
};
```

We are inheriting from `FEdMode`. The `EM_MarsEditorMode` static variable will be our unique identifier to our editor mode, and we will use this when registering the

DOI: 10.1201/9781003511748-2

editor mode. We also declared an `Enter` and `Exit` function for our mode. Then we implement `UsesPropertyWidgets` and return true. This means that when we are in our editor mode, we allow the editor to display widgets for any properties that has the `MakeEditWidget` meta flag specified. Since I prefer my editor modes to function as close to the Selection mode as possible, I prefer to allow these property widgets, but if you are making a more complex editor mode it could be a good idea to disable this.

Now let us implement the cpp file, in /Plugins/MarsEditor/Source/MarsEditor/Private/EditorMode create MarsEditorMode.cpp. Fill the file with this code.

```
#include "MarsEditorMode.h"

const FEditorModeID FMarsEditorMode::EM_MarsEditorMode =
TEXT("EM_MarsEditorMode");

void FMarsEditorMode::Enter()
{
  FEdMode::Enter();
}

void FMarsEditorMode::Exit()
{
  FEdMode::Exit();
}
```

The only thing of note is that we set our editor mode ID. You can set this to anything you want, the only important thing is that it doesn't collide with any of the other editor modes so make it something unique. We follow the Unreal standard here with the EM_ prefix and then the name of our editor mode. The `Enter/Exit` functions are empty now, but we will be adding things here later. Now we have an empty editor mode, but we still need to register it. We will do this in our plugin module. Go to MarsEditorModule.cpp and add these includes.

```
#include "EditorModeRegistry.h"
#include "EditorMode/MarsEditorMode.h"
```

And then in `StartupModule()` add this code.

```
void FMarsEditorModule::StartupModule()
{
  FEditorModeRegistry::Get().RegisterMode<FMarsEditorMode>
(FMarsEditorMode::EM_MarsEditorMode, FText::FromString("Mars
Editor Mode"), FSlateIcon(), true, 200);
}
```

This function registers our editor mode. We give it our unique identifier, a name, an icon (empty currently), make it visible and give it a priority. Usually, you want to make your editor mode visible, so it appears in the editor mode list directly. But it's possible to hide it and make it visible whenever you want, maybe when opening a specific map or when having a specific asset in a map for example. The priority determines where in the list our mode shows up. The lower the priority the higher up in the list it will appear.

Here's the values of the other default editor modes.

- Selection – 0
- Landscape – 300
- Foilage – 400
- Mesh Paint – 600
- Modeling – 5000
- Fracture – 6000
- Brush Editing – 7000
- Animation – 8000

That is why our priority value of 200 places us on the second place.

We are now ready to compile our code, however this will give us an unresolved external symbol error. This is because we are trying to use some code from another module, but we have not defined that our own module depends on those modules. We define this in MarsEditor.Build.cs in /Plugins/MarsEditor/Source/MarsEditor/. Open the file and find the `PrivateDependencyModuleNames` field, here is where we will need to add the new modules we have started using, so let us add `"EditorFramework"` and `"UnrealEd"`. The private include section should now look like this.

```
PrivateDependencyModuleNames.AddRange(
  new string[]
  {
    "CoreUObject",
    "Engine",
    "Slate",
    "SlateCore",
    "EditorFramework",
    "UnrealEd"
  }
  );
```

Now if you can compile and run the editor and you will see our new editor mode in the second place. We also automatically get a shortcut to our mode. Pressing shift + 2 will open our mode and we will get an empty window for our mode.

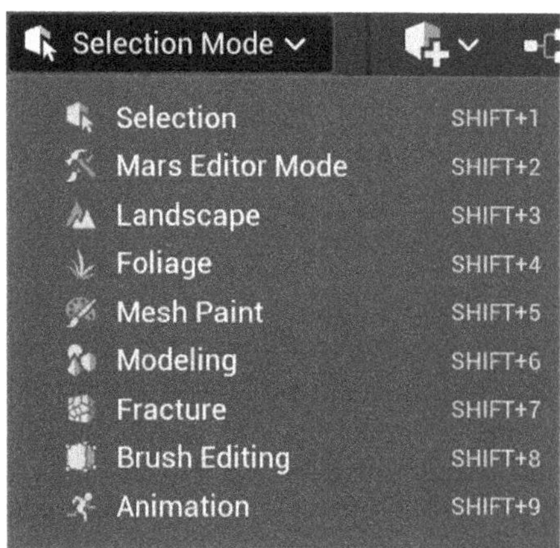

STYLE SET

Before we move on let us set up a custom icon for our editor mode. We will do this by creating our own slate style set and registering our icon in it. Throughout this book we will be needing icons for a lot of different things, not just our editor mode. We will be creating this style set in our plugin module class and not in our editor mode class.

So, in MarsEditor.h let us add the following in our class

```
class FMarsEditorModule : public IModuleInterface
{
  //...
  void RegisterStyleSet();
  void UnregisterStyleSet();
static FName GetStyleSetName() { return
FName("MarsModuleStyleSet"); }
private:
  TSharedPtr< FSlateStyleSet > StyleSet;
};
```

We also need a forward declaration of `FSlateStyleSet`, so add `class FSlateStyleSet;` above the class. It's always a good idea to forward declare in our headers instead of including the .h file needed since it keeps the compiling times down. It's just one file now, but it's a good habit to try and use forward declarations as much as possible and keep the includes in the .cpp files. In a full project this can really make a difference. We make `GetStyleSetName` static since we will be accessing this from other places where we might not have a pointer to our module class or at least don't want to dig one out.

Now in MarsEditor.cpp file we first need to add the Register/Unregister call in Startup/ShutdownModule

```
void FMarsEditorModule::StartupModule()
{
  RegisterStyleSet();
  //...
}

void FMarsEditorModule::ShutdownModule()
{
  UnregisterStyleSet();
}
```

Then we need to implement RegisterStyleSet.

```
#include "Styling/SlateStyleRegistry.h"
void FMarsEditorModule::RegisterStyleSet()
{
  StyleSet = MakeShareable(new FSlateStyleSet
    (GetStyleSetName()));
```

```
  StyleSet->SetContentRoot(FPaths::ProjectPluginsDir() /
TEXT("MarsEditor/Resources"));

  const FVector2D Icon40x40(40.0f, 40.0f);
  const FVector2D Icon20x20(20.0f, 20.0f);

#define IMAGE_BRUSH( RelativePath, … ) FSlateImageBrush(
StyleSet->RootToContentDir( RelativePath, TEXT( ".png" ) ),
__VA_ARGS__ )
  StyleSet->Set("MarsEditor.EditorMode", new IMAGE_
BRUSH("MarsEditorMode", Icon40x40));
  StyleSet->Set("MarsEditor.EditorMode.Small", new IMAGE_
BRUSH("MarsEditorMode", Icon20x20));

  FSlateStyleRegistry::RegisterSlateStyle(*StyleSet.Get());
}
```

First thing we do is create a new slate style set and give it our style set name. Next up we will define where our content root folder will be, we want to point this to a folder called Resources located in our plugin folder. So adjacent to our Source folder. You can name this folder something else if you want to, but it's always a good idea to follow the standard way of doing things.

The normal usage of icons in Unreal is to have one normal sized and one small icon of each icon. We create two vectors to have this size information, again we are going with the standard Unreal values here. We then define a little macro to help us and then we register our two first icon. We use the same actual png file for both the normal and small size, we just register it with a different name and a different size vector. This is the standard way of doing it in Unreal and you will find this exact code copied all over the place. This will add this icon /Plugins/MarsEditor/Resources/MarsEditorMode.png to our style set. Finally, we actually register the style set.

Now we also need to unregister ourselves if our module was shutdown. Time to implement UnregisterStyleSet.

```
void FMarsEditorModule::UnregisterStyleSet()
{
  if (StyleSet.IsValid())
  {
    FSlateStyleRegistry::UnRegisterSlateStyle(*StyleSet.
Get());
    ensure(StyleSet.IsUnique());
    StyleSet.Reset();
  }
}
```

We just unregister it and then delete our style set. Now we can add our new icon to our editor mode register call like this.

```
void FMarsEditorModule::StartupModule()
{
 FEditorModeRegistry::Get().RegisterMode<FMarsEditorMode>
(FMarsEditorMode::EM_MarsEditorMode, FText::FromString("Mars
Editor Mode"), FSlateIcon(GetStyleSetName(), "MarsEditor.
EditorMode", "MarsEditor.EditorMode.Small"), true, 200);
};
```

As I mentioned, we will be adding more icons to our style set later and you can also add a lot of other things to the style set, icons, sounds, fonts, colours. It is a container for all properties for how your slate widgets will look. Now we can launch the editor, and we have our own editor mode we can enter and exit. It's time to add something useful to it!

OUR FIRST TOOL

Now it's time to finally start creating some tools. But what tools should we create? What is even possible to do? When you start out making new tools in the editor it can be hard to know what is possible to do and how much work it is. One of the goals with this book is to help you give that context. To show you some useful tools and how they are implemented. But something to keep in mind is if it can be hard for you to know what is possible and the amount of work it is, that also goes for the people you make the tools for. So having some easy, useful tools also serves a purpose in starting a discussion with the people you are making the tools for, so they can see what is possible to do. This also means that it really is a never-ending discussion, or at least until you run out of time on the project. As your project progresses, so can the requirements on what needs to be implemented change. Sometimes it can be hard to see what the big-time sinks are in a workflow before it has been tested a bit.

This is worth keeping in mind and to keep having a discussion with your designer/artists who you are making the tool for; their answers might change after a while and after seeing some of the other tools you have created. Or the tools you have already created might need some tweaking. It's always a good idea to check in every now and then about current and future needs, but also how the tools already created are used. Especially if you create a tool then don't receive any feedback on it. it's probably a sign that it's not being used for some reason. It could be lack of knowledge or that it's not working, either way following up is important.

Anyways, enough ranting, time to start with implementing our very first tools. We will start with creating some different tools in our editor modes to get us started and give us an idea on what is possible, and we will make a mix of tools, some more designer oriented and some more artist oriented. Then it will hopefully be easier to see what is possible and have an idea of how much time it will take to implement new features.

MATERIAL COPY/PASTE

Our first tool will be quite simple but still speed up artists work quite a bit. We will add a way to copy and paste materials by clicking on them. The idea is simple, hold down a button and click the right mouse button on a static mesh to copy the material you click, then hold down the same button and left click to paste the material onto the static mesh you click on. We will default the button to hold down to M (as in Material), but we of course want the user to be able to rebind it to whatever key they prefer, so we will look into how to do this in Unreal Engine.

While we could place this functionality straight into our editor mode, we will put it in a class and put that class in our editor mode instead. It's always a good practice to compartmentalize our logic. We will be adding more tools into the editor mode so it would get quite big and messy if we didn't. And if we have multiple editor modes, say one for artists and one for designers we might have some tools we want to have in both editor modes. For our first tool we will also start on a helper library where we will put functionality we will use in other parts of the book.

Before we start with our helper class, let us create the input command we need for our material copy/paste tool. We want to hold down M while using the mouse buttons to trigger the copy/paste. We want the M key to be rebindable so our users can change the key binding, we need to create a command for it and register it. For this we first need to create our command class. Create MarsEditorCommands.h in /Plugins/MarsEditor/Source/MarsEditor/Public/ and add this code in it.

```
#pragma once

#include "CoreMinimal.h"
#include "Framework/Commands/Commands.h"

class FMarsEditorCommands : public
TCommands<FMarsEditorCommands>
{
public:

  FMarsEditorCommands();

  // TCommands<> interface
  virtual void RegisterCommands() override;

public:
  TSharedPtr< FUICommandInfo > MaterialTool;
};
```

We inherit from the templated class `TCommands`, we add a `RegisterCommands` function and then our actual command. This is all that is needed for the header. Now let us create MarsEditorCommands.cpp in /Plugins/MarsEditor/Source/MarsEditor/Private/ and add the following code.

```
#include "MarsEditorCommands.h"

#define LOCTEXT_NAMESPACE "FMarsEditorCommands"

FMarsEditorCommands::FMarsEditorCommands()
: TCommands< FMarsEditorCommands >("MarsEditor",
  FText::FromString(TEXT("Mars Editor Commands")),
```

```
  NAME_None,
  FMarsEditorModule::GetStyleSetName())
 {
 }

void FMarsEditorCommands::RegisterCommands()
{
    UI_COMMAND(MaterialTool, "Material tool", "Button to hold
down while left/middle mouse clicking to copy/paste material
from static mesh actors", EUserInterfaceActionType::None,
    FInputChord(EKeys::M));
}
#undef LOCTEXT_NAMESPACE
```

First thing we do is add the `LOCTEXT_NAMESPACE` define. This is used in Unreal's localization system to help set up localizable `FText`. Usually, I ignore this and just create the `FText` manually since the tools I create will never be localized anyways. However, in this case we need it since the `UI_COMMAND` macro we will use to create our command makes use of it.

In the constructor all we need to do is supply a name for our command class, a description and then for parent context we don't send in anything. If we are doing something more complex and split up our commands in several different classes, we can send in a parent here. Children and parents are not allowed to share bindings, so it's a way to enforce that there's no collision between keys. Last parameter is our style set name; this is used for any icons we might use.

In `RegisterCommands` is where we register our commands with the `UI_COMMAND` macro. In the `UI_COMMAND` we first send in our variable, then the display name of our command followed by a description, this is what the user will see (and search on) in the editor settings when rebinding keys. Then we can give some context on how this command will be used, if it's a button or toggle. For a simple keyboard shortcut `None` is fine here (we will look into other usage here in another chapter). Then we can give it a default keyboard binding in the `FInputChord` struct. It's perfectly fine to leave this empty, that just means we must bind it in the editor before we can use. But for most commands we will want a default binding.

Now that we have our command class, we just need to register it, we will do this in our module class `FMarsEditorModule`. In `StartupModule()` add the following line.

```
void FMarsEditorModule::StartupModule()
{
  RegisterStyleSet();
  FMarsEditorCommands::Register();
  //...
};
```

And in `ShutdownModule()` the unregister call.

```
void FMarsEditorModule::ShutdownModule()
{
  //...
  FMarsEditorCommands::Unregister();
};
```

Now that we have our command ready you can rebind it in the editor. Start the editor and go to Edit > Editor Preferences > Keyboard Shortcuts > Mars Editor Commands and you will see our material tool command there, you can rebind it to whatever you want now.

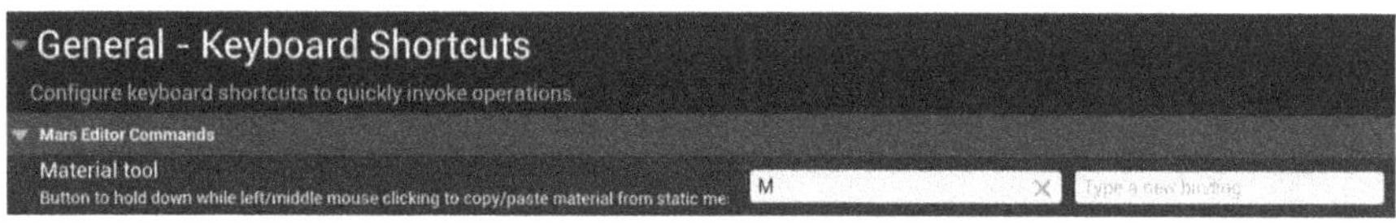

Now we can continue with creating our helper class that will handle the copy/pasting of the material. Create MarsEditorMaterialCopyPasteTool.h in /Plugin/MarsEditor/Source/MarsEditor/Public/EditorMode/ and add this code to it.

```
#pragma once

#include "CoreMinimal.h"

class FEditorViewportClient;
class HHitProxy;
class UStaticMeshComponent;
class UMaterialInterface;
struct FViewportClick;

class FMarsEditorMaterialCopyPasteTool
{
public:
  bool HandleClick(FEditorViewportClient* _viewportClient,
HHitProxy* _hitProxy, const FViewportClick& _click);


private:
  void CopyMaterial(int _materialIndex, const
UStaticMeshComponent* _meshComponent);
  void PasteMaterial(int _materialIndex, UStaticMeshComponent*
_meshComponent);

  TWeakObjectPtr<UMaterialInterface> Material = nullptr;
};
```

We start with the forward declarations we need, as I mentioned before using forward declarations instead of includes in the .h files lead to faster compile times. We then create a class that will handle our logic. This is not a `UCLASS()` though, in fact our editor mode is not a `UCLASS()` either. This means that we cannot use Unreal's reflection system for our member variables and that's why we store our material in a `TWeakObjectPtr` instead of using a `UPROPERTY()` for it. The `HandleClick` function will come from our editor mode, we will just pass the call on from the editor mode to our helper class. Then we have some internal functions to help with the copy/pasting.

Let us take a look at the implementation of this, create MarsEditor MaterialCopyPasteTool.cpp in /Plugin/MarsEditor/Source/MarsEditor/Private/Editor Mode/ and start with adding this code.

```
#include "EditorMode/MarsEditorMaterialCopyPasteTool.h"

#include "EngineUtils.h"
#include "MarsEditorCommands.h"

bool FMarsEditorMaterialCopyPasteTool::HandleClick
(FEditor ViewportClient* _viewportClient, HHitProxy*
_hitProxy, const FViewportClick& _click)
{
  if (_click.GetEvent() == IE_Released)
  {
    FInputEventState inputState(GEditor->GetActiveViewport(),
_click.GetKey(), _click.GetEvent());
    const FInputChord& primaryChord = *FMarsEditorCommands::
Get().MaterialTool->GetActiveChord(EMultipleKeyBindingIndex::
Primary);
    const FInputChord& secondaryChord =
*FMarsEditorCommands::Get().MaterialTool->GetActiveChord
(EMultipleKeyBindingIndex::Secondary);
    bool mateialMode = primaryChord.IsValidChord()
&& inputState.IsButtonPressed(primaryChord.Key)
|| secondaryChord.IsValidChord() && inputState.
IsButtonPressed(secondaryChord.Key);
    if (mateialMode)
    {
      //TODO add copy/paste code here
    }
  }
  return false;
}
```

The `HandleClick` function is one of the input related functions we have from our editor mode. We will simply pass on all the data from the editor mode into our helper class. Not only does this function have information about the click event, like 2D position in the viewport, what kind of click (it can tell you if it was a double click or if we just released the mouse button for example). We use this click event to create an `FInputEventState`, this struct allows us to check if the button for our material command is pressed down also. First, we get our command and then get the input chord from it, both the primary and secondary. This is because Unreal allows the user to have two different bindings for each command. We then check if any of the chords are pressed in the input state, if it is we can go on with the second part of this function. Replace the "`//TODO add copy/paste code here`" comment with the following code.

```
if (HActor* actorProxy = HitProxyCast< HActor >(_hitProxy))
{
  AVolume* volume = Cast< AVolume >(actorProxy->Actor);
  if (volume == nullptr)
  {
    if (_click.GetKey() == EKeys::RightMouseButton)
    {
      const UStaticMeshComponent* meshComponent =
Cast< UStaticMeshComponent >(actorProxy->PrimComponent);
      if (meshComponent != nullptr)
      {
        CopyMaterial(actorProxy->MaterialIndex,
meshComponent);
        return true;
      }
    }
    else if (_click.GetKey() == EKeys::LeftMouseButton)
    {
      const UStaticMeshComponent* meshComponent =
Cast< UStaticMeshComponent >(actorProxy->PrimComponent);
      if (meshComponent != nullptr)
      {
        PasteMaterial(actorProxy->MaterialIndex,
const_cast<UStaticMeshComponent*>(meshComponent));
        return true;
      }
    }
  }
}
```

The `HHitProxy` struct we got with our function contains the information we need about what we clicked on in our world. It has the information about what actor, component and material index we clicked on, and we will need all of these things. The first things we do is check if we clicked on an `AVolume` and then ignore it. This is because if we are trying to copy or paste a material onto an `AVolume`, it is very likely that it's a mistake. If it's a right mouse button we are clicking with, we call our copy function and then we return true. Returning true in `HandleClick` means that we have handled the click, and we want to consume the input, so no other system will get it. If we don't do anything with the input, we will return false and let other systems handle it. If it's a left mouse button click, we call our paste material function.

Now unfortunately the hitproxy struct we received with this function has a const pointer to the component (but interestingly not to the actor the component belongs to). So, we have to cast this constness away so we can edit the component. This is safe to do here, but if you prefer to avoid the const cast you can get the actor we clicked on from the hit proxy and loop through all components and look for a match, the result will be the same though, we will edit this component.

When checking what mouse button we are clicking with we are using the `EKeys` struct, which is located in the `InputCore` module, thus we must add it in our MarsEditor.Build.cs file in the `PrivateDependencyModuleNames` array, we must also add `"UnrealEd"` and `"EditorFramework"`

Next up is our `CopyMaterial` function.

```
void FMarsEditorMaterialCopyPasteTool::CopyMaterial(int
_materialIndex, const UStaticMeshComponent* _meshComponent)
{
  Material = _meshComponent->GetMaterial(_materialIndex);
}
```

The function is very simple, we just get the material from the static mesh component. Our PasteMaterial function will also be quite simple.

```
void FMarsEditorMaterialCopyPasteTool::PasteMaterial(int
_materialIndex, UStaticMeshComponent* _meshComponent)
{
  if (UMaterialInterface* material = Material.Get())
  {
    _meshComponent->SetMaterial(_materialIndex, material);
  }
}
```

If we have a valid material, we simple apply it to the static mesh component. We need to do one last things before the tool is functional. In MarsEditorMode.h we need to add our helper class (and the include for it).

```
#include "EditorMode/MarsEditorMaterialCopyPasteTool.h"

class FMarsEditorMode : public FEdMode
{
//...
  virtual bool HandleClick(FEditorViewportClient*
_viewportClient, HHitProxy* _hitProxy, const FViewportClick&
_click) override;
private:
  FMarsEditorMaterialCopyPasteTool CopyMaterial;
};
```

We need to override `HandleClick` in our editor mode since this is the input we will pass into our helper class. Let's take a look at the .cpp file.

```
bool FMarsEditorMode::HandleClick(FEditorViewportClient*
_viewportClient, HHitProxy* _hitProxy, const FViewportClick&
_click)
```

```
{
  if (CopyMaterial.HandleClick(_viewportClient, _hitProxy,
_click))
  {
    return true;
  }
  return FEdMode::HandleClick(_viewportClient, _hitProxy,
_click);
}
```

That's all we need, just pass on the input to our helper class and then if our tool did something, we return true to consume this click so no other tool does anything with it. Alright, compile it and test it. Remember that you must enter our editor mode (shift + 2) before you can use the tool. Try to copy/paste some materials between different static mesh actors. The tool is functional. But the tool is not done, it is lacking two very important things that every single tool we make *must* have. It is missing *Undo/Redo* support and *User Feedback.*

UNDO/REDO SUPPORT

Tools without Undo/Redo are always painful and frustrating to work with, since mistakes will always happen and in fact the faster our tools are, the more people will work with it and more mistakes they will make. Every single tool we make *must* have undo/redo support in my opinion. Unless our tool has undo/redo support the tool is simple not finished yet. When we make a tool, it is very easily to skip this, but for people who actually use the tool it will make a huge difference, and they should always be able to rely on it working. Likewise, you should always demand reliable undo/redo support in tools you use.

Thankfully adding undo/redo support is very easy and straightforward in Unreal and the built-in system for this is easy to work with and works very well. Let's modify our `PasteMaterial` function so it looks like this.

```
#include "ScopedTransaction.h"
//...
void FMarsEditorMaterialCopyPasteTool::PasteMaterial(int
_materialIndex, UStaticMeshComponent* _meshComponent)
{
  if (UMaterialInterface* material = Material.Get())
  {
    FScopedTransaction transaction(FText::FromString("Paste a
material onto clicked actor"));
    _meshComponent->GetOwner()->Modify();
    _meshComponent->SetMaterial(_materialIndex, material);
  }
}
```

The simplest way to add undo/redo support is to use the `FScopedTransaction` helper struct. It will start an undo/redo transaction when it's created and finish the transaction when it goes out of scope. The only variable it takes is a `FText` that should describe what this action is. This text will be visible for the user in the undo history window (Edit > Undo History).

Before we do the actual modification on our component, we must call `Modify()` on the actor it belongs to. This will store a snapshot of the object that Unreal will use to figure out what has changed when the `FScopedTransaction` goes out of scope and end the undo/redo transaction. And now we have working undo/redo support for out material copy/paste tool. As you can see adding support for this in Unreal Engine is very easy so there's really no excuse to not have it in all our tools.

USER FEEDBACK

Currently we do not have any user feedback on any of the steps at all. How can the user know that they did actually copy the material they clicked? When something goes wrong, how can they figure out why it is not working as they expect it to?

Good user feedback makes the tool easier to work with and removes frustration from it, but it also saves your time. If people can figure out quickly on their own why it's not working, they will not have to ask you for help, thus saving both of you from an interruption. Or if there's a problem, they will have more information about the problem if you implement good feedback, thus saving your time on error searching.

Feedback can come in many forms, from small notification widgets in the corner, to a popup requesting user input, to widgets that are permanently on screen or in a new window. For each tool we have to consider which method fits it. We want it to be informative, but not cumbersome. It needs to provide useful information without providing too much information, so people start to ignore it. This can be quite hard, especially since we will not work with the tool daily so our instincts can be quite wrong and what is useful and interesting information for us might be obvious to the people using the tool, and the other way around. Since we know the inner workings of the tool information, what we might consider obvious might not be to the user.

Also, if a tool has to little feedback, it can be hard to get feedback on the tool itself. It's always easier to get feedback on things that are visible then on things that do not exist. Because of this I think it's very important to constantly ask the people that are using the tool if it is working as expected, are they missing anything with the tool or is something annoying to use? And every single time someone asks for help with the tool, consider how the feedback can be improved so they can solve their issues on their own. You should also check in with the people using the tool after a couple of weeks after you make the tool for them, once they have had time to use the tool their experience might have changed, and they can have discovered small things that are annoying with the tool. Our goal is to make the tool as useful as possible, that means removing as much friction as possible.

Since feedback is of such importance we will be creating some helper functions for it, we will be using them a lot throughout this book. But we also want to expose these helpers to Blueprint, so we can make use of them in any blutilities we create.

While making blutilities are outside the scope of this book, a lot of same concepts apply to them as to our tools.

Unreal has built in support for several types of different feedback types already, however using them could be made a little bit easier thus we will streamline their usage a bit in our own helper library.

For this tool I think the slate notification manager is a good choice. It's a small popup in the lower right corner that is not too intrusive and can easily be ignored, but it can quite clearly signal error vs success. This is the feedback I use the most often for my tools, both code-based ones and Blueprint-based ones. Since we will be using it a lot, we want it to be just one function to call but also be exposed to Blueprint, since it's quite nice to be able to use it in blutilities also.

In fact, we will probably want to use it from our game project also sometime in the future. But we will also be using things from our game project in our plugin in the future as well. But obviously our plugin module cannot have a dependency on our game if our game has a dependency on our plugin, we will get a circular dependency. We need to consider our plugin structure a bit here. One solution is to place the feedback functionality in the game project, then our plugin can have a dependency on the game and that would work. While this solution would work and might be good enough for you, it does make it a bit harder to move the code to another project in the future (or if your plugin is used by multiple projects at the same time).

A better way around this is to create a new module in our plugin. Our plugin is called MarsEditor and is placed in /Plugins/MarsEditor/, but in this plugin we have a module also called MarsEditor placed at /Plugins/MarsEditor/Source/MarsEditor/. Our plugin can have multiple modules for different purposes. We will now add a new module called MarsShared, it will be placed in /Plugins/MarsEditor/Source/MarsShared/. This way not only can we have different dependencies on the different modules, but they can also be of different types. Since MarsEditor will never be used by the game project, it can be an editor only module. But our shared module will be used by both our editor module (MarsEditor) and our game, thus it needs to be a Runtime type.

While it might seem like a lot of work to set up a new module in our plugin just to be able to use this feedback function from the game and Blueprints, it is worth it. It's not only important that our tools are good for our users, but we also want them to be as easy as possible to write the correct way, if it's a hassle to use the feedback functions people will skip using them. Besides, it's not a lot of work needed to set up a new module at all.

Shared Module

Let's start with editing MarsEditor.uplugin and add our new module there. Change the `Modules` section to the following.

```
"Modules": [
  {
    "Name": "MarsEditor",
    "Type": "Editor",
    "LoadingPhase": "Default"
  },
  {
    "Name": "MarsShared",
    "Type": "Runtime",
    "LoadingPhase": "Default"
  }
]
```

As mentioned before, we are going to call our new module MarsShared and we want it to be a Runtime type since we want to be able to use it from our game as well. Next up we need to create MarsShared.Build.cs in /Plugins/MarsEditor/Source/MarsShared/ and add the following code in it.

```
using UnrealBuildTool;
public class MarsShared : ModuleRules
{
  public MarsShared(ReadOnlyTargetRules Target) : base(Target)
  {
    PCHUsage = ModuleRules.PCHUsageMode.
UseExplicitOrSharedPCHs;

    PublicDependencyModuleNames.AddRange(
      new string[]
      {
        "Core",
        "NetCore",
      }
      );

    PrivateDependencyModuleNames.AddRange(
     new string[]
      {
        "ApplicationCore",
        "CoreUObject",
        "Engine",
        "Slate",
      }
      );
  }
}
```

Just some standard includes we will need in it. Last thing we need to do is create our module class, even though we can leave it empty for now (we will be extending it in later chapters though). In /Plugins/MarsEditor/Source/MarsShared/Public/ add MarsSharedModule.h and add the following code in it.

```
#pragma once

#include "CoreMinimal.h"
#include "Modules/ModuleManager.h"

class FMarsSharedModule : public IModuleInterface
{
};
```

That's it, we don't need to implement anything in this module right now. Now it's time to add MarsSharedModule.cpp in /Plugins/MarsEditor/Source/MarsShared/Private/ and add the following code.

```
#include "MarsSharedModule.h"

IMPLEMENT_MODULE(FMarsSharedModule, MarsShared)
```

All we need is that macro and our module is created. It's a bit of overhead for our current usage of this, but as I said before, we will be extending this later.

Now we can finally create our library, add MarsSharedLibrary.h here /Plugins/MarsEditor/Source/MarsShared/Public/ and add the following code in it.

```
#pragma once

#include "Kismet/BlueprintFunctionLibrary.h"

#include "MarsSharedLibrary.generated.h"

UENUM(BlueprintType)
enum class EMarsNotificationType : uint8
{
  Fail,
  Success,
};

UCLASS()
class MARSSHARED_API UMarsSharedLibrary : public
UBlueprintFunctionLibrary
{
  GENERATED_BODY()

public:
  UFUNCTION(BlueprintCallable, Category = "Util")
  static void AddNotification(FString _header, FString
_description, EMarsNotificationType _type, float
_expireDuration = 2.0f,
float _fadeOutDuration = 2.0f);
};
```

Nothing too surprising here, we inherit from `UBlueprintFunctionLibrary` so we can make use of it in Blueprints and make sure our new function is `BlueprintCallable`. We also have to create our own enum that we expose to Blueprint, since the enum used internally by the slate notification manager is not exposed to Blueprints and exposing it would lead to quite a few engine changes. In this case I think it's better to avoid doing engine changes since we can quite easily work around it. Note that we must also add `MARSEDITOR_API` to the class. Without this we will be unable to access this class in other modules.

Alright, let us take a look at the implementation now. Add MarsSharedLibrary.cpp in /Plugins/MarsEditor/Source/MarsShared/Private/ and add the following code.

```
#include "MarsSharedLibrary.h"

#include "Framework/Notifications/NotificationManager.h"
#include "Widgets/Notifications/SNotificationList.h"

void UMarsSharedLibrary::AddNotification(FString _header,
FString _description, EMarsNotificationType _type, float
_expireDuration, float _fadeOutDuration)
{
  FNotificationInfo info(FText::FromString(_header));
  info.SubText = FText::FromString(_description);
  info.ExpireDuration = _expireDuration;
  info.FadeOutDuration = _fadeOutDuration;

  FSlateNotificationManager& notificationManager =
FSlateNotificationManager::Get();
  TSharedPtr< SNotificationItem > notification =
notificationManager.AddNotification(info);
  switch (_type)
  {

  case EMarsNotificationType::Fail:
    notification->SetCompletionState(SNotificationItem::
ECompletionState::CS_Fail);
    break;
  case EMarsNotificationType::Success:
    notification->SetCompletionState(SNotificationItem::
ECompletionState::CS_Success);
    break;
  }
}
```

We set up the struct the notification manager wants and then translated our enum to the enum the managers use. We have simplified the call quite a bit, we will only need one line of code, which is quite nice since we will use this a lot and when we use it, we don't have to know about what struct to fill in, just one function with some strings and float parameters.

There is a third type which we have not exposed here. You can also do a pending notification, which will show a spinning icon. But we have to save the notification item we get and update it when we are done, which certainly is possible, but our helper function ends up not really helping in that case and exposing it to Blueprint is also a challenge. So, we ignore this case for out helper function.

Now we just need to add some notifications to our tool, we should add one to every possible failure. In other words, we add one to every single "if" case we have and also one for when we succeed. Let's take a look at the Copy/Paste functions with the added notifications.

```
#include "MarsSharedLibrary.h"
void FMarsEditorMaterialCopyPasteTool::CopyMaterial(int
_materialIndex, const UStaticMeshComponent* _meshComponent)
{
  Material = _meshComponent->GetMaterial(_materialIndex);
  if (Material != nullptr)
  {
    UMarsSharedLibrary::AddNotification("Copied Material",
FString::Printf(TEXT("Copied material %s!"),
*Material->GetName()), EMarsNotificationType::Success);
  }
  else
  {
    UMarsSharedLibrary::AddNotification("Copied Material",
"Failed getting material", EMarsNotificationType::Fail);
  }
}


void FMarsEditorMaterialCopyPasteTool::PasteMaterial(int
_materialIndex, UStaticMeshComponent* _meshComponent)
{
  if (UMaterialInterface* material = Material.Get())
  {
    FScopedTransaction transaction(FText::FromString("Paste a
material onto clicked actor"));
    _meshComponent->GetOwner()->Modify();
    _meshComponent->SetMaterial(_materialIndex, material);
    UMarsSharedLibrary::AddNotification("Pasted Material",
FString::Printf(TEXT("Pasted material %s!"),
*material->GetName()), EMarsNotificationType::Success);
  }
  else
  {
    UMarsSharedLibrary::AddNotification("Pasted Material",
FString::Printf(TEXT("We do not have a copied material!")),
EMarsNotificationType::Fail);
  }
}
```

We add a notification if we fail or succeed. This way we now have pretty good feedback on our tool when it's used. We can improve it even further by adding some fail notifications inside the `HandleClick` function also, specifically if the user clicks on a `AVolume` we don't do anything, that is an excellent place for a failure notification.

Since we are now using our `MarsShared` module from `MarsEditor`, we must add a dependency for it. In `MarsEditor.Build.cs` add `"MarsShared"` in the `PrivateDependencyModuleNames` array.

Engine Edit

If you tried to use the middle mouse button instead of the left or right button, you will notice it didn't work (at least as of Unreal 5.4.1, maybe this bug is fixed in later versions). If we debug this, we will find out that the middle mouse button click is consumed in `FLevelEditorViewportClient::ProcessClick` by this piece of code

```
if (Click.GetKey() == EKeys::MiddleMouseButton && !Click.
IsAltDown() && !Click.IsShiftDown())
{
  LevelViewportClickHandlers::ClickViewport(this, Click);
  return;
}
```

If the input is middle mouse button and alt and shift is not pressed down, the input is sent to the viewport click handlers and then we stop executing. So even if they do not consume it, we will still stop evaluating the click. If we look inside `ClickViewport` we see it only handles the middle mouse button if control is held down.

So, this is clearly a bug in the engine, so let us fix it.

```
//ENGINE MOD START - Fix for middle mouse button is consumed
even if ClickViewport do not consume it.
//LevelViewportClickHandlers::ClickViewport(this, Click);
//return;
if (LevelViewportClickHandlers::ClickViewport(this, Click))
{
  return;
}
//ENGINE MOD END
```

The fix is quite easy, `ClickViewport` already returns if it consumes the input or not.

Of note here is all marking we did for our engine edit, I explained this in the in the Code Standard paragraph, but it's worth re-iterating. Once you get comfortable doing engine edits, you can quite easily end up with many off them and will then have to deal with that when you upgrade the engine. Clearly marking your changes makes it a lot easier to merge over all edits into the new engine versions. One common type of engine edits to make is to pull in fixes from future version of Unreal Engine before the full release, clearly marking that it's a fix from that specific version will make it easier to know that there's no need to merge that fix over.

Conclusion

Now our first tool is complete and functional and is a quite useful little tool for artists to speed up their workflow. We covered a lot of things for this first tool, we set up two modules in our plugin, we covered user feedback and made a helper library for it, we added undo/redo support, we looked into how to let the user rebind the keys for our command. We took the time to sperate this functionality from our tool so it will be easier for us to re-use for future tools. When making tools it's always good to consider what parts should be separated so we can re-use them for other functionality later.

Our next tool is going to be a lot faster to make since we already have all these things now. The more tools we have, the more building blocks we will have for other future tools and of course the more knowledge we will have about what systems we have to work with.

REIMPORT ASSET FROM ACTOR

Our next tool will allow us to re-import a static mesh from our selected actor. Unreal already has support for re-importing an asset in the content browser, so we have that functionality we can use. But there is no easy way to reload an asset (or assets) from an actor placed in the world. Our tool will take the selected actor and re-import the static mesh from it.

We want this to trigger from a keyboard shortcut command. In the last tool we looked at how to add commands that can be rebound by the user, but we only polled that command when the mouse was clicked, this time we will hook up a callback that will trigger when our command is pressed.

Let's start with adding our new command, go to MarsEditorCommands.h and add the following variable.

```
TSharedPtr< FUICommandInfo > ReimportActorAsset;
```

And in MarsEditorCommands.cpp add the following inside `RegisterCommands`.

```
UI_COMMAND(ReimportActorAsset, "Reimport actor asset",
"Re-imports the first static mesh component from the selected
actor", EUserInterfaceActionType::None,
FInputChord(EKeys::R, EModifierKey::Control));
```

The only difference from last time is that we added a modifier key in the default binding. You can add any combination of the modifier keys here (Controls, Alt and Shift).

Now let's create the helper class for our tool. Start with creating MarsEditorReimportAssetTool.h in /Plugin/MarsEditor/Source/MarsEditor/Public/EditorMode/ and add the following code.

```
#pragma once

#include "CoreMinimal.h"

class FUICommandList;

class FMarsEditorReimportAssetTool
{
public:
  void Init(TWeakPtr< FUICommandList > _commandList);
private:
  void ReimportAssetFromSelectedActor();
};
```

Unlike our material copy/paste tool, this time we will need a command list passed into us, this is where we will register our callback, which will be the `ReimportAssetFromSelectedActor` function. We will create this command list later, for now create MarsEditorReimportAssetTool.cpp in /Plugin/MarsEditor/Source/MarsEditor/Private/EditorMode/ and start with adding the following code.

```
#include "EditorMode/MarsEditorReimportAssetTool.h"

#include "MarsEditorCommands.h"

void FMarsEditorReimportAssetTool::Init(TWeakPtr<
FUICommandList > _commandList)
{
  FUICommandList* commandList = _commandList.Pin().Get();
  commandList->MapAction(FMarsEditorCommands::Get().
ReimportActorAsset,
    FExecuteAction::CreateLambda(
      [this]()
      {
        ReimportAssetFromSelectedActor();
      }),
    FCanExecuteAction());
}
```

In the command list we bind our command (`ReimportActorAsset`) to a `FExecuteAction` lambda, that just calls our function. `FExecuteAction` is a delegate, and you can bind a number of things to it like normally (Lambdas, UFunctions, and so on). After this we also pass in a `FCanExecuteAction` that we leave empty, this means it will default to true, meaning our action can always be executed. We could add some validation here if we wanted and, in some cases, it makes sense to have validation. But something to consider when we add validation in the `FCanExecuteAction` delegate is that if we return false here, the key input will not be consumed and might then trigger another command if the key input has multiple bindings.

For our command we set Control + R as the default binding, this is the same binding as toggling realtime mode on/off, which for most people isn't very useful. So, if we return false in our can execute delegate, realtime mode will be toggled. But if we instead always return true in the can execute delegate and instead do any validation inside our function the input will be consumed, and we can handle feedback on this ourselves. In other words, for commands like this I think it's better to always consume the input, even if we don't do anything. The user triggered the command with intent, we don't want to risk anything else to trigger. Now the command list can also be used for other types of command, like buttons, but we will cover more of that in later chapters. Ok, time to look at the actual reimport function.

```
#include "EditorReimportHandler.h"
#include "MarsSharedLibrary.h"
//...

void FMarsEditorReimportAssetTool::
ReimportAssetFromSelectedActor()
{
  AActor* currentSelectedActor = UMarsSharedLibrary::
GetSelectedActor();
  if (currentSelectedActor != nullptr)
  {
    UStaticMeshComponent* staticMeshComponent
= currentSelectedActor->GetComponentByClass
< UStaticMeshComponent >();
    if (staticMeshComponent != nullptr)
    {
      TArray< UObject* > assets;
      assets.Emplace(staticMeshComponent->GetStaticMesh());
      FReimportManager::Instance()->
ValidateAllSourceFileAndReimport(assets, true);
    }
    else
    {
      UMarsSharedLibrary::AddNotification("Re-import actor",
"The selected actor must have a static mesh component",
EMarsNotificationType::Fail);
    }
  }
  else
  {
    UMarsSharedLibrary::AddNotification("Re-import
actor", "You must have only 1 actor selected",
EMarsNotificationType::Fail);
  }
 }
```

First, we get the selected actor, more on this helper function soon. Once we have the selected actor, we get the first `UStaticMeshComponent` we can find in it and from that component we get the actual static mesh asset. This asset we then trigger a reimport on through the `FReimportManager`. This function takes an array of assets to reimport so we could get the assets from all static mesh components on our actor in case there are multiple. We can also go through all selected actors and add them if we wanted. I'll leave that up to you how you want this function to be implemented. Of course, we also add some notifications popups for all possible fail states in this function.

Let's add the helper function for getting the selected actors and while we are at it, we will also add one for getting all selected actors, we are going to need it in the future. We are going to place these helper functions in our shared module because we might want to use them from our game code in the future. Add the following function declarations in MarsSharedLibrary.h.

```
class MARSSHARED_API UMarsSharedLibrary : public
UBlueprintFunctionLibrary
{
  //...
  static AActor* GetSelectedActor();
  static void GetSelectedActors(TArray< AActor* >& _actors);
};
```

And then the following include and functions definitions in the .cpp file.

```
#if WITH_EDITOR
#include "Selection.h"
#endif //WITH_EDITOR

AActor* UMarsSharedLibrary::GetSelectedActor()
{
#if WITH_EDITOR
  TArray< AActor* > selectedActors;
  USelection* selection = GEditor->GetSelectedActors();
  if (selection != nullptr)
  {
    selection->GetSelectedObjects(selectedActors);
  }
  AActor* currentSelectedActor = nullptr;
  if (selectedActors.IsEmpty() == false)
  {
    currentSelectedActor = selectedActors.Last();
  }
  return currentSelectedActor;
#else //WITH_EDITOR
  return nullptr;
#endif //WITH_EDITOR
}
```

```
void UMarsSharedLibrary::GetSelectedActors
(TArray< AActor* >& _actors)
{
#if WITH_EDITOR
 USelection* selection = GEditor->GetSelectedActors();
 if (selection != nullptr)
 {
  selection->GetSelectedObjects(_actors);
 }
#endif
}
```

Both functions are very simple, we can just get the selection from `GEditor` and from that selection we can get an array of all selected actors. Our helper function just saves a few lines of code, but that does make the code where we use it more readable, I think, and this is a very common operation to do when writing tools. Since the MarsShared module is a runtime module, we need to do have some if defines for when we are compiling the editor vs when we are compiling the game.

We also must add a module dependency in MarsShared.Build.cs.

```
public class MarsShared : ModuleRules
{
  public MarsShared(ReadOnlyTargetRules Target) : base(Target)
  {
    //...
    if (Target.bBuildEditor == true)
    {
     PrivateDependencyModuleNames.AddRange(
       new string[]
       {
          "UnrealEd",
        }
        );
    }
  }
}
```

Just like with the code we added, we need to make our module dependency only happen when we compile the editor, since the UnrealEd module will not compile for non-editor builds.

Now the only thing left is to create our command list where we registered our callback. We will create our command list in our editor mode, this way our command is only active in our editor mode. If we want it to always be active, we could register it in our module class, `FMarsEditorModule`, instead. Open MarsEditorMode.h and add the following code inside of the `FMarsEditorMode` class.

```
virtual bool InputKey(FEditorViewportClient* _viewportClient,
FViewport* _viewport, FKey _key, EInputEvent _event) override;
private:
TSharedPtr< FUICommandList > CommandList;
FMarsEditorReimportAssetTool ReimportAsset;
```

The InputKey function is where we will check if the command list should trigger any of its callbacks. We also need to add an include file to our helper class.

```
#include "EditorMode/MarsEditorReimportAssetTool.h"
```

Next, add the following code in FMarsEditorMode::Enter().

```
CommandList = MakeShareable(new FUICommandList);
ReimportAsset.Init(CommandList);
```

This is all we need to do to create our command list, finally we just need to implement the InputKey function like this.

```
bool FMarsEditorMode::InputKey(FEditorViewportClient*
_viewportClient, FViewport* _viewport, FKey _key,
EInputEvent _event)
{
  return CommandList->ProcessCommandBindings(_key,
FSlateApplication::Get().GetModifierKeys(), false);
}
```

We pass the input into the command list, which will trigger any callback if possible, and just return the result of this. If we triggered any callbacks we will consume the input, otherwise it will be passed on to other systems.

That is it, as promised this tool was a lot faster to build then the first one, even if we did extent our helper library a little bit. The tool itself is quite simple but can speed up the workflow a little for artist. Both of our tools so far have been artist focused; the next tool will be more gameplay focused.

SPAWNER TOOL

The next tool we will create will have three things it can do. Place our actor in the world with the settings we want, select all actors matching our current settings and finally apply our current settings on our selection. The details of how the spawn point actor functions aren't important, we will just focus on the tools to place them faster with some settings and also to easily apply settings on a selection. For this tool we will need to create a slate widget where we can change some settings and click on some buttons, we will also extend the right click menu when clicking on our test actor (the right click menu is called context menu in Unreal and I will refer to it like that from now on). Before we start with the tool, we need to add a spawner actor in our game project (I'm calling my game project Mars). Let's create MarsSpawner.h in our game project and add the following code.

```
#pragma once

#include "CoreMinimal.h"

#include "MarsSpawner.generated.h"

UENUM(BlueprintType)
enum class EClasses : uint8
{
```

```
  Pilot,
  Navigator,
  Commander,
  Gunner,
  Max UMETA(Hidden),
};

UENUM(BlueprintType)
enum class ETeams : uint8
{
  Red,
  Blue,
  Max UMETA(Hidden),
};

UCLASS()
class MARS_API AMarsSpawner : public AActor
{
  GENERATED_BODY()
public:
  UPROPERTY(EditAnywhere, BlueprintReadOnly)
  EClasses Class = EClasses::Gunner;

  UPROPERTY(EditAnywhere, BlueprintReadOnly)
  ETeams Team = ETeams::Red;
};
```

That's all we need for our purposes. Just an actor with a couple of enums on it that we will create tools for setting. Of course, since we want to use this in our MarsEditor module we must also add a dependency to it in MarsEditor.Build.cs.

```
    PrivateDependencyModuleNames.AddRange(
      new string[]
      {
        //…
        "Mars",
      }
      );
```

First thing we will do is add a command for each of the three actions we want our tool to do. Open MarsEditorCommands.h and add the following variables.

```
  TSharedPtr< FUICommandInfo > SpawnerToolPlacement;
  TSharedPtr< FUICommandInfo > SpawnerToolSelectSimilar;
  TSharedPtr< FUICommandInfo > SpawnerToolApplySettingsOnActor;
```

Then in the .cpp file add the following lines in RegisterCommands().

```
  UI_COMMAND(SpawnerToolPlacement, "Spawner Tool Placement",
"Button to hold down while left mouse clicking to place AI
spawners", EUserInterfaceActionType::None,
```

```
FInputChord(EKeys::X));
  UI_COMMAND(SpawnerToolSelectSimilar, "Spawner Tool Select
Similar", "Select all spawners with current settings",
EUserInterfaceActionType::None,
FInputChord());
  UI_COMMAND(SpawnerToolApplySettingsOnActor, "Spawner Tool
Apply Settings", "Apply current settings on all spawners",
EUserInterfaceActionType::None,
FInputChord());
```

We only give our placement tool a default binding. The other two commands we leave empty, these two commands we are going to add to the context menu (the right click menu) on our spawner actor. Now let's start with our helper class for this tool. In /Plugins/MarsEditor/Source/MarsEditor/Pulic/EditorMode/ create MarsEditor SpawnerPlacerTool.h and add the following code.

```
#pragma once

#include "CoreMinimal.h"
#include "Mars/MarsSpawner.h"


class FEditorViewportClient;
class HHitProxy;
struct FViewportClick;

class FMarsEditorSpawnerPlacerTool
{
public:
  void Init(TWeakPtr< FUICommandList > _commandList);
  void UnInit();
  bool HandleClick(FEditorViewportClient* _viewportClient,
HHitProxy* _hitProxy, const FViewportClick& _click);

  void ApplySettingsOnSelection();
  bool SelectSpawnersMatching(ETeams _team, EClasses _class);

  ETeams SelectedTeam = ETeams::Red;
  EClasses SelectedClass = EClasses::Commander;

private:
  TSharedRef<FExtender> GetLevelViewportContextMenuExtender
(const TSharedRef<FUICommandList> _commandList, const
TArray<AActor*> _actors);
  FDelegateHandle LevelEditorExtenderDelegateHandle;

TSharedPtr<FUICommandList> SpawnerCommandList;
};
```

We follow the same pattern as in the earlier tool so this should look familiar by now. We have our `Init` function, but this time we also have an `UnInit`, our `HandleClick`, then we have some functions for the commands we have created.

Then the team and classes variables are what we will later change when we add some UI to the tool, these are the settings we apply on our newly created spawner, set on our selection or find all spawner with identical settings.

Then we have our callback for extending the context menu and a delegate handle to it. Finally, we have a command list, these are the commands that we will add into the context menu. Time to start looking at the implementation of all this. In /Plugins/MarsEditor/Source/MarsEditor/Private/EditorMode/ create MarsEditorSpawnerPlacerTool.cpp and start adding this code.

```
#include "EditorMode/MarsEditorSpawnerPlacerTool.h"

#include "Editor.h"
#include "SEditorViewport.h"
#include "EngineUtils.h"
#include "LevelEditor.h"
#include "ScopedTransaction.h"
#include "Kismet/GameplayStatics.h"
#include "Mars/MarsSpawner.h"
#include "MarsEditorSettings.h"
#include "MarsSharedLibrary.h"

void FMarsEditorSpawnerPlacerTool::Init
(TWeakPtr< FUICommandList > _commandList)
{
  SpawnerCommandList = MakeShareable(new FUICommandList);
  SpawnerCommandList->MapAction(
    FMarsEditorCommands::Get().SpawnerToolSelectSimilar,
    FExecuteAction::CreateLambda([this]
      {
        AMarsSpawner* spawner = Cast< AMarsSpawner>(UMarsShare
dLibrary::GetSelectedActor());
        if (spawner != nullptr)
        {
          SelectSpawnersMatching(spawner->Team,
spawner->Class);
        }
    }));
  SpawnerCommandList->MapAction(
FMarsEditorCommands::Get().
SpawnerToolApplySettingsOnActor,
    FExecuteAction::CreateLambda([this]
      {
        ApplySettingsOnSelection();
      }));
  FUICommandList* editorModeCommandList = _commandList.Pin().
Get();
  editorModeCommandList->Append(SpawnerCommandList.
ToSharedRef());
```

```
  FLevelEditorModule& levelEditorModule =
FModuleManager::Get().LoadModuleChecked<FLevelEditorModule>
("LevelEditor");
  TArray<FLevelEditorModule::FLevelViewportMenuExten
der_SelectedActors>& menuExtenders = levelEditorModule.
GetAllLevelViewportContextMenuExtenders();
  menuExtenders.Add(FLevelEditorModule::FLevelViewportMenuExte
nder_SelectedActors::CreateRaw(this, &FMarsEditorSpawnerPlacer
Tool::GetLevelViewportContextMenuExtender));
  LevelEditorExtenderDelegateHandle = menuExtenders.Last().
GetHandle();

}
```

Lots of includes! Not all of these are needed for the Init function of course, but they will be used in the other functions. There are several different things going on here. First thing we do is create our own command list and map our callback to our commands in it. The reason we create our own command list for this is that we will use this command list when extending the context menu later on. While we didn't set any default keyboard buttons for these two commands, the user might do it on their own so we also append our command list to the editor modes command list, since that one will be checked against the key input and trigger the callback for that if possible. We could also call `ProcessCommandBindings` on our command list on our own also of course.

The last thing we do is add our callback function to the level viewport context menu extender in the level editor module. The lever editor module has extenders for a lot of different kinds of context menus. Take a look in LevelEditor.h for the other context menu extenders you can use. Ok, the `Init` function is done, so let's take a look at the `UnInit` function.

```
void FMarsEditorSpawnerPlacerTool::UnInit()
{
  FLevelEditorModule& levelEditorModule =
FModuleManager::Get().LoadModuleChecked<FLevelEditorModule>
("LevelEditor");
  TArray<FLevelEditorModule::FLevelViewportMenuExtender
_SelectedActors>& menuExtenders = levelEditorModule.
GetAllLevelViewportContextMenuExtenders();
 menuExtenders.RemoveAllSwap([&](const FLevelEditorModule::
FLevelViewportMenuExtender_SelectedActors& _delegate) -> bool
    {
      return _delegate.GetHandle() ==
LevelEditorExtenderDelegateHandle;
    });
 }
```

Of course, we need to remove our context menu extender. Not much more to say about that really so let's move on to the actual context menu extender.

```
TSharedRef<FExtender> FMarsEditorSpawnerPlacerTool::GetLevel
ViewportContextMenuExtender(const TSharedRef<FUICommandList>
_commandList, const TArray<AActor*> _actors)
{
  TSharedRef<FExtender> extender = MakeShareable(new
FExtender);
  bool foundSpawner = false;
for( AActor* actor : _actors)
{

  if (Cast<AMarsSpawner>(actor) != nullptr)
  {
    foundSpawner = true;
    break;
  }
}
 if (foundSpawner)
  {
    extender->AddMenuExtension("ActorTypeTools",
EExtensionHook::After, SpawnerCommandList, FMenuExtension
Delegate::CreateLambda(
    [this, _actors](FMenuBuilder& _menuBuilder)
    {
      _menuBuilder.BeginSection("SpawnerTool", FText::
FromString("Spawner"));
      _menuBuilder.AddMenuEntry(FMarsEditorCommands::Get().
SpawnerToolSelectSimilar);
      _menuBuilder.AddMenuEntry(FMarsEditorCommands::Get().
SpawnerToolApplySettingsOnActor);
      _menuBuilder.EndSection();
    }));
  }
  return extender;
}
```

There's quite a bit going on here that we need to go through. First thing is the input parameter, we get a command list here of the other commands already in the context menu, which isn't super useful really, I haven't found a single use case for it. Then we have a list of the selected actors, which is much more useful, and we are using this to make sure there's at least one spawner in our selection. If there's not, we don't want to add our spawner specific commands.

Once we have made sure we have a spawner we add a menu extension to our extender object. The first parameter in the menu extension is which extension hook you want to place your command around. There are two hook you can use here, ActorUETools and ActorTypeTools. ActorUETools is for commands that can be used for all actors. ActorTypeTools is for commands that are only used for specific actors, which is what we want to use here. The second parameter controls where around the hook you want your commands, before or after. In the third parameter we send in our command list, this is needed so the system will know about our callbacks we added. The final parameter is a delegate where we will actually add our commands to the context menu. Here we hook up a lambda and then inside it we start a new section for our commands and then we add the two commands we want in the menu builder.

Now if we right click on one of our spawner actors (when in our editor mode!) we will see our commands in the context menu. If you have bound a keyboard shortcut to them, you will also see that next to them.

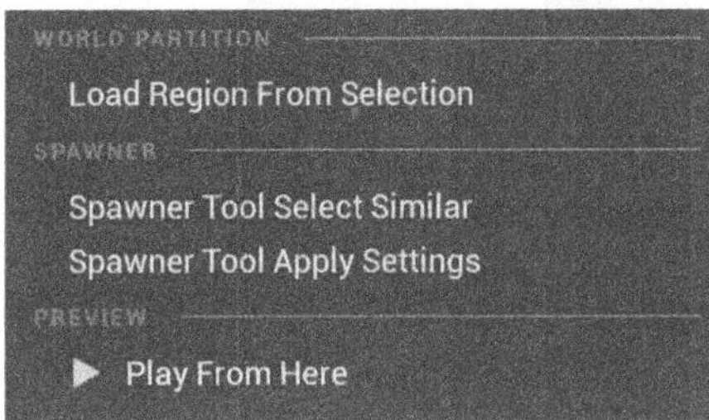

Of course we haven't implemented our functions yet, so clicking them does nothing yet. Let's take a look at the implementation of those functions next.

```
void FMarsEditorSpawnerPlacerTool::ApplySettingsOnSelection()
{
  TArray< AActor* > selectedActors;
  UMarsSharedLibrary::GetSelectedActors(selectedActors);
  if (selectedActors.IsEmpty() == false)
  {
    FScopedTransaction transaction(FText::FromString("Apply
settings on spawners"));
    int changedActors = 0;

    for (AActor* actor : selectedActors)
    {
     AMarsSpawner* spawner = Cast< AMarsSpawner>(actor);
     if (spawner != nullptr)
     {
       spawner->Modify();
       spawner->Class = SelectedClass;
       spawner->Team = SelectedTeam;
       spawner->MarkPackageDirty();
       ++changedActors;
     }
    }
    if (changedActors > 0)
    {
      FString str = FString::Printf(TEXT("Changed %i
spawners"), changedActors);
      UMarsSharedLibrary::AddNotification("Apply settings",
str, EMarsNotificationType::Success);
      return;
"if(changeActors > 0)"
    }
  }
```

```
  UMarsSharedLibrary::AddNotification("Apply settings", "No
valid selection", EMarsNotificationType::Fail);
}
```

We go through all our selected actors and if they are a spawner, we change the class and team settings on them (we cannot change these values yet, but we will soon look into that). Of course, we make sure undo/redo will work and add some notifications about the result of the operations as well. Our next function is for selecting all of our spawners that has the same team and class setting. Let's take a look at the code.

```
bool FMarsEditorSpawnerPlacerTool::SelectSpawnersMatching
(ETeams _team, EClasses _class)
{
  FScopedTransaction transaction(FText::FromString("Select
matching spawners"));
  int selectedActors = 0;
  GEditor->SelectNone(true, true, false);
  TArray< AActor* > listOfActors;
  UGameplayStatics::GetAllActorsOfClass
(GEditor->GetEditorWorldContext().World(),
AMarsSpawner::StaticClass(), listOfActors);
  for (int indexActor = 0; indexActor < listOfActors.Num();
++indexActor)
  {
    AMarsSpawner* spawner = Cast<AMarsSpawner>(listOfActors
[indexActor]);
    if (spawner != nullptr)
    {
      if (spawner->Team == _team && spawner->Class == _class)
      {
        GEditor->SelectActor(spawner, true, false);
        ++selectedActors;
      }
    }
  }
  GEditor->NoteSelectionChange();
  if (selectedActors > 0)
  {
    UMarsSharedLibrary::AddNotification("Select matching
spawners", FString::Printf(TEXT("Selected %i spawners"),
selectedActors), EMarsNotificationType::Success);
    return true;
  }
  UMarsSharedLibrary::AddNotification("Select matching
spawners", FString("Failed finding any matching spawners"),
EMarsNotificationType::Fail);
  return false;
}
```

Ok let's go through this code. The first thing we do of course is set up our undo buffer with `FScopedTransaction`, nothing new here. Then we clear the current selection in the editor, since we will be adding new actors to the selection, we need to clear it out first. Next, in order to get all the actors from the world, we must get the world from the editor world context. This will return the actual editor world. Unreal Engine can have multiple instances of a world, one for the actual editor and one for when you are playing in the editor. Which world we use matters, for this tool we want the editor world. We rarely want our tools to change the game world, since those changes will be discarded once we stop playing anyway. However, this does mean we can make our tool work on the game world if we would want, which can be nice for some types of debug tools.

Moving on, once we have a list of our spawners we check if they are a match, if they are we select them. But we do not trigger the notify about our selection change (the third parameter is false). This is important since we will do more selection, we do not want to trigger this notify over and over for performance reasons, once we are done marking up all our selections, we manually trigger a notify selection change with `NoteSelectionChange`. Sometimes it's better to manually handle selection notifications like this, since they have a lot of side effects (the details panel can refresh, gizmo position updates, the actor itself might be doing things when selection changes and so on) and it we have a very large selection this can eat up a lot of time. If we do it manually it's very important that we do not miss the selection notify in any case, since it can lead to some quite weird behaviours (the details panel being connected to the last selected actor and things like that). Finally, we have some notifications for the user about how the selection went.

Now the last things to look into is how we will actually spawn an actor when clicking in the viewport.

```
bool FMarsEditorSpawnerPlacerTool::HandleClick
(FEditorViewportClient* _viewportClient, HHitProxy* _hitProxy,
const FViewportClick& _click)

{
  if (_click.GetEvent() == IE_Released)
  {
    FInputEventState inputState(GEditor->GetActiveViewport(),
_click.GetKey(), _click.GetEvent());
    const FInputChord& primaryChord =
*FMarsEditorCommands::Get().SpawnerToolPlacement->
GetActiveChord(EMultipleKeyBindingIndex::Primary);
   const FInputChord& secondaryChord =
*FMarsEditorCommands::Get().SpawnerToolPlacement->
GetActiveChord(EMultipleKeyBindingIndex::Secondary);
   bool spawnerMode = primaryChord.IsValidChord()
&& inputState.IsButtonPressed(primaryChord.Key)
|| secondaryChord.IsValidChord() && inputState.
IsButtonPressed(secondaryChord.Key);
    if (spawnerMode)
    {
```

```
      if (_click.GetKey() == EKeys::LeftMouseButton)
      {
         FScopedTransaction transaction(TEXT("SpawnSpawner"),
FText::FromString("Create Spawner"), nullptr);
         const UMarsEditorSettings* editorSettings =
GetDefault< UMarsEditorSettings >();
         AMarsSpawner* newSpawner= Cast< AMarsSpawner >
(GEditor->GetEditorWorldContext().World()->
SpawnActor(editorSettings->SpawnerClass,
&GEditor->ClickLocation));
         if (newSpawner != nullptr)
         {
           newSpawner->Team = SelectedTeam;
           newSpawner->Class = SelectedClass;
         }
         GEditor->SelectNone(true, true, false);
         GEditor->SelectActor(newSpawner, true, true);
         return true;
       }
     }
   }
   else if( _click.GetEvent() == IE_DoubleClick)
   {
     AMarsSpawner* spawner = Cast< AMarsSpawner>(UMarsShared
Library::GetSelectedActor());
     if (spawner != nullptr)
     {
       SelectSpawnersMatching(spawner->Team, spawner->Class);
       return true;
     }
   }
   return false;
}
```

The input handling is exactly like in the material copy/paste tool, we just check the chords from a different command. Then spawning a new actor is as simple as calling `SpawnActor`, again we just need to make sure we are doing it on the editor world. For the class type we could have passed in AMarsSpawner::StaticClass(), but since we might want to create a BP class also, we get the spawner class from a settings file instead. We will go through this settings class soon. We don't get the click position from the `FViewportClick` event as one might expect, this is because it only has the 2D position on the viewport, not the 3D position in the world. That's why we have to get it from the editor engine instead. Once we have spawned our actor, we apply our settings on it, then we deselect everything and select our new actor.

After our spawn functionality we listen for a double click event, and if we have a double click and a spawner selected, we select all spawners matching it. It's a nice little bonus functionality which can be quite useful, depending on your project.

Let's create the settings file next, in /Plugins/MarsEditor/Source/MarsEditor/Public/ create the file MarsEditorSettings.h and add the following code.

```
#pragma once

#include "CoreMinimal.h"

#include "MarsEditorSettings.generated.h"

class AMarsSpawner;

UCLASS(Config = MarsEditorSettings, defaultconfig)
class MARSEDITOR_API UMarsEditorSettings : public UObject
{
  GENERATED_BODY()

public:

  UPROPERTY(config, EditAnywhere, Category = "Editor Mode")
  TSubclassOf< AMarsSpawner > SpawnerClass;
};
```

The key here is the config keyword we set in the `UCLASS` field. The value if this keyword will be used to the config name and it will now load all `UPROPERTY` variables at construction time. Since we want this property to be shared between all user, we also add the `defaultconfig` keyword. We will soon create a settings file that is local per user.

```
#include "MarsEditorSettings.h"
void FMarsEditorModule::StartupModule()
{
 //...
 if (ISettingsModule* settingsModule = FModuleManager::
GetModulePtr<ISettingsModule>("Settings"))
 {
  settingsModule->RegisterSettings("Editor", "Mars",
"MarsSettings", FText::FromString(TEXT("Mars Editor
Settings")),
   FText::FromString("Mars plugin editor settings."),
GetMutableDefault< UMarsEditorSettings >());
 }
}
```

You can find the setting by going to Edit > Editor Preferences… > Mars Editor Settings.

Toolkit and Our Own Widgets

Our tool is working well, but we are unable to actually change the settings we are using. For this we need to create a widget where the user can change our values. We will do this by creating the UI we want with Slate, if you have never used Slate before it can be a bit overwhelming. A lot of code is required to do anything in it as you will see. Teaching Slate is out of scope for this book, so I will not be explaining every little thing we do, just the big picture of it. There are plenty of resources online if you want to get a better understanding of how Slate works. But you can get pretty far without a deeper knowledge of it. Let's start with creating the widget for our editor mode. In /Plugins/MarsEditor/Source/MarsEditor/Public/EditorMode/ create MarsEditorModeWidget.h and add the following code.

```
#pragma once

class FMarsEditorMode;

class SMarsEditorWidget : public SCompoundWidget
{
public:
  SLATE_BEGIN_ARGS(SMarsEditorWidget) {}
  SLATE_END_ARGS();

  void Construct(const FArguments& _args);

private:
  void SetupSpawnerWidgets();
  TSharedPtr< SExpandableArea > SpawnerExpandableArea;
  TSharedPtr< SHorizontalBox > SpawnerToolTeam;
  TSharedPtr< SHorizontalBox > SpawnerToolClass;
  TSharedPtr< SHorizontalBox > SpawnerToolButtons;

  FMarsEditorMode* GetEdMode() const;
};
```

Creating a widget requires some special SLATE_* macros. Since we do not expose any parameters for the construction of our widget this is all that is needed. But if we wanted to, we could add parameters with `SLATE_ARGUMENT/SLATE_EVENT` macros in between the Begin/End macro. It's not needed for our use case though. We are only going to add a widget for our spawner tool, so we have shared pointer to a `SExpandableArea`, which will be our actual widget, and we have a setup function that will create it.

Let's take a look at the end result before we go through the next variables.

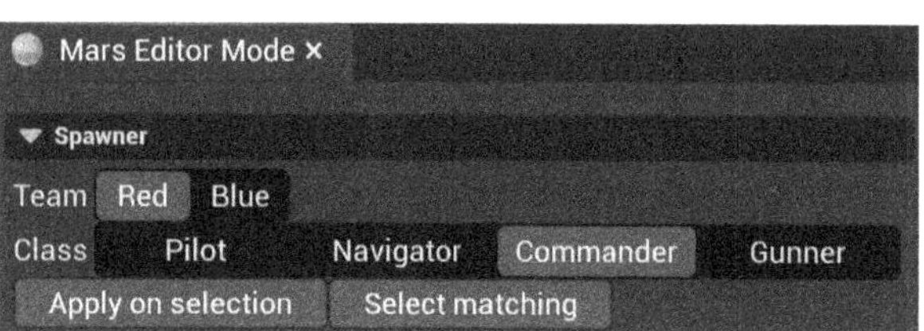

First, we have an expandable area, which is a widget the user can collapse so all the content inside of it is hidden. This becomes very useful when we start getting more tools, they will quite quickly eat up a lot of screen space. After that we have three lines of widgets, the first for the selection of the team, the second for the class and the last line with some buttons for the functionality we created for the tool. Since slate code is very verbose, as you will soon see, it really helps to break it down into smaller pieces like this. Let's take a look at the implementation. In /Plugins/MarsEditor/Source/MarsEditor/Private/EditorMode/ create MarsEditorModeWidget.cpp and add the following code.

```
#include "EditorMode/MarsEditorModeWidget.h"

#include "Widgets/Input/SSegmentedControl.h"

#include "MarsEditorUserSettings.h"
#include "Mars/MarsSpawner.h"

void SMarsEditorWidget::Construct(const FArguments& _args)
{
  SetupSpawnerWidgets();

  ChildSlot[
    SNew(SScrollBox)
      + SScrollBox::Slot()
      [
        SpawnerExpandableArea.ToSharedRef()
      ]
  ];
 }

FMarsEditorMode* SMarsEditorWidget::GetEdMode() const
{
  return
(FMarsEditorMode*)GLevelEditorModeTools().GetActiveMode
(FMarsEditorMode::EM_MarsEditorMode);
}
```

In the `Construct` function we first call our setup function (we will implement it soon) and then we add a `SScrollBox` with our spawner tool widget inside of it to the `ChildSlot`. If we had another tool, we would just add another `SScrollBox` slot and the widget for that tool. Once we have multiple tools, we can still swap them around quite easily with this structure. Then we have the `GetEdMode` helper, we will be using this a bit soon and it saves us some precious space. Ok time to look at SetupSpawnerWidget. Since there are plenty of resources that explain how Slate works, I will not dig too deep into how this code works. And frankly you do not need to understand how the code works under the hood, just how to use it. Anyways, let's start taking a look at our widgets.

```
void SMarsEditorWidget::SetupSpawnerWidgets()
{
  SAssignNew(SpawnerToolTeam, SHorizontalBox)
```

```
    + SHorizontalBox::Slot()
    .AutoWidth()
    .VAlign(VAlign_Center)
    [
      SNew(STextBlock)
        .Text(FText::FromString("Team "))
    ]
    + SHorizontalBox::Slot()
    .AutoWidth()
    .VAlign(VAlign_Center)
    [
      SNew(SSegmentedControl<uint32>)
        .SupportsMultiSelection(false)
        .Values_Lambda([this]()
          {
          TArray<uint32> values;
          FMarsEditorMode* editorMode = GetEdMode();
          if (editorMode != nullptr)
          {
            values.Add(static_cast<uint32>
            (editorMode->SpawnerTool.SelectedTeam));
           }
           return values;
        })
          .OnValuesChanged_Lambda([this](TArray<uint32>
          _newTeams)
        {
          FMarsEditorMode* editorMode = GetEdMode();
          if (editorMode != nullptr && _newTeams.IsEmpty() ==
          false)
          {
            editorMode->SpawnerTool.SelectedTeam =
            static_cast<ETeams>(_newTeams[0]);
          }
       })
       + SSegmentedControl<uint32>::Slot
(static_cast<uint32>(ETeams::Red))
        .Text(FText::FromString("Red"))
        + SSegmentedControl<uint32>::Slot(static_cast<uint32>
(ETeams::Blue))
        .Text(FText::FromString("Blue"))
    ];
//TODO: More code goes here
```

This is the first line of our widget. We create a horizontal box and first we add a simple `STextBlock` as a header, then following that we add a `SSegmentedControl` widget. This widget supports multiselection, meaning the user can click on several options at the same time. Not something we want for this tool, so we disable that. Then we hook up a lambda for getting the value, which we get from our spawner tool helper class by digging it out from the editor more. Then we do the same, but for when the value is changed, we set it back into our class. Finally, we add our two values to the segment controller, Red and Blue. We could of course use another type of widget if we wanted, like the `SComboBox` (a dropdown widget). But we will make use of that one later in the book. Next line is really the same thing, but for choosing the class instead of the team, let's take a look at it.

```
SAssignNew(SpawnerToolClass, SHorizontalBox)
  + SHorizontalBox::Slot()
  .AutoWidth()
  .VAlign(VAlign_Center)
  [
    SNew(STextBlock)
      .Text(FText::FromString("Class "))
  ]
  + SHorizontalBox::Slot()
  .AutoWidth()
  .VAlign(VAlign_Center)
  [
    SNew(SSegmentedControl<uint32>)
      .SupportsMultiSelection(false)
      .Values_Lambda([this]()
      {
        TArray<uint32> values;
        FMarsEditorMode* editorMode = GetEdMode();
        if (editorMode != nullptr)
        {
          values.Add(static_cast<uint32>
          (editorMode->SpawnerTool.SelectedClass));
        }
        return values;
      })
      .OnValuesChanged_Lambda([this](TArray<uint32> _newTeams)
      {
        FMarsEditorMode* editorMode = GetEdMode();
        if (editorMode != nullptr && _newTeams.IsEmpty() ==
        false)
        {
          editorMode->SpawnerTool.SelectedClass =
          static_cast<EClasses>(_newTeams[0]);
        }
       })
       + SSegmentedControl<uint32>::Slot(static_cast<uint32>
       (EClasses::Pilot))
       .Text(FText::FromString("Pilot"))
       + SSegmentedControl<uint32>::Slot(static_cast<uint32>
       (EClasses::Navigator))
       .Text(FText::FromString("Navigator"))
       + SSegmentedControl<uint32>::Slot(static_cast<uint32>
       (EClasses::Commander))
       .Text(FText::FromString("Commander"))
```

```
        + SSegmentedControl<uint32>::Slot(static_cast<uint32>
        (EClasses::Gunner))
        .Text(FText::FromString("Gunner"))
];
```

Not much to say about it that we didn't already cover. Let's move on.

```
SAssignNew(SpawnerToolButtons, SHorizontalBox)
    + SHorizontalBox::Slot()
    .AutoWidth()
    .VAlign(VAlign_Center)
    [
      SNew(SButton)
        .Text(FText::FromString(TEXT("Apply on selection")))

        .ToolTip(FSlateApplication::Get().MakeToolTip(FText::
FromString(TEXT("Applies current settings on selection"))))
        .HAlign(HAlign_Center)
        .OnClicked_Lambda([this]()
        {
          FMarsEditorMode* editorMode = GetEdMode();
          if (editorMode != nullptr)
          {
            editorMode->SpawnerTool.
ApplySettingsOnSelection();
          }
          return FReply::Handled();
        })
    ]
    + SHorizontalBox::Slot()
    .AutoWidth()
    .VAlign(VAlign_Center)
    [
      SNew(SButton)
        .Text(FText::FromString(TEXT("Select matching")))

        .ToolTip(FSlateApplication::Get().MakeToolTip
(FText::FromString(TEXT("Finds and selects all spawners
matching settings"))))
        .HAlign(HAlign_Center)
        .OnClicked_Lambda([this]()
        {
          FMarsEditorMode* editorMode = GetEdMode();
          if (editorMode != nullptr)
          {
            editorMode->SpawnerTool.SelectSpawnersMatching
(editorMode->SpawnerTool.SelectedTeam, editorMode-
>SpawnerTool.SelectedClass);
          }
          return FReply::Handled();
        })
    ];
```

The next horizontal box we set up is for the buttons. We create two buttons, give them a name and a tooltip. Then when clicking them we simple call our functions in our helper class. Almost done, now we just need to add the horizontal widgets into an expandable area widget.

```
  const UMarsEditorUserSettings* editorUserSettings =
GetDefault< UMarsEditorUserSettings >();
  SAssignNew(SpawnerExpandableArea, SExpandableArea)
    .BorderBackgroundColor(FLinearColor(0.4f, 0.4f, 0.4f,
1.0f))
    .Padding(4.0f)
    .InitiallyCollapsed(editorUserSettings->SpawnerExpanded)
    .OnAreaExpansionChanged_Lambda([this](const bool&
_isExpanded)
    {
      UMarsEditorUserSettings* editorUserSettings =
GetMutableDefault< UMarsEditorUserSettings >();
      if (editorUserSettings != nullptr)
      {
        editorUserSettings->SpawnerExpanded = !_isExpanded;
        editorUserSettings->SaveConfig();
      }
    })
    .AreaTitle(FText::FromString("Spawner"))
    .BodyContent()
    [
      SNew(SScrollBox)
        + SScrollBox::Slot()
        [
        SpawnerToolTeam.ToSharedRef()
        ]
        + SScrollBox::Slot()
        [
        SpawnerToolClass.ToSharedRef()
        ]
        + SScrollBox::Slot()
        [
          SpawnerToolButtons.ToSharedRef()
        ]
    ];
}
```

The expandable area widget allows the user to collapse the entire widget, and we can place whatever widget we want inside it, in the `BodyContent` field. Now once we have several tools, each with their own expandable area widget, it would be quite nice to save their collapse status for each user, so they can keep their favourite tool expanded and collapse everything else. Let's create the settings class, in /Plugins/MarsEditor/Source/MarsEditor/Public/ create MarsEditorUserSettings.h and add the following code.

```
#pragma once

#include "CoreMinimal.h"

#include "MarsEditorUserSettings.generated.h"

UCLASS(config = MarsEditorUserSettings)
class UMarsEditorUserSettings : public UObject
{
  GENERATED_BODY()

public:

  UPROPERTY(config)
  bool SpawnerExpanded = true;
};
```

Like the settings file we created before, but we skipped the `defaultconfig` keyword to make this setting file local instead of shared.

```
#include "MarsEditorUserSettings.h"
void FMarsEditorModule::StartupModule()
{
 //...
 if (ISettingsModule* settingsModule = FModuleManager::GetModu
lePtr<ISettingsModule>("Settings"))
 {
  //...
settingsModule->RegisterSettings("Editor", "Mars",
"MarsUserSettings", FText::FromString(TEXT("Mars Editor User
Settings")),
 FText::FromString("Mars plugin user settings"), GetMutableDef
ault<UMarsEditorUserSettings>());
 }
}
```

```
#pragma once
#include "EditorModeManager.h"
#include "Toolkits/BaseToolkit.h"
#include "EditorMode/MarsEditorMode.h"
#include "EditorMode/MarsEditorModeWidget.h"

class FEdMode;
class SWdiget;

class FMarsEditorModeToolkit : public FModeToolkit
{
public:
 virtual void Init(const TSharedPtr<IToolkitHost>&
_toolkitHost, TWeakObjectPtr<UEdMode> _owningMode) override;
 virtual TSharedPtr< SWidget > GetInlineContent() const
override;
 virtual FEdMode* GetEditorMode() const override;
```

```
 virtual FName GetToolkitFName() const override;
 virtual FText GetBaseToolkitName() const override;
private:
 TSharedPtr< SMarsEditorWidget > EditorModeWidget;
};

#include "EditorMode/MarsEditorModeToolkit.h"
void FMarsEditorModeToolkit::Init
(const TSharedPtr<IToolkitHost>& _toolkitHost,
TWeakObjectPtr<UEdMode> _owningMode)
{
 SAssignNew(EditorModeWidget, SMarsEditorWidget);
 FModeToolkit::Init(_toolkitHost, _owningMode);
}
TSharedPtr< SWidget > FMarsEditorModeToolkit::
GetInlineContent() const
{
 return EditorModeWidget;
}
FEdMode* FMarsEditorModeToolkit::GetEditorMode() const
{
 return GLevelEditorModeTools().GetActiveMode(FMarsEditorMode::
EM_MarsEditorMode);
}
FName FMarsEditorModeToolkit::GetToolkitFName() const
{
 return FName("MarsEditorMode");
}
FText FMarsEditorModeToolkit::GetBaseToolkitName() const
{
 return FText::FromString("MarsEditorMode Toolkit");
}
```

We are almost done now, our toolkit and the widget for it is done, but we still need to add it and our helper tool to our editor mode class. In MarsEditorMode.h add the following include and variable in the class.

```
#include "EditorMode/MarsEditorSpawnerPlacerTool.h"
//...
FMarsEditorSpawnerPlacerTool SpawnerTool;
```

That's all for the .h file, we need to do a bit more in the .cpp file however.

```
#include "EditorMode/MarsEditorModeToolkit.h"

void FMarsEditorMode::Enter()
{
  FEdMode::Enter();

  if (!Toolkit.IsValid())
```

```
  {
    Toolkit = MakeShareable(new FMarsEditorModeToolkit);
    Toolkit->Init(Owner->GetToolkitHost());
  }

  CommandList = MakeShareable(new FUICommandList);

  ReimportAsset.Init(CommandList);
  SpawnerTool.Init(CommandList);
}
```

Here we create our toolkit, which will create our widget and assign that to our editor mode's toolkit. Then we also initialize our helper class.

```
void FMarsEditorMode::Exit()
{
  FEdMode::Exit();

  SpawnerTool.UnInit();
}
```

For this helper class we also needed to do some cleanup, so we add the uninitialize function in our Exit function.

```
bool FMarsEditorMode::HandleClick(FEditorViewportClient* _
viewportClient, HHitProxy* _hitProxy, const FViewportClick&
_click)
{
  if (CopyMaterial.HandleClick(_viewportClient, _hitProxy,
_click))
  {
    return true;
  }
  else if (SpawnerTool.HandleClick(_viewportClient, _hitProxy,
_click))
  {
    return true;
  }
  return FEdMode::HandleClick(_viewportClient, _hitProxy,
_click);
}
```

Finally, we also add it in our `HandleClick` function. That's it, we are finally done! Try out the tool now. We can quickly place multiple spawners with the settings we want and find all matching our setting with just one button click. We added several tools to our editor mode and created a good foundation for our future tool by creating another module, some helper libraries and multiple settings files.

FEdMode vs UEdMode

We have one last thing to discuss before we are done with this chapter. The editor mode we created inherited from `FEdMode`, however there is also an `UEdMode`. This can be quite confusing since their names are extremely similar and at a first glance, they might look very similar, but they have some big differences. The biggest is that `UEdMode` can make use of Unreal's reflection system. This means you can have `UPROPERTY` straight in your class and it will be exposed to the user without having to do your own slate code. Sounds great right? The drawback with this is that it's a lot more setup needed, your tool will need to be split up into several classes and by default you can't even click on things in the viewport. Personally, I prefer using `FEdMode`, especially when starting with doing editor mode. It's faster to get up and running. However, if you are going to do a bigger editor mode that is not a collection of random tools, but doing something very specific (like the mesh painting mode) it can make sense to base it on `UEdMode`. That said a lot of advanced editor modes are based on `FEdMode`, like the landscape editor mode. They both have their pros and cons. If you are curious, do explore `UEdMode` and try it out.

2 Toolbar

The editor mode is a great place to put functionality that not everyone needs, or at least not all the time. But some of the tools we will make we want to always be accessible; in this chapter we will extend the toolbar with our own buttons and menus.

We will extend the toolbar with four different tools, showing different ways of adding buttons and menus to the toolbar. We will extend the tools menu at the top of the editor with one of our tools as well.

BugItGo

The BugItGo command in Unreal will teleport the camera to a specific coordinate. It's very useful when reporting or dealing with bugs, having a coordinate that leads directly to the issue saves a lot of time. While you can just type it into the console, we will make two buttons for it to make it even easier to use. The first button will copy the current position into the clipboard so you can easily send the coordinate to someone. The second button will read the clipboard and teleport the camera to that position. A small, but very useful tool.

The first thing we will need to do is add our commands. They can go in the same command file as we put out editor mode commands, since we didn't make those commands specific for the editor mode but registered them from our module class. Add the following two variables in `FMarsEditorCommands`.

```
TSharedPtr< FUICommandInfo > BugItGoCopy;
TSharedPtr< FUICommandInfo > BugItGoPaste;
```

Then in the .cpp file set up the commands like this.

```
  UI_COMMAND(BugItGoCopy, "BugItGo Copy", "Copies the current
camera location and rotation to the clipboard", EUserInterface
ActionType::Button, FInputChord());
  UI_COMMAND(BugItGoPaste, "BugItGo Paste", "Moves the
camera to the current BugItGo location and rotation in the
clipboard", EUserInterfaceActionType::Button, FInputChord());
```

Very similar to how we did it in the editor mode, however this time we specify we want these commands to be a button command type. This lets Unreal know we want this to be displayed as a normal button, and we want a callback when the user clicks on it. There are other types of buttons you can specify here also (ToggleButton

DOI: 10.1201/9781003511748-3

and RadioButton for example) and we will cover some of these types later in this chapter.

Just like with the tools in the editor mode we will place these tools in their own small helper classes as well. Start with creating MarsEditorBugItGo.h in /Plugins/MarsEditor/Source/MarsEditor/Public/Toolbar/ and add the following code.

```
#pragma once

class FUICommandList;

class FMarsEditorBugItGo
{
public:
  void Init(TSharedPtr< FUICommandList >& _menuCommands);
  void RegisterMenus(TSharedPtr< FUICommandList >&
_menuCommands);

  void BugItGoCopy();
  void BugItGoPaste();
};
```

Very similar pattern as in our editor mode tool helper classes. We have the `Init` function that takes a command list, and we have our two Copy/Paste functions that will do the actual work. But then we have a `RegisterMenus` function also. This is because we need to do the actual registering to the toolbar at a later point then when our module is initialized. This will happen a bit later then our `Init` function. Let's start looking at the implementation of this class. In /Plugins/MarsEditor/Source/MarsEditor/Private/Toolbar/ add MarsEditorBugItGo.cpp and add the following code.

```
#include "Toolbar/MarsEditorBugItGo.h"

#include "Subsystems/UnrealEditorSubsystem.h"
#include "HAL/PlatformApplicationMisc.h"
#include "MarsSharedLibrary.h"

void FMarsEditorBugItGo::Init(TSharedPtr< FUICommandList >&
_menuCommands)
{
  _menuCommands->MapAction(
    FMarsEditorCommands::Get().BugItGoCopy,
    FExecuteAction::CreateRaw(this, &FMarsEditorBugItGo::
BugItGoCopy),
    FCanExecuteAction());

  _menuCommands->MapAction(
    FMarsEditorCommands::Get().BugItGoPaste,
    FExecuteAction::CreateRaw(this, &FMarsEditorBugItGo::
BugItGoPaste),
    FCanExecuteAction());
}
```

Just like we did in the editor mode tools we map our callback to the commands. We leave the `FCanExecuteAction` callback empty this time also. We could add one for the paste command if we wanted to and then check if we have a valid string in the clipboard. This way our button would be greyed our when the use does not have a valid string to teleport to. However, this function will be called a lot and since we need to do some string operations on the buffer in the clipboard it can cause some performance issues, because of this I do not think it's worth it in this case so we leave the callback empty, meaning we can always execute our command.

Next up is registering our commands to the toolbar where we want them.

```
void FMarsEditorBugItGo::RegisterMenus(TSharedPtr<
FUICommandList >& _menuCommands)
{
  UToolMenu* toolbarMenu = UToolMenus::Get()
->ExtendMenu("LevelEditor.LevelEditorToolBar.PlayToolBar");
  {
    FToolMenuSection& section = toolbarMenu->FindOrAddSection
("MarsPluginTools");
    {
     FToolMenuEntry& entryCopy = section.AddEntry
(FToolMenuEntry::InitToolBarButton(FMarsEditorCommands::Get().
BugItGoCopy));
     entryCopy.Icon = FSlateIcon(FMarsEditorModule::GetStyle
SetName(), "MarsEditor.CameraCopy", "MarsEditor.CameraCopy.
Small");
     entryCopy.StyleNameOverride = FName("Toolbar.
BackplateLeft");
     entryCopy.SetCommandList(_menuCommands);

     FToolMenuEntry& entryPaste = section.AddEntry
(FToolMenuEntry::InitToolBarButton(FMarsEditorCommands::Get().
BugItGoPaste));
   entryPaste.Icon = FSlateIcon(FMarsEditorModule::GetStyle
SetName(), "MarsEditor.CameraPaste", "MarsEditor.CameraPaste.
Small");
     entryPaste.StyleNameOverride = FName("Toolbar.
BackplateRight");
     entryPaste.SetCommandList(_menuCommands);
    }
  }
}
```

There's a bit more going on here that we need to go through. In the first line we are getting the menu we want to extend. There are a lot of menus in Unreal we can choose to extend. You can do a search on `UToolMenus::Get()->RegisterMenu(` to find all menus that register themselves. We can extend any off them if we want to. After that we find the `MarsPluginTools` section. We create our own section here so we don't risk any other plugins getting mixed up with us, if we want, we can also create different sections for different tools we create, if we need to separate them a bit if we end up with too many tools.

Next up, we create our entry and add it to our section. Then comes the most important part, we use a helper function for getting our command setup for the toolbar. This is what controls the behaviour of what we are adding, should it be a button? A dropdown? A submenu? Or we can add our own widget here if we want to do something custom. We will cover more functions here later in this chapter to see what is possible. After this we set what icon (and from what styleset) we should use and then what style we want to use. Here I'm adding my own icon, we will cover how to add these icons soon. There are plenty of useful styles that already exists in the editor, so here I will be using the left/right backplate (there's also a centre of course) to group my two buttons together. If we wanted to, we could create our completely own style for this. That would not only let us control the look of our button, but also the behaviour when we hover over the icon or press it. But for now, we will stick with the default styles.

Finally, we set the command list, where we added what callback should be connected to what command. This is how the button will know what callback to call. Now we have our two commands as button in the toolbar, and they will be nicely grouped together since we went with the backplate style for them. Next up is our copy function.

```
void FMarsEditorBugItGo::BugItGoCopy()
{
  FVector location;
  FRotator rotation;
  UUnrealEditorSubsystem* unrealEditorSubsystem = GEditor
->GetEditorSubsystem< UUnrealEditorSubsystem >();
  unrealEditorSubsystem->GetLevelViewportCameraInfo(location,
rotation);

  FString consoleBugIt = FString::Printf(TEXT("BugItGo %f %f
%f %f %f %f"), location.X, location.Y, location.Z, rotation.
Pitch,
    rotation.Yaw, rotation.Roll);

  FPlatformApplicationMisc::ClipboardCopy(*consoleBugIt);

  UMarsFeedbackLibrary::AddNotification("Copy BugItGo",
consoleBugIt, EMarsNotificationType::Success);
}
```

Thankfully Unreal has all the helpers we need to get the viewport location and to copy a string into the clipboard. We use these helpers to get the location and the rotation and build our BugItGo string and then copy that into the clipboard. Of course, we also show a notification for the user that we have succeeded. We always want feedback on our tools! Lastly, we have the paste function.

```
void FMarsEditorBugItGo::BugItGoPaste()
{
  FString clipboard;
```

```
  FPlatformApplicationMisc::ClipboardPaste(clipboard);

  if (clipboard.RemoveFromStart(TEXT("BugItGo ")) == false)
  {
    UMarsSharedLibrary::AddNotification("Paste BugItGo",
"Not a valid BugItGo string in the clipboard",
EMarsNotificationType::Fail);
    return;
  }
  FVector location;
  FRotator rotation;
  TArray< float > values;

  // Split the string
  while (!clipboard.IsEmpty())
  {
    FString newString;
    clipboard.Split(TEXT(" "), &newString, &clipboard);

    if (newString.IsEmpty())
    {
     clipboard.Reset();
     newString = clipboard;
    }

    values.Emplace_GetRef() = FCString::Atof(*newString);
    if (values.Num() >= 6)
    {
      break;
    }
  }
  bool validPos = false;
  if (values.Num() >= 3)
  {
    location = FVector(values[0], values[1], values[2]);
    validPos = true;
  }
  if (values.Num() >= 6)
  {
    rotation = FRotator(values[3], values[4], values[5]);
  }
  if (validPos)
  {
    UUnrealEditorSubsystem* unrealEditorSubsystem =
GEditor->GetEditorSubsystem< UUnrealEditorSubsystem >();
    unrealEditorSubsystem->SetLevelViewportCameraInfo
(location, rotation);
  }
  else
  {
    UMarsSharedLibrary::AddNotification("Paste BugItGo",
"We failed to find a valid position in the clipboard",
EMarsNotificationType::Fail);
```

```
    }
}
```

There's a bit more going on here since we need to dig out the position and rotation from a string and there's several error cases we need to handle and give feedback to the user, so they know why nothing happened when they click the button if we failed to find a valid BugItGo string. Currently this function only handles BugItGo strings, but it could certainly be extended to handle other type of string. For example, of you copy a position in Unreal you get it like this X=42.0 Y=42.0 Z=42.0, which this function currently doesn't handle. I will leave it to you to extend it to handle that case however!

We are almost done, but we must edit MarsEditorModule a bit. Add the following code to the header.

```
#include "Toolbar/MarsEditorBugItGo.h"
//...
class FMarsEditorModule : public IModuleInterface
{
  //...
  void RegisterMenus();
private:
  TSharedPtr< FUICommandList > MenuCommands;
  FMarsEditorBugItGo BugItGo;
};
```

Just like we have a command list in our editor mode, we will also have one here in our module. Now let's go to the cpp file.

```
void FMarsEditorModule::StartupModule()
{
  //...
  MenuCommands = MakeShareable(new FUICommandList);

  BugItGo.Init(MenuCommands);

UToolMenus::RegisterStartupCallback(FSimpleMulticastDelegate
::FDelegate::CreateRaw(this, &FMarsEditorModule::RegisterMenu
s));
}
```

We create our new command list and pass it in our Init function for our `BugItGo` helper class. Then we register to get a callback when the engine is ready to receive menu registrations. We cannot do it here inside of `StartupModule`, it's too early in the initialization process.

```
void FMarsEditorModule::RegisterMenus()
{
  FToolMenuOwnerScoped ownerScoped(this);

  BugItGo.RegisterMenus(MenuCommands);
```

```
}
```

FToolMenuOwnerScoped is a helper for making sure everything we register gets the correct owner set, everything we register until it goes out of scope will get our module as an owner. We are almost done, but we must also register the two new icons we have started using. In RegisterStyleSet add the following lines right after where we added the editor mode icons.

```
  StyleSet->Set("MarsEditor.CameraCopy", new IMAGE
_BRUSH("CameraCopy", Icon40x40));
  StyleSet->Set("MarsEditor.CameraCopy.Small", new IMAGE
_BRUSH("CameraCopy", Icon20x20));

  StyleSet->Set("MarsEditor.CameraPaste", new IMAGE
_BRUSH("CameraPaste", Icon40x40));
  StyleSet->Set("MarsEditor.CameraPaste.Small", new IMAGE
_BRUSH("CameraPaste", Icon20x20));
```

This will register CameraCopy.png and CameraPaste.png in /Plugins/MarsEditor/Resources/. Now there is only one last thing to do, we must add two new modules in our MarsEditor.Build.cs since we have started using them in our plugin. So, add the following lines in PrivateDependencyModuleNames.

```
"ApplicationCore",
"TooMenus"
```

That's it, you can compile and test it out! The tool itself is quite easy, but useful and we have learned how to add our own buttons to the toolbar.

EDITOR LIGHT

The next tool we will add is an editor light, a light that follow the camera so we can more easily see what we are working on if it's a dark level. We will also add a drop-down menu to our light button with some settings that we are going to save between sessions. As with the BugItGo buttons, the first thing we need to do is add our new command, so in MarsEditorCommands.h add this.

```
TSharedPtr< FUICommandInfo > EditorLight;
```

And then in the cpp file add this

```
UI_COMMAND(EditorLight, "Toggle Editor Light", "Toggles a
light attached to editor camera on/off", EUserInterfaceAction
Type::ToggleButton, FInputChord());
```

This time we are making use of the ToggleButton type, since we want to toggle the light on and off and with this type of button, it will show the state for us. We will create a little helper class to handle the light, just like we did with the BugItGo functionality. Create MarsEditorLight.h in /Plugins/MarsEditor/Source/MarsEditor/Public/Toolbar/ and add the following code

```
#pragma once

class SWidget;
class FUICommandList;
class APointLight;

class FMarsEditorLight
{
public:
  void Init(TSharedPtr< FUICommandList >& _menuCommands);
  void Shutdown();
  void RegisterMenus(TSharedPtr< FUICommandList >&
_menuCommands);

  void SetEditorLight(bool _on);
  void ToggleEditorLight() { SetEditorLight(
!IsEditorLightOn() ); }
  bool IsEditorLightOn() const { return EditorLight !=
nullptr; }
  bool EditorLightTick(float _deltaTime);
  TSharedRef< SWidget > GenerateEditorLightOptionMenuContent();

  void OnMapChanged( UWorld* _world, EMapChangeType _type );

private:
  TObjectPtr< APointLight > EditorLight;
  FTSTicker::FDelegateHandle EditorLightTickHandle;
};
```

There are more functions here then you might have expected. We will soon go through them one by one. But first a note on our EditorLight pointer. Since our class is not a UCLASS() we cannot use UPROPERTY() to hold our editor light variable like this.

```
  UPROPERTY()
  APointLight* EditorLight;
```

This is how we would normally store a pointer like this in Unreal, but this is only safe in a UCLASS(), which our helper class is not. This means we must be a bit more careful with our pointer handling so we don't end up using a dangling pointer, that's why we need to use TObjectPtr instead. Now create MarsEditorLight.cpp in /Plugins/MarsEditor/Source/MarsEditor/Private/Toolbar/ and add the following code.

```
#include "Toolbar/MarsEditorLight.h"

#include "Engine/PointLight.h"
#include "Components/PointLightComponent.h"
```

```
#include "Components/BillboardComponent.h"
#include "LevelEditorViewport.h"
#include "Widgets/Input/SSpinBox.h"
#include "MarsEditorCommands.h"
#include "MarsEditorUserSettings.h"

void FMarsEditorLight::Init(TSharedPtr< FUICommandList >&
_menuCommands)
{
  _menuCommands->MapAction(
    FMarsEditorCommands::Get().EditorLight,
    FExecuteAction::CreateRaw(this, &FMarsEditorLight::
ToggleEditorLight),
    FCanExecuteAction(),
    FIsActionChecked::CreateRaw(this, &FMarsEditorLight::
IsEditorLightOn));

  FLevelEditorModule& levelEditor = FModuleManager::
LoadModuleChecked<FLevelEditorModule> ("LevelEditor");
  levelEditor.OnMapChanged().AddRaw(this, &FMarsEditorLight::
OnMapChanged);
}
```

As you might have expected, we start with registering our callback we want to connect to our command. However, this time we are adding a function for if we are active or not since we have defined ourselves as a togglable button earlier, this function is what will be used to determine what state our button should be in. Again, we leave the `CanExecuteAction` empty, meaning we can always execute. Then we register a callback for it we change map, this is because we need to cleanup our light if it's active before we switch map. Since we registered the map change callback, we also need to remove it when shutting down.

```
void FMarsEditorLight::Shutdown()
{
  if (FLevelEditorModule* levelEditor = FModuleManager::
GetModulePtr<FLevelEditorModule>("LevelEditor"))
  {
    levelEditor->OnMapChanged().RemoveAll(this);
  }
}
```

And the function for changing maps.

```
void FMarsEditorLight::OnMapChanged(UWorld* _world,
EMapChangeType _type)
{
  SetEditorLight(false);
}
```

We simple turn off our light, which will destroy it, we must clean everything up to avoid crashes. Next up, registering our button to the toolbar menu.

```
void FMarsEditorLight::RegisterMenus(TSharedPtr<
FUICommandList >& _menuCommands)
{
  UToolMenu* toolbarMenu = UToolMenus::
Get()->ExtendMenu("LevelEditor.LevelEditorToolBar.PlayToolBar");
  {
    FToolMenuSection& section = toolbarMenu->FindOrAddSection
("MarsPluginTools");
    {
      FToolMenuEntry& entry = section.AddEntry(FToolMenuEntry
::InitToolBarButton(FMarsEditorCommands::Get().EditorLight));
      entry.Icon = FSlateIcon(FMarsEditorModule::GetStyleSet
Name(), "MarsEditor.EditorLight", "MarsEditor.EditorLight.
Small");
      entry.StyleNameOverride = FName("Toolbar.
BackplateLeft");
      entry.SetCommandList(_menuCommands);
      {
        FUIAction menuAction;
        menuAction.CanExecuteAction = FCanExecuteAction();

        FToolMenuEntry comboEntry = FToolMenuEntry::
InitComboButton("EditorLightOptions", menuAction,
         FOnGetContent::CreateRaw(this, &FMarsEditorLight::
GenerateEditorLightOptionMenuContent),
         FText(), FText::FromString(TEXT("Editor Light
Options")));

        comboEntry.StyleNameOverride = FName("Toolbar.
BackplateRightCombo");
        section.AddEntry(comboEntry);
      }
    }
  }
}
```

We start with adding our button, with icon and the command list for the callback connected to the command. But then we also create a new UI action that we use to register a new combo button with. Combo button is Unreals name for a button the pops another widget when you click on it. In this case we want a dropdown menu to open when we click this button, where we will place some settings. We give it our callback for this, `GenerateEditorLightOptionMenuContent`, in the `FOnGetContent` parameter. Finally, we give this button the style of `BackplateRightCombo`, this will give our button three small dots, like the Play/Stop/Eject toolbar buttons have.

Before we take a look at the dropdown menu creation, let's finish the light creation first.

```
void FMarsEditorLight::SetEditorLight(bool _on)
{
  if (_on == IsEditorLightOn())
  {
    return;
  }
  if (_on)
  {
    if (!EditorLightTickHandle.IsValid() && GEditor)
    {
      EditorLightTickHandle = FTSTicker::GetCoreTicker().
AddTicker(
        FTickerDelegate::CreateRaw(this, &FMarsEditorLight::
EditorLightTick));

      FEditorViewportClient* editorViewClient =
GCurrentLevelEditingViewportClient;
      if (editorViewClient)
      {
        UWorld* world = GEditor->GetEditorWorldContext().
World();
        FActorSpawnParameters spawnParams;
        spawnParams.ObjectFlags &= ~RF_Transactional;
        spawnParams.ObjectFlags |= RF_Transient;
        spawnParams.bTemporaryEditorActor = true;
        spawnParams.bCreateActorPackage = false;
        spawnParams.bHideFromSceneOutliner = true;
        spawnParams.bNoFail = true;

        EditorLight = world->SpawnActor< APointLight
>(editorViewClient->GetViewLocation(), FRotator::ZeroRotator,
spawnParams);


        EditorLight->PointLightComponent->LightColor =
FColor::White;
        EditorLight->PointLightComponent->CastShadows = false;
        EditorLight->PointLightComponent->
VolumetricScatteringIntensity = 0.0f;
        EditorLight->PointLightComponent->Mobility =
EComponentMobility::Movable;
        EditorLight->bIsEditorOnlyActor = true;

        UBillboardComponent* billboard = EditorLight->Get
ComponentByClass<UBillboardComponent>();
        if (billboard != nullptr)
        {
         billboard->SetVisibility(false);
        }
```

```
        const UMarsEditorUserSettings* settings = GetDefault<
UMarsEditorUserSettings >();
        EditorLight->PointLightComponent->SetIntensity
(settings->PointLightIntensity);
        EditorLight->PointLightComponent->SetAttenuationRadius
(settings->PointLightAttenuationRadius);
      }
    }
  }
  else
  {
    if (EditorLightTickHandle.IsValid())
    {
      FTSTicker::GetCoreTicker().RemoveTicker(EditorLightTick
Handle);
      EditorLightTickHandle.Reset();
    }
    if (EditorLight != nullptr)
    {
      EditorLight->Destroy(false, false);
      EditorLight = nullptr;
    }
  }
}
```

The first thing we do before creating our new light, is to register a new tick function. We will not actually attach the light to the viewport but rather move our light every tick to the current viewport. We then spawn a new light actor into our editor world, and we make sure this actor is temporary and will not be saved in our world in any way. We do this by giving it the `RF_Transient` flag, marking it as a temporary editor actor and also making sure we will not create a package for this actor. Then we also hide the actor from the outliner and finally set the spawn params to not allow failure. Then we spawn the actor and then set up some settings on the light component.

Once the light is spawned, we give it a colour, make sure it doesn't cast shadows and that it's movable, mark it as an editor only actor and finally we hide the billboard component on the light. Then we set the intensity and attenuation radius on it, but from our settings class. This is because we will allow the user to change these settings, and we want to save them between sessions. Then when turning off the light we just destroy it and unregister our tick function.

Before we continue on, let's add the setting variables to our settings files. Open MarsEditorUserSettings.h and add the following variables.

```
UPROPERTY(config)
float PointLightIntensity = 5000.0f;

UPROPERTY(config)
float PointLightAttenuationRadius = 3000.0f;
```

Now let's continue with our editor light helper class.

```
bool FMarsEditorLight::EditorLightTick(float _deltaTime)
{
  if (EditorLight != nullptr)
  {
    const FEditorViewportClient* editorViewClient =
GCurrentLevelEditingViewportClient;
    if (editorViewClient != nullptr)
    {
      EditorLight->SetActorLocation(editorViewClient
->GetViewLocation());
      EditorLight->SetActorRotation(editorViewClient
->GetViewRotation());
    }
  }
  return true;
}
```

Every tick, we simple set the light to our viewport position so it always follows the camera. The return true means we want to continue ticking. Time to look at how we will create our dropdown menu with settings. Like before we will split the widget up into smaller pieces so it's a bit more manageable.

```
TSharedRef< SWidget > FMarsEditorLight::
GenerateEditorLightOptionMenuContent()
{
TSharedPtr< SSpinBox<float> > intensitySpinBox;
SAssignNew(intensitySpinBox, SSpinBox<float>)
  .MinDesiredWidth(100.0f)
  .MinValue(100.0f)
  .MaxValue(20000.0f)
  .MinFractionalDigits(0)
  .MaxFractionalDigits(0)
  .OnValueChanged_Lambda([this](float _intensity)
  {

   UMarsEditorUserSettings* settings = GetMutableDefault<
UMarsEditorUserSettings >();
   settings->PointLightIntensity = _intensity;
   if (EditorLight != nullptr)
   {
     EditorLight->PointLightComponent->SetIntensity
(_intensity);
     if (FViewport* viewport = GEditor->GetActiveViewport())
     {
       viewport->InvalidateDisplay();
     }
   }
  })
```

```
  .OnValueCommitted_Lambda([this](float _intensity,
ETextCommit::Type _commitInfo)
  {
    UMarsEditorUserSettings* settings = GetMutableDefault<
UMarsEditorUserSettings >();
    settings->SaveConfig();
  })
  .Value_Lambda([this]() -> float
  {
    const UMarsEditorUserSettings* settings = GetDefault<
UMarsEditorUserSettings >();
    return settings->PointLightIntensity;
  });
```

We start with setting up a spin box for the intensity of our light. A spin box is a widget that allows the user to not just type in a number but also drag on the spinbox with the mouse to change the value. We give the widget a desired width, a min and max value. We also specify we don't want any fractional digits; they don't really help since the numbers are so large. Then we have a lambda for when the value in the spinbox changes. We set the value in our settings file, but we do not save the file. This is for performance reasons, saving the config file takes time and will lead to small freezes when using the mouse to update the value. We do however invalidate our viewport so it will re-render. This is so that we can see the changes of our value without having to click on the viewport to cause it to refresh.

When the value is committed, in other words when we have released the mouse button and stopped dragging it around, we do save the value to the config file. Lastly, we have a lambda to return our current value.

```
  TSharedPtr< SSpinBox<float> > radiusSpinBox;
  SAssignNew(radiusSpinBox, SSpinBox<float>)
    .MinDesiredWidth(100.0f)
    .MinValue(100.0f)
    .MaxValue(16384.0f)//Taken from LocalLightComponent.h
    .MinFractionalDigits(0)
    .MaxFractionalDigits(0)
    .OnValueChanged_Lambda([this](float _radius)
    {
      UMarsEditorUserSettings* settings = GetMutableDefault<
UMarsEditorUserSettings >();
      settings->PointLightAttenuationRadius = _radius;
      if (EditorLight != nullptr)
      {
        EditorLight->PointLightComponent->SetAttenuationRadius
(_radius);
        if (FViewport* viewport = GEditor->
GetActiveViewport())
        {
          viewport->InvalidateDisplay();
        }
```

```
      }
    })
    .OnValueCommitted_Lambda([this](float _radius, 
ETextCommit::Type _commitInfo)
    {
      UMarsEditorUserSettings* settings = GetMutableDefault< 
UMarsEditorUserSettings >();
      settings->SaveConfig();
    })
    .Value_Lambda([this]() -> float
    {
      const UMarsEditorUserSettings* settings = GetDefault< 
UMarsEditorUserSettings >();
      return settings->PointLightAttenuationRadius;
    });
```

The spinbox for the radius is almost identical, it's just working on a different variable

```
  TSharedRef< SWidget > lightSettings = SNew(SVerticalBox)
    + SVerticalBox::Slot()
    .AutoHeight()
    .Padding(5.0f)
    .VAlign(VAlign_Top)
    [
      SNew(SHorizontalBox)
        + SHorizontalBox::Slot()
        .AutoWidth()
        .Padding(3)
        [
          SNew(STextBlock)
            .Text(FText::FromString("Intensity: "))
        ]
        + SHorizontalBox::Slot()
        .AutoWidth()
        [
          intensitySpinBox.ToSharedRef()
        ]
    ]
    + SVerticalBox::Slot()
    .AutoHeight()
    .Padding(5.0f)
    .VAlign(VAlign_Top)
    [
      SNew(SHorizontalBox)
        + SHorizontalBox::Slot()
        .AutoWidth()
        .Padding(3)
        [
          SNew(STextBlock)
            .Text(FText::FromString("Radius: "))
```

```
        ]
        + SHorizontalBox::Slot()
        .AutoWidth()
        [
          radiusSpinBox.ToSharedRef()
        ]
    ];
  return lightSettings;
}
```

Finally, we create a vertical box and for each vertical slot we add a horizontal box where we add a text block, our header, and then our spinbox.

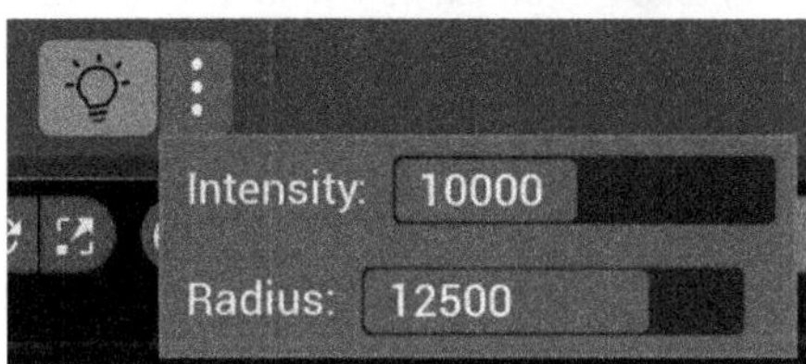

We are almost done, but we must still add our helper class to our module. Edit MarsEditorModule.h with this code.

```
#include "Toolbar/MarsEditorLight.h"

class FMarsEditorModule : public IModuleInterface
{
  //...
  FMarsEditorLight EditorLight;
  //...
};
```

Then in the .cpp file we need to add the following code.

```
void FMarsEditorModule::StartupModule()
{
  //...
  EditorLight.Init(MenuCommands);
}

void FMarsEditorModule::ShutdownModule()
{
  EditorLight.Shutdown();
  //...
}

void FMarsEditorModule::RegisterMenus()
{
  //...
```

```
  EditorLight.RegisterMenus(MenuCommands);
}
void FMarsEditorModule::RegisterStyleSet()
{
  //...
  StyleSet->Set("MarsEditor.EditorLight", new IMAGE_
BRUSH("EditorLight", Icon40x40));
  StyleSet->Set("MarsEditor.EditorLight.Small", new IMAGE_
BRUSH("EditorLight", Icon20x20));
  //...
}
```

Now our editor light is ready to be used! We have a nice toggle button for it in the toolbar and we can change settings on the light in a dropdown menu.

GAME SETTINGS

For our next tool, we will add some settings to the toolbar that will control the game. We will be adding an option for starting with god mode enabled and one option to choose which class to start with. Of course, neither option will actually do anything since we will not care about the actual implementation of god mode or starting class, we will just do the settings for this so we can read it from the game project. First thing we will do is create a settings file, just like with MarsEditorUserSettings, but that will be placed in our game project. We will place it there because we want to be able to access it from both the game project and from our editor module. Let's start with setting up this settings file so we have some data to work with. In /Source/Mars/Settings/ create MarsGameSettings.h and add the following code.

```
#pragma once

#include "CoreMinimal.h"

#include "Mars/MarsSpawner.h"

#include "MarsGameSettings.generated.h"

UCLASS(config = EditorPerProjectUserSettings)
class MARS_API UMarsGameSettings : public UObject
{
public:
  GENERATED_BODY()

  UPROPERTY(config, EditAnywhere, Category = "Cheat")
  bool StartWithGodMode = false;

  UPROPERTY(config, EditAnywhere, Category = "Cheat")
  EClasses SelectedClass = EClasses::Commander;
};
```

It's just like our editor settings file; we make it per user since we don't want to share these settings between people. Since we will be accessing this settings file from our editor module, we must add `MARS_API` to it. For the starting class we re-use the class enum we created for our spawner actor.

Let's move on to our helper class in our editor module. In /Plugins/MarsEditor/Source/MarsEditor/Public/Toolbar/ create MarsEditorGameSettings.h and add the following code.

```
#pragma once

class FMarsEditorGameSettings
{
public:
  void RegisterMenus();
private:
  TSharedRef< SWidget > GenerateOptionMenuContent();
  void GenerateSubMenuWidget(FMenuBuilder& _inMenuBuilder);
};
```

Just like our other tool, we will start with a `RegisterMenus` call where we will add ourselves to the toolbar. Then we have a function, `GenerateOptionMenuContent`, for the actual dropdown menu followed by a function, `GenerateSubMenuWidget`, for the submenu we will be creating. Time to look at the implementation. In /Plugins/MarsEditor/Source/MarsEditor/Private/Toolbar/ create MarsEditorGameSettings.cpp and start adding the following code.

```
#include "Toolbar/MarsEditorGameSettings.h"

#include "Mars/Settings/MarsGameSettings.h"

void FMarsEditorGameSettings::RegisterMenus()
{
  UToolMenu* toolbarMenu = UToolMenus::Get()->
ExtendMenu("LevelEditor.LevelEditorToolBar.PlayToolBar");
  FToolMenuSection& section = toolbarMenu->FindOrAddSection
("MarsPluginTools");
  {
    FUIAction menuAction;
    menuAction.CanExecuteAction = FCanExecuteAction();

    FToolMenuEntry comboEntry = FToolMenuEntry::InitCombo
Button("MarsEditor.Settings", menuAction,
      FOnGetContent::CreateRaw(this,
&FMarsEditorGameSettings::
GenerateOptionMenuContent),
      FText(), FText::FromString(TEXT("Mars Settings")));

    comboEntry.Icon = FSlateIcon(FMarsEditorModule::GetStyleSet
Name(), "MarsEditor.Settings", "MarsEditor.Settings.Small");
    section.AddEntry(comboEntry);
  }
}
```

Very similar to the editor light button we did, but this time we will not use the backplate style, since we only have one button and they are used to group a bunch of buttons together. This will give us our icon with a small arrow pointing down instead. Let's move on to the widgets for the dropdown.

```
TSharedRef< SWidget > FMarsEditorGameSettings::
GenerateOptionMenuContent()
{
  FMenuBuilder menuBuilder(false, nullptr);
  FUIAction godModeAction(
    FExecuteAction::CreateLambda([]()
    {
      UMarsGameSettings* settings = GetMutableDefault<
UMarsGameSettings >();
      settings->StartWithGodMode =
!settings->StartWithGodMode;
      settings->SaveConfig();
    }),
    FCanExecuteAction(),
    FIsActionChecked::CreateLambda([]()
    {
      const UMarsGameSettings* settings = GetDefault<
UMarsGameSettings >();
      return settings->StartWithGodMode;
    })
  );
  menuBuilder.AddMenuEntry(FText::FromString("God Mode"),
    FText::FromString("Toggle god mode on/off"),
    FSlateIcon(),
    godModeAction,
    NAME_None,
    EUserInterfaceActionType::ToggleButton);

  menuBuilder.AddSeparator();

  menuBuilder.AddSubMenu(FText::FromString("Starting class"),
FText::FromString("Select starting class"),
    FNewMenuDelegate::CreateRaw(this, &FMarsEditorGameSettings
::GenerateSubMenuWidget),
    false, FSlateIcon(), false);

  return menuBuilder.MakeWidget();
}
```

This time we are using the `FMenuBuilder` class to set up our menu, instead of manually creating all widgets like last time. This helper class has some useful helpers to make this process easier. We start with creating an action for checking godmode on/off. This action simple reads and changes the setting file we just created. We then add this action with the menubuilder and mark our action as a toggle button; this will give it a nice little checkbox. We then add a little separator; these are useful to keep your menus easier to navigate if they start getting lots of entries in them. In this little test menu, it's a bit of overkill though. Anyway, after that we use the menu builder to add a submenu.

The submenu takes a name, a tooltip and a delegate to the actual function that will be generating the widget for it. But it also takes a couple of bools that control how it will work. The first of the bools controls if we need to click the submenu to open it, or if hovering with the mouse is enough. We want to open the submenu on hover so we send in false, the next bool controls if the submenu should close automatically when we click in it. This would make sense if the thing we click on start an action of some sort, but since we are just changing settings, we want the submenu to remain open, thus we send in false here also. Ok let's look at the code to generate the submenu widget.

```
void FMarsEditorGameSettings::GenerateSubMenuWidget
(FMenuBuilder& _inMenuBuilder)
{
  for (int i = 0; i < (int)EClasses::Max; ++i)
  {
    EClasses currentClass = static_cast<EClasses>(i);
    FString currentClassName;
    switch (currentClass)
    {
    case EClasses::Pilot: currentClassName = FString("Pilot");
break;
    case EClasses::Navigator: currentClassName =
FString("Navigator"); break;
    case EClasses::Commander: currentClassName =
FString("Commander"); break;
    case EClasses::Gunner: currentClassName =
FString("Gunner"); break;
    }

    FUIAction selectClassAction(
      FExecuteAction::CreateLambda([currentClass]()
      {
        UMarsGameSettings* settings = GetMutableDefault<
UMarsGameSettings >();
        settings->SelectedClass = currentClass;
        settings->SaveConfig();
      }),
      FCanExecuteAction(),
      FIsActionChecked::CreateLambda([currentClass]()
      {
        const UMarsGameSettings* settings = GetDefault<
UMarsGameSettings >();
        return settings->SelectedClass == currentClass;
      })
    );
    _inMenuBuilder.AddMenuEntry(
      FText::FromString(currentClassName),
```

```
            FText::FromString(currentClassName),
            FSlateIcon(),
            selectClassAction,
            NAME_None,
            EUserInterfaceActionType::RadioButton
        );
    }
}
```

For submenus, we get a menu builder passed into us instead of having to return a widget. We loop through our enum and for each enum value we add a widget to the menu builder. We create an UI action that simply selects and saves our choice and also returns if this entry is selected. Then we add the entry to the menu builder. We skip the icon, but if we had icons for our classes, we should add them here also. Finally, we choose `RadioButton` as action type instead of a `ToggleButton`, the radio button style is supposed to be used for options that are mutually exclusive, which our starting class is since we can only have one. We could have used checkboxes here, but that goes against Unreal's standard. It's always better to have a consistent look into our tools.

We are almost done; we just need to add our helper class and icon to our module. Start with adding the following code to MarsEditor.h

```
#include "Toolbar/MarsEditorGameSettings.h"

class FMarsEditorModule : public IModuleInterface
{
  //...
  FMarsEditorGameSettings GameSettings;
};
```

And then the following code in the .cpp file.

```
void FMarsEditorModule::RegisterMenus()
{
  //...
  GameSettings.RegisterMenus();
}
void FMarsEditorModule::RegisterStyleSet()
{
  //...
  StyleSet->Set("MarsEditor.Settings", new IMAGE_
BRUSH("Settings", Icon40x40));
  StyleSet->Set("MarsEditor.Settings.Small", new IMAGE_
BRUSH("Settings", Icon20x20));
  //...
}
```

That is it! Now we have a working dropdown menu with a submenu in it that changes settings in our game project. This makes it very easy to set up common debug option you might need when developing your game like starting with god mode enabled.

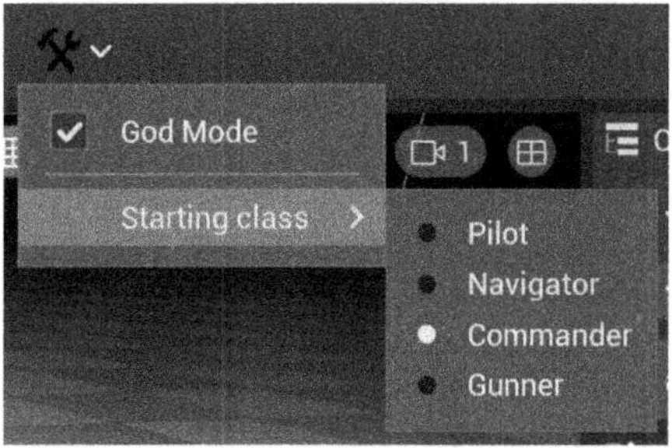

COMPILE ALL BLUEPRINTS

The next tool we will add is just going to be a button we can click. When we click it, we will go through and compile each Blueprint in the project. Unreal already has a commandlet that does this, so we will be launching that as an external process and read data back from it and use that to show the error in the message log and make the error clickable so you can quickly find them in the content browser. We will also add progress bar, since if we have a big project with several hundreds or thousands of Blueprints this operation will take several minutes.

So, first off, we need to add our command to FMarsEditorCommands.h.

```
TSharedPtr< FUICommandInfo > CompileAllBPs;
```

And the following code in RegisterCommands in the .cpp file.

```
UI_COMMAND(CompileAllBPs, "Compile All Blueprints", "Compiles
all blueprints in project and displays any errors", EUserInter
faceActionType::Button, FInputChord());
```

Nothing new here, just a simple button. Next up we will create our helper class. In /Plugins/MarsEditor/Source/MarsEditor/Public/Toolbar/ create MarsEditor CompileAllBP.h and add the following code.

```
#pragma once

class FUICommandList;

class FMarsEditorCompileAllBPs
{
public:
  void Init(TSharedPtr< FUICommandList >& _menuCommands);
  void RegisterMenus(TSharedPtr< FUICommandList >&
_menuCommands);

  void CompileAllBPs();
};
```

Same pattern as earlier helper classes. Now in /Plugins/MarsEditor/Source/MarsEditor/Private/Toolbar/ create MarsEditorCompileAllBP.cpp and add the following code.

```
#include "Toolbar/MarsEditorCompileAllBP.h"
#include "Misc/ScopedSlowTask.h"
void FMarsEditorCompileAllBPs::Init(TSharedPtr< FUICommandList
>& _menuCommands)
{
  _menuCommands->MapAction(
    FMarsEditorCommands::Get().CompileAllBPs,
    FExecuteAction::CreateRaw(this, &FMarsEditor
CompileAllBPs:: CompileAllBPs),
    FCanExecuteAction() );
}
```

Just like before, we map our callback function to our action. Next up is our RegisterMenu function.

```
void FMarsEditorCompileAllBPs::RegisterMenus(TSharedPtr<
FUICommandList >& _menuCommands)
{
  FSlateIcon compileIcon(FMarsEditorModule::GetStyleSetName(),
"MarsEditor.CompileAllBPs", "MarsEditor.CompileAllBPs.Small");
  UToolMenu* toolbarMenu = UToolMenus::
Get()->ExtendMenu("LevelEditor.LevelEditorToolBar.PlayToolBar");
  {
    FToolMenuSection& section = toolbarMenu->FindOrAddSection
("MarsPluginTools");
    FToolMenuEntry& entry = section.AddEntry(FToolMenuEntry::
InitToolBarButton(FMarsEditorCommands::Get().CompileAllBPs));
    entry.Icon = compileIcon;
    entry.SetCommandList(_menuCommands);
  }

  UToolMenu* toolMenu = UToolMenus::Get()->ExtendMenu
("LevelEditor.MainMenu.Tools");
  {
    FToolMenuSection& section = toolMenu->AddSection
("MarsPluginTools", FText::FromString("Mars Plugin Tools"));
    section.AddMenuEntryWithCommandList(FMarsEditorCommands
::Get().CompileAllBPs, _menuCommands, TAttribute<FText>(),
TAttribute<FText>(), compileIcon);
  }
}
```

The first part is just like our earlier tool, we get the toolbar menu and add our button to our section. Hower this time we also get the Tools menu in the main menu and add a section and our action to it. It's the same method, but instead of adding it in the toolbar, we have now added it in the tool's menu.

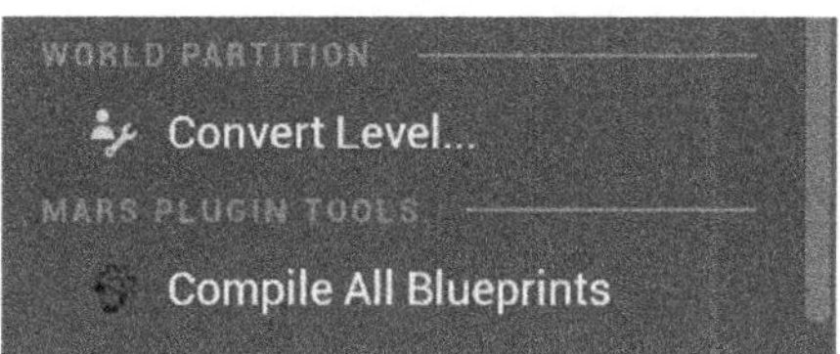

Now it's time to start looking into how we launch the compile all Blueprints commandlet. Let's begin with launching the commandlet and waiting on it to finish.

```
void FMarsEditorCompileAllBPs::CompileAllBPs()
{
  FString projFilePath = FPaths::GetProjectFilePath();
  FString unrealEditor = FPlatformProcess::ExecutablePath();
  FString params = projFilePath + " -run=CompileAllBlueprints
-IgnoreFolder=/Engine -unattended";

  void* pipeRead = nullptr;
  void* pipeWrite = nullptr;
  if (!FPlatformProcess::CreatePipe(pipeRead, pipeWrite))
  {
    return;
  }

  FProcHandle proc = FPlatformProcess::CreateProc
(*unrealEditor, *params, true, true, true, nullptr, 0,
nullptr, pipeWrite);

  FString stringOutput;
  if (proc.IsValid())
  {
    //TODO - Add progress bar
    do
    {
      FString thisRead = FPlatformProcess::ReadPipe(pipeRead);
      stringOutput += thisRead;

      //TODO - Update progress bar

      FPlatformProcess::Sleep( 0.5f );
    } while (FPlatformProcess::IsProcRunning(proc));

    //TODO - Replace with error code
  }

  FPlatformProcess::ClosePipe(pipeRead, pipeWrite);
  FPlatformProcess::CloseProc(proc);
}
```

Lot of things happening here, and we are not even displaying the results or progress yet! Let's walk through it step by step. We start with setting up what exe we want to launch and what parameters we want. In order to launch a commandlet we need to launch a new editor process, so we get the path to our executable. Then for the parameters we need our project path first. After the that we say we want to run the CompileAllBlueprints commandlet (which is a commandlet the engine comes with) by specifying it with -run=NameOfCommandlet. do note the space before the -run part, we need to separate the project path from our other parameters. -IgnoreFolder is a parameter for the commandlet, we can pass in multiple folders here (just separate them with a ,). We chose to ignore all engine Blueprints here. We will never change them so no need to waste time on compiling them. Then we also add the -unattended parameter which will stop any popups from being generated by our commandlet and is a global parameter.

We also need to create a read/write pipe to our process we will launch. It's through these pipes we will read and write data. In our case we will not be doing any writing of data to the commandlet but only read back data from it. We still need to create and hook up both pipes however.

After this we start the process, we give it the exe path and parameters we want to start. We specify we want the commandlet to be completely hidden.

Then as long as the process is running, we read all output from it and put it in our `stringOutput` variable, once the process is finished we close our read/write pipes and the process. The commandlet now runs, but we have no feedback on that it is running, and we don't show the result of it. Let's start with showing any errors we have from it, replace the "`//TODO - Replace with error code`" comment with the following code.

```
  TArray< FString > logFileAsArray;
  stringOutput.ParseIntoArrayLines(logFileAsArray);

  TArray< TSharedRef< FTokenizedMessage > > errorMessages;
  for (const FString& logLine : logFileAsArray)
  {
    if (logLine.Contains(TEXT("LogBlueprint: Error:"),
ESearchCase::IgnoreCase) ||
      logLine.Contains(TEXT("was pruned because its Exec pin
is not connected"), ESearchCase::IgnoreCase))
    {
      TSharedRef< FTokenizedMessage > message = FTokenized
Message::Create(EMessageSeverity::Error);
      FString messagePart;
      FString assetPart;

      if (logLine.Split(TEXT("from Source: "), &messagePart,
&assetPart))
      {
        message->AddToken(FAssetNameToken::Create(assetPart));
        messagePart.Split(TEXT("[Compiler] "), nullptr,
&messagePart);
        message->AddToken(FTextToken::Create(FText::FromString
(messagePart)));
      }
      else
      {
```

```
        message->AddToken(FTextToken::Create(FText::FromString
(logLine)));
      }

      // Do not add duplicate messages
      if (!errorMessages.ContainsByPredicate(
        [&](const TSharedRef< FTokenizedMessage >& _candidate)
        {
          return _candidate->ToText().CompareTo
(message->ToText()) == 0;
        }))
      {
        errorMessages.Add(message);
      }
    }
  }
  FMessageLog messageLog = FMessageLog("BlueprintLog");
  messageLog.NewPage(FText::FromString("Compile all
blueprints"));
  messageLog.AddMessages(errorMessages);
  messageLog.Open(EMessageSeverity::Error, true);
```

We start with breaking our huge string into an array, with one line for each element. Then we go through this array and see if the string contains “LogBlueprint: Error:” or a warning about someone using an exec pin that is not connected (this really should be an error and not a warning), feel free to add other warnings you want to catch easier here. In order to add our error lines with meta data so the user can click on them we are using the `FTokenizedMessage` struct, we are specifying it should be an error, but we could also post warnings or infos. We can also add a link to the actual asset, so when we click the error message it will navigate to the asset in the content browser. This is what we do if we can find the path, which we can if we have “`from Source:`” in our string, we also tidy up the string a bit by removing the “`[Compiler]`” string since it’s just taking up space. If we cannot find this string, we just add the error message directly without any link to our asset.

Error message tends to be generated multiple times for each error, so we make sure to not add duplicates to our `errorMessages` variable. Then we create a new page in the message log, this is so if we run the commandlet multiple times we get a new page for them, so we don’t look at old error messages by mistake. Finally, we add our errors to the message log and then we open it, we specify we want to open it even if we didn’t have any errors, an empty message log is better feedback that we succeeded then nothing.

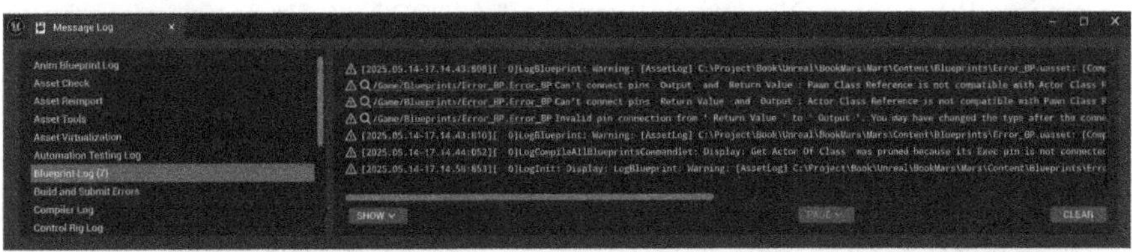

Only thing missing now is some feedback while the commandlet is running. We will be using the `FScopedSlowTask` for this, which will provide us with a popup with a progress bar we can update, we can also use this to get a cancel button so we could abort our execution if the user started it by mistake. Now in order for us to know our progress, we must know how many Blueprints we are going to compile and when each Blueprint is done. The commandlet prints a string for every Blueprint it compiles, but it never lists how many Blueprints it *will* compile. We need to fix this with a small engine modification in `UCompileAllBlueprintsCommandlet::BuildBlueprints`. Simply add these lines of code at the top of the function.

```
  //#MARS ENGINE MOD START - Print number of BPs so we can
have a functional progress bar
  UE_LOG(LogCompileAllBlueprintsCommandlet, Display,
TEXT("Blueprints to compile: %i"), BlueprintAssetList.Num());
  //#AMRS ENGINE MOD END
```

This is the function that goes through all the gathered Blueprint assets, loads them, and then compiles them. In here it already prints a line for each individual Blueprint it loads and compiles. Now that we are printing how many Blueprints will be loaded and compiled, we will have the information we need to display a progress bar. Step one is to open the progress bar and set up some variables we will need, replace the "`//TODO - Add progress bar here`" with the following code.

```
    FScopedSlowTask slowTask(100.0f, FText::
FromString("Scanning all blueprints… patience please"));
    slowTask.MakeDialog(true, false);

    int blueprintsToCompile = -1;
    int blueprintsCompiled = 0;
    float progressPerBP = 0.0f;
    const FString blueprintsToCompileStr("Blueprints to
compile: ");
    const FString blueprintsLoadingAndCompilingStr("Loading
and Compiling: ");
```

First, we create our scoped task variable, and we specify we want to do 100.0f units of work, this number can be anything. If we knew how many Blueprints, we were compiling we could use that, but we don't know that yet so we will go with 100 so we can calculate our percentage progress easily. We also give it a start string to display. Next up we call `MakeDialog` on our scoped task, this is what actually open the dialog, and we specify that we want a cancel button on it, but we don't want it if we are in a PIE session. Now we will replace `"//TODO - Update progress bar"` with the following code.

```
float progress = 0.0f;
if (blueprintsToCompile == -1)
{
  int index = thisRead.Find(blueprintsToCompileStr);
```

```
  if (index != INDEX_NONE)
  {
    FString numStr = thisRead.RightChop(index +
blueprintsToCompileStr.Len());
    blueprintsToCompile = FCString::Atoi(*numStr);
    progressPerBP = 100.0f / static_cast<float>
(blueprintsToCompile);
  }
}
//No else case because we might have some progress on the
frame we start compiling, so we need to check directly
if (blueprintsToCompile != -1)
{
  int index = INDEX_NONE;
  while ((index = thisRead.Find(blueprintsLoadingAndCompiling
Str)) != INDEX_NONE)
  {
   blueprintsCompiled++;
   progress += progressPerBP;
   thisRead = thisRead.RightChop(index + blueprints
LoadingAndCompilingStr.Len());
  }
}
FString msg;
if ( blueprintsToCompile >= 0 )
{
  msg = FString::Format(TEXT("Compiling {0} out of {1}
blueprints"), { blueprintsCompiled, blueprintsToCompile });
}
else
{
  msg = TEXT("Scanning all blueprints… patience please");
}
slowTask.EnterProgressFrame(progress, FText::FromString(msg));
if (slowTask.ShouldCancel())
{
  FPlatformProcess::TerminateProc(proc, true);
}
```

Every loop we read the output from the commandlet and get it back in our string. We can get multiple lines in this string, so we need to keep that in mind when we analyse it. First thing we do is look for the string output we added to the commandlet about how many Blueprints will be loaded and compiled, once we have that we know how much progress each single Blueprint is. Every frame we check how many Blueprints were compiled, then call EnterProgressFrame with that value, this will fill up the progress bar in the popup for us. We also change the string we display depending on our progress and status. Finally, we check if the user has pressed the cancel button and terminate our external process if needed.

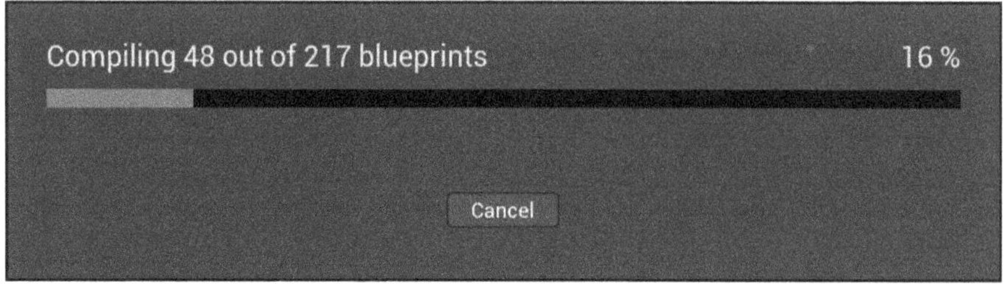

We are almost done, now we must just add our helper class to our module and register our icon. Add the following code in MarsEditor.h

```
#include "Toolbar/MarsEditorCompileAllBP.h"
class FMarsEditorModule : public IModuleInterface
{
  //...
  FMarsEditorCompileAllBPs CompileAllBPs;
};
```

And then the following code in the .cpp file.

```
void FMarsEditorModule::StartupModule()
{
  //...
  CompileAllBPs.Init(MenuCommands);
}
void FMarsEditorModule::RegisterMenus()
{
  //...
  CompileAllBPs.RegisterMenus(MenuCommands);
}
void FMarsEditorModule::RegisterStyleSet()
{
  //...
  StyleSet->Set("MarsEditor.CompileAllBPs", new IMAGE_
BRUSH("CompileAllBPs", Icon40x40));
  StyleSet->Set("MarsEditor.CompileAllBPs.Small", new IMAGE_
BRUSH("CompileAllBPs", Icon20x20));
  //...
}
```

That is it! Now by pressing this button you can verify any code or Blueprint changes you have made and make sure you didn't miss a Blueprint that could break the build.

3 Editor Windows

Now it's time to create our own editor windows. An editor window is a great place to present our own information, and it can be used for anything. I find them to be the most useful for presenting information in a specialized way and I'll be showing two different windows doing this. One for showing all pickups placed in the world, allowing us to quickly get an overview of how many pickups and of what type we have, the other window will show all spawners in a world. Of course, displaying information is all good, but we will also add support for editing the actors directly from our windows.

PICKUP WINDOW

Let us begin with considering what we want from a window listing all pickups in the world. We could just list all the pickups we have in the world in a big list, but there will be a lot of pickups of the same type, probably with very similar names. Instead, we will sort them after type. We also want to quickly navigate to them so we can edit them any way we want. Clicking them should select them in the editor and move the camera to them. I'll stop there since this is our first window we will be making, but we could easily keep on adding more functionality to it.

The important part is that we want to group all pickups of the same type, so a tree list view makes sense. We will have each pickup type as the parent entry and when extended we can show all placed instanced of that pickup. As before, we will be creating a small helper class that will handle the registration and the opening of our window. But then we will also be creating our own slate class that will contain the tree list, and the functionality related to it (sorting, selecting entries, expanding/collapsing and so on).

Before we get started with our window, we are going to need a code class for our pickup. We will not bother with any functionality since we do not need it for our purposes, but we must have at least a class. We need to create a pickup class in our game project, I will place my class in /Source/Mars/ in MarsPickup.h with the following code in it.

```
#pragma once

#include "CoreMinimal.h"

#include "MarsPickup.generated.h"

UCLASS()
class MARS_API AMarsPickup : public AActor
{
  GENERATED_BODY()
};
```

DOI: 10.1201/9781003511748-4

If your game project has a different name (it probably does) remember to replace MARS_API with whatever your project is named. The idea is that we will create several Blueprint classes inheriting from this class and then group all instance of each pickup actor under the same node in the tree view. So, one Blueprint class for a shotgun, one for a pistol and so on. The end result will look like this.

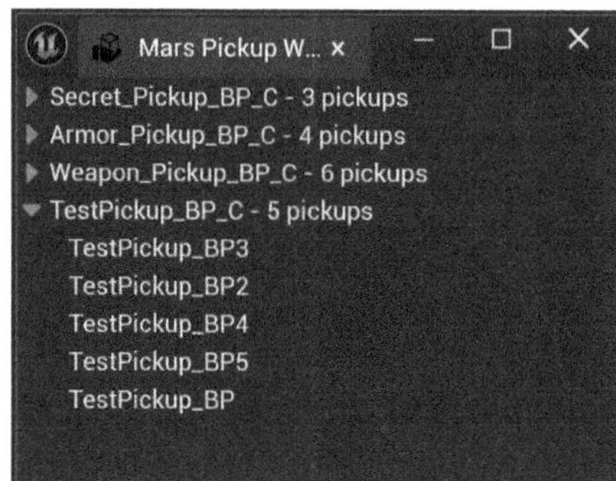

Now that we have what we need to get started with our editor window. Let's create our helper class that will handle the registration and opening of our windows. In /Plugins/MarsEditor/Source/MarsEditor/Public/Windows/ create MarsEditor Windows.h and add the following code.

```
#pragma once

class FMarsEditorWindows
{
public:
  void Init();
  void Shutdown();

  TSharedRef<SDockTab> OnSpawnPickupTab(const FSpawnTabArgs&
_tabArgs);
  static const FName PickupWindowName;
};
```

We have a Init and Shutdown function, then we have a function that will spawn our window, it returns a SDockTab. This slate widget will handle all docking for our window, so you can place it with other windows and get tabs automatically. Last, we have our name identifier for our window. Time to look at the .cpp file for this. In /Plugins/MarsEditor/Source/MarsEditor/Private/Windows/ create MarsEditor Windows.cpp and add the following code.

```
#include "Windows/MarsEditorWindows.h"

#include "WorkspaceMenuStructure.h"
#include "WorkspaceMenuStructureModule.h"
#include "Widgets/Docking/SDockTab.h"

#include "Windows/Pickup/MarsPickupTreeViewWidget.h"

const FName FMarsEditorWindows::PickupWindowName =
TEXT("MarsPickupWindow");
void FMarsEditorWindows::Init()

{
  TSharedRef<FWorkspaceItem> marsGroup = WorkspaceMenu::
GetMenuStructure().GetLevelEditorCategory()->AddGroup(
  FText::FromString("Mars Editor Windows"),
  FSlateIcon(FMarsEditorModule::GetStyleSetName(),
"MarsEditor.EditorMode", "MarsEditor.EditorMode.Small"));

  FGlobalTabmanager::Get()->RegisterNomadTabSpawner
(PickupWindowName, FOnSpawnTab::CreateRaw(this, &FMarsEditor
Windows::OnSpawnPickupTab))
   .SetDisplayName(FText::FromString("Mars Pickup Window"))
   .SetGroup(marsGroup)
   .SetIcon(FSlateIcon(FMarsEditorModule::GetStyleSetName(),
"MarsEditor.WindowPickup"));
}
```

While we could add ourselves to a main menu just like we did with the `CompileAllBP` tool, there's another way to do it also for editor windows like this. We will add our own group to the window menu and then register our editor windows to that group. This will put all our editor windows in the same submenu in the window menu. We will also get a small checkbox next to our editor window entry whenever it is opened. We do this by using the `WorkspaceMenu` class to get the window menu (it's called `GetLevelEditorCategory`) then we add our group to this window. We give our group a name and an icon.

Next up we need to register our window with the global tab manager, when we do that, we give it our `marsGroup`, this will place the entry in our submenu. If we wanted to, we can add ourselves manually to the window entry in the menu bar with the `UToolMenu` like we did for the `CompileAllBP` tool we created, then we just need to replace `SetGroup(marsGroup)` with `.SetMenuType(ETabSpawnerMenuType::Hidden)` on the call to `RegisterNomadTabSpawner`. We must also add a couple of new dependencies for our module. In `MarsEditor.Build.cs` add `"WorkspaceMenuStructure"` to `PrivateDependencyModuleNames`.

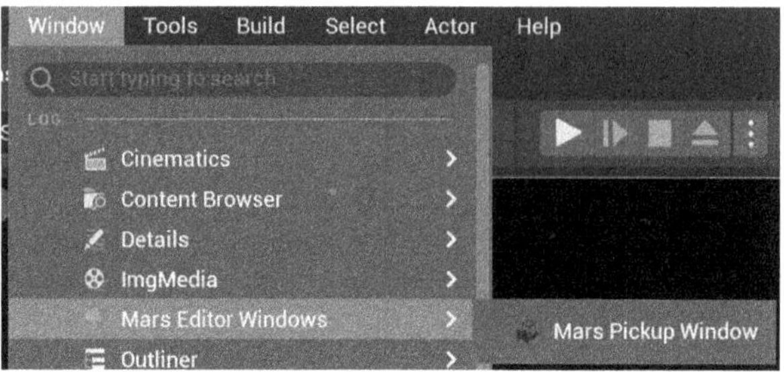

Next up the shutdown function.

```
void FMarsEditorWindows::Shutdown()
{
  FGlobalTabmanager::Get()->UnregisterNomadTabSpawner
(PickupWindowName);
}
```

Really simple, we just unregister our window from the global tab manager. Now onto the function that will actually create our window.

```
TSharedRef<SDockTab> FMarsEditorWindows::OnSpawnPickupTab
(const FSpawnTabArgs& _tabArgs)
{
  return SNew(SDockTab)
     .TabRole(ETabRole::NomadTab)
     [
      SNew(SMarsPickupTreeViewWidget)
     ];
}
```

`SMarsPickupTreeViewWidget` is our widget for the window which we will implement next, we will be implementing this soon. `SDockTab` is the container we will place our widget in, this will let Unreal dock our windows, automatically creating tabs if needed which is very useful. We specify that we want our window to be a nomad tab, meaning we are a standalone window that can be moved around freely, and we can be docked to other windows in the editor. This gives us all window docking logic for free.

TreeView

With the helper class out of the way, it's time to start with the actual widget for our window. We will be making use of a tree view widget Unreal already has. It's important to understand that the actual data and the widget are completely separated from each other. This means that we can use whatever data we want and Unreal's tree view widget can handle all the UI for us.

In /Plugins/MarsEditor/Source/MarsEditor/Public/Windows/Pickup/ create Mars PickupTreeViewWidget.h and start adding the following code, we will be doing this step by step this time since there's a bit more going on in this header file.

```
#pragma once

#include "Widgets/Views/STreeView.h"
#include "Widgets/Views/STableRow.h"

struct FPickupData : public TSharedFromThis<FPickupData>
{
  UClass* Class;
  TWeakObjectPtr<AActor> Pickup;
  TArray<TSharedPtr<FPickupData> > Children;
};

typedef TSharedPtr<FPickupData> FPickupDataPtr;
```

This struct is what will be used for our tree, every single node in our tree view will be represented by one instance of this struct. Our struct inherits from `TSharedFromThis` with itself as a parameter, this is a common pattern in a lot of slate code since we pass data around as shared pointers, this template trick makes that a bit easier. First variable in our struct is a `UClass` variable. This is where we will store what class the pickup actually is, and we will use this to know which parent node we should place each pickup under in our tree.

Next is a weak pointer to the actual instance of the pickup actor and finally we have an array of `FPickupData`, this is where we will add every child to the nodes. If things are a bit hard to grasp right now that is ok, it will become clearer when we start filling in and using this data. Finally, we have a define for a shared pointer to our struct to make our lives a bit easier since this is how we will use this struct most of the time, this is also a common pattern in Unreal. Now it's time to look at our actual widget class.

```
class SMarsPickupTreeViewWidget : public SCompoundWidget
{
public:
  SLATE_BEGIN_ARGS(SMarsPickupTreeViewWidget)
    {}
  SLATE_END_ARGS()

  ~SMarsPickupTreeViewWidget();
  void Construct(const FArguments& _args);
  //TODO - TreeView functions and variables goes here
};
```

Since our widget will not be needing any slate arguments, the declaration is quite simply, we inherit from `SCompoundWidget`, set up our slate arguments (which are none) and then we add our construct function, which is what will actually create the widget and fill it with things. We also add the destructor, since we will be doing some cleanup in it. But since we know we will be adding a tree view widget, we will need some functions and data for it.

```
private:
  TSharedPtr< STreeView< FPickupDataPtr > > TreeWidget;
  TArray<FPickupDataPtr> TreeViewData;
public:
  void OnGetChildren(FPickupDataPtr _item, TArray<
FPickupDataPtr >& _children) const;
  TSharedRef<ITableRow> OnGenerateRow(FPickupDataPtr _item,
const TSharedRef<STableViewBase>& _tableViewBase) const;
  void OnSelectionChanged(FPickupDataPtr _pickup,
ESelectInfo::Type _info);
```

The `TreeWidget` variable is where we will store our tree view widget. This widget will not have any actual data in it. The data structure is separated from the widgets. In `TreeViewData` is where we store our actual data. In this array each element will be each pickup type we have. Each element will then have an array of all the instances of that pickup.

Then we have three functions that are used by the tree view widget. The first function, `OnGetChildren,` is responsible for returning the children to the passed in item. This is so the widget will know which nodes in our tree view should be expanded or not. If the node has children it will be expandable, if not it's a leaf node and cannot be expanded.

The second function, `OnGenerateRow,` is used for creating the widget for the row connected to the passed in item. This means we can make each row look completely different depending on the data for it, so we have a lot of flexibility with the tree view widget.

The last function, `OnSelectionChanged`, is called whenever we click on an item in the tree view so we can do any logic we wish when this happens. We will be selecting the actor in the level editor and moving to camera to the actor.

Only thing missing is some functions for updating our widget when actors are added/deleted.

```
public:
  void OnLevelActorAdded(AActor* _actor);
  void OnLevelActorRemoved(AActor* _actor);
private:
  void AddActor(AActor* _actor);
```

First two functions we will connect to some editor delegates, so we find out whenever an actor is added or removed. `AddActor` will be our internal helper function for adding an actor to our tree view data and updating the tree view widget, this is where we will be building up our tree view structure.

Time to move on to the .cpp file. In /Plugins/MarsEditor/Source/MarsEditor/Private/Windows/Pickup/ create MarsPickupTreeViewWidget.cpp and start adding the following code.

```
#include "Windows/Pickup/MarsPickupTreeViewWidget.h"

#include "Kismet/GameplayStatics.h"
#include "Widgets/Views/SHeaderRow.h"

#include "Mars/MarsPickup.h"

void SMarsPickupTreeViewWidget::Construct(const FArguments&
_args)
{
  GEditor->OnLevelActorAdded().AddRaw(this, &SMarsPickupTree
ViewWidget::OnLevelActorAdded);
  GEditor->OnLevelActorDeleted().AddRaw(this, &SMarsPickupTree
ViewWidget::OnLevelActorRemoved);

  TArray<AActor*> pickups;
  UGameplayStatics::GetAllActorsOfClass(GEditor->
GetEditorWorldContext().World(),AMarsPickup::StaticClass(),
pickups);
  for (AActor* actor : pickups)
  {
     AddActor(actor);
  }

  ChildSlot
  [
    SAssignNew(TreeWidget, STreeView< FPickupDataPtr >)
      .TreeItemsSource(&TreeViewData)
      .OnGenerateRow(this, &SMarsPickupTreeViewWidget::
OnGenerateRow)
      .OnGetChildren(this, &SMarsPickupTreeViewWidget::
OnGetChildren)
      .OnSelectionChanged( this, &SMarsPickupTreeViewWidget::
OnSelectionChanged)
      .SelectionMode(ESelectionMode::Single)
  ];
}
```

First of we sign up our callbacks to the actor added/removed delegates. There's a bunch of other delegates that are useful here also, but for this window these are all we need. These two delegates will fire whenever an actor is added or removed in the current opened level. Next up we find all `AMarsPickup` actors and call our `AddActor` function, we will look at this add function a bit later, but this is where we will build up the tree structure

After adding all actors to our data structure, we create the tree. We make sure to save this widget in a variable also with `SAssignNew`, instead of just creating it with `SNew`. The first three function calls on the tree widgets are mandatory; the widget will not work without them.

- TreeItemsSource is the data for all the nodes in the tree, we will be filling this in soon.

- OnGenerateRow is the function that will create the widget for every row in the tree, we are responsible for generating this widget on our own.
- OnGetChildren will return the children (if any) to a specific node in our tree.

That's all we must set up, but we will also set up two optional arguments.

- OnSelectionChanged allow us to do things whenever we change our selection in the tree, we move the camera to the selected actor.
- SelectionMode controls if we can only select one item at a time, or make multiple items, for this window I think it makes sense with only allowing one item to be selected.

Now let's take a look at how we actually create our node tree, AddActor is the function responsible for this.

```
void SMarsPickupTreeViewWidget::AddActor(AActor* _actor)
{
  //Create the node for this actor
  FPickupDataPtr pickupDataChild = MakeShared<FPickupData>();
  pickupDataChild->Pickup = _actor;

  //Find our parent node if we have one
  FPickupDataPtr* existingParent = TreeViewData.
FindByPredicate([_actor](const FPickupDataPtr& _other)
  { return _actor->GetClass() == _other->Class; }
  );

  if (existingParent != nullptr)
  {
    //Add our new node to the parent node
    FPickupDataPtr parent = *existingParent;
    parent->Children.Add(pickupDataChild);
  }

  else
  {
    //Create parent node and set it up, then add our new node
to it.
    FPickupDataPtr pickupDataParent =
MakeShared<FPickupData>();
    pickupDataParent->Class = _actor->GetClass();
    pickupDataParent->Children.Add(pickupDataChild);

    TreeViewData.Add(pickupDataParent);
  }

  if (TreeWidget != nullptr)
  {
    TreeWidget->RebuildList();
  }
}
```

The goal with this function is to add one node for each type of pickup we have (one for shotgun, pistol and so on). Then in each of these nodes we will add all instances of the pickups in the `Children` array.

We start with creating a new node for this actor. Then we try to find a parent node to this actor. If we found one, we simply add ourselves to the parent node's `Children` array.

However, if we did not find a parent node, we create the parent node and set the `Class` type on it, then add our node to the `Children` before adding the parent node to `TreeViewData`.

Last, we call rebuild on `TreeWidget` if needed. This function rebuilds the entire list and makes sure the widget and data are in sync. Since we build up our data before we construct the widget, we make sure the widget exists before refreshing. If we haven't created it yet, there's no need to refresh it.

This will give is a simple tree structure, one level deep. The tree view widget does support multiple levels, so we could build a more complex tree if we wanted to. For example, we could separate armour and weapon pickups in our tree. Now let's look at the callback from the editor delegates.

```
void SMarsPickupTreeViewWidget::OnLevelActorAdded(AActor*
_actor)
{
  if (Cast<AMarsPickup>(_actor))
  {
    AddActor(_actor);
  }
}
```

The actor added callback is quite simple, we just call the `AddActor` function we just created if it's a pickup actor. Now when an actor is removed, we have to the same thing as when we add one, but in reverse. So first we need to remove the actor from its parent node, then if the parent node is empty, we need to remove it also.

```
void SMarsPickupTreeViewWidget::OnLevelActorRemoved(AActor*
_actor)
{
  if (Cast<AMarsPickup>(_actor))
  {
    //Find our parent node
    FPickupDataPtr* existingParent = TreeViewData.
FindByPredicate([_actor](const FPickupDataPtr& _other)
      { return _actor->GetClass() == _other->Class; }
    );
    if (existingParent != nullptr)
    {
      //Find our child node and remove it
      FPickupDataPtr parent = *existingParent;
      int index = parent->Children.IndexOfByPredicate([_actor]
(const FPickupDataPtr& _other)
        { return _actor == _other->Pickup; }
      );
```

```
        if (index != INDEX_NONE)
        {
          parent->Children.RemoveAt(index);
        }
        //Finally remove the parent node if it's empty
        if (parent->Children.IsEmpty())
        {
          TreeViewData.RemoveSingle(parent);
        }
        TreeWidget->RebuildList();
      }
    }
}
```

There is one case where the added/removed delegates to not trigger and that is when an actor is added/removed from an undo/redo. So, if we add a pickup, then undo it our tree will be out of sync. There is a delegate we can use for this however, `FEditorDelegates::PostUndoRedo`, this delegate will notify us that an undo has happened. But the problem with that delegate is that it does not have any information about what happened in the undo/redo operation. We have no way to know what actually happened in the undo/redo operation and to what actors. We could still use this and just regenerate our entire tree, but on levels with lots of actors loaded this can be quite expensive and we will also loose the current selection and expansion state of the tree (or we have to save that and try to restore it). But we should also consider that most undo/redo operations will not be related to our pickups.

Another option is to just let the user handle this manually, meaning we can add a button that manually refreshes our entire window. For the next window we will be looking at adding buttons where we can do things like this. Depending on what window you are making, you might want to listen to the undo/redo delegate and do some refreshing of your window, it all depends on what you are doing. For this window we will just accept that the list can get out of sync in these cases. Closing and re-opening the window will fix this however.

Next up is the function for returning the children for each node, in our simple tree it's very straightforward, we just have to return the `Children` variable.

```
void SMarsPickupTreeViewWidget::OnGetChildren(FPickupDataPtr
_item, TArray< FPickupDataPtr >& _children) const
{
  _children = _item->Children;
}
```

Now we will create the widget for each row. For the parent nodes, we want to display the name pickup class, but also how many pickups we have so we get a better overview. For the child nodes the name of the pickup is all we need.

```
TSharedRef<ITableRow> SMarsPickupTreeViewWidget::OnGenerate
Row(FPickupDataPtr _item, const TSharedRef<STableViewBase>&
_tableViewBase) const
{
  FString pickupName("Invalid");
  if (_item->Pickup.IsValid())
  {
    pickupName = _item->Pickup->GetActorLabel();
  }
  else if (_item->Class != nullptr)
  {
    pickupName = FString::Printf(TEXT("%s - %i pickups"),
*_item->Class->GetName(), _item->Children.Num());
  }
  return SNew(STableRow<TSharedPtr<FName>>, _tableViewBase)
   .Padding(FMargin(2.0f))
   [
     SNew(STextBlock)
     .Text(FText::FromString(pickupName))
   ];
}
```

A simple `STextBlock` is good enough for us now, in the next window we will look into making something more complex here. We are almost done with the widget class now, but we need to implement the selection changed function. Whenever the user clicks on an item in our window, we want to select that actor in the level editor viewport and move the camera to show that actor.

```
void SMarsPickupTreeViewWidget::OnSelectionChanged
(FPickupDataPtr _pickup, ESelectInfo::Type _info)
{
  if (_pickup != nullptr)
  {
    FScopedTransaction transaction(FText::FromString("Pickup
window selection change"));
    GEditor->SelectNone(false, false, false);
    if (_pickup->Pickup.IsValid())
    {
      GEditor->SelectActor(_pickup->Pickup.Get(), true, true);

      GEditor->MoveViewportCamerasToActor(*_pickup->Pickup.
Get(), false);

      const FLevelEditorModule& levelEditorModule = FModule
Manager::LoadModuleChecked< FLevelEditorModule >("LevelEditor");
      const TSharedPtr< SDockTab > levelEditorTab =
levelEditorModule.GetLevelEditorInstanceTab().Pin();
      if (levelEditorTab.IsValid())
      {
        levelEditorTab->DrawAttention();
      }
```

```
        }
        else
        {
          for (FPickupDataPtr pickupData : _pickup->Children)
          {
            if (pickupData->Pickup.IsValid())
            {
              GEditor->SelectActor(pickupData->Pickup.Get(), true,
              false);
            }
          }
          GEditor->NoteSelectionChange();
        }
    }
}
```

The `_info` parameter contains information about how the selection happened (key press, mouse click, navigation or directly from code). We don't care about why so we can ignore it, but you might want to only move the camera to the actor is selected with a mouse click and not when navigated through with the arrow keys for example.

First thing we do is create an undo/redo buffer. Since we change the selection, we want the user to be able to undo it. This might seem unnecessary, but if you have a big selection and click on our window by mistake it's nice to be able to undo it and get your original selection back. Then we clear the current selection (in the editor, not in our tree). I specifically say I do not want to do a notify here which might seem strange at first. But we will be doing a notify when we select our new actor(s) and doing the notify can be very expensive if we have a lot of things listening on them and/or a lot of actors in our selection. It's always good practice to try and only do one notify when doing selection changes, so we keep our window as performant and responsive as possible.

If we selected a child node, we select that actor (and notify) and move the viewport cameras to that actor, Unreal has a nice helper function for this we use. Then we get the level editor widget and call `DrawAttention` on it. This will give the viewport focus.

However, if it's a parent node we clicked on, we select each child (without notifying) and do a manual notify once we are done with our selection changes. This is nice way to quickly find all pickups of a specific type.

Last thing we need to do is some cleanup; we need to remove ourselves from the editor delegates when our window is closed.

```
SMarsPickupTreeViewWidget::~SMarsPickupTreeViewWidget()
{
  GEditor->OnLevelActorDeleted().RemoveAll(this);
  GEditor->OnLevelActorAdded().RemoveAll(this);
}
```

We are almost done, but we must still add our helper class to our module. Edit MarsEditor.h with this code.

```
#include "Windows/MarsEditorWindows.h"

class FMarsEditorModule : public IModuleInterface
{
  //...
  FMarsEditorWindows Windows;
  //...
};
```

Then in the .cpp file we need to add the following code.

```
void FMarsEditorModule::StartupModule()
{
  //...
  Windows.Init();
}

void FMarsEditorModule::ShutdownModule()
{
  Windows.Shutdown();
  //...
}
void FMarsEditorModule::RegisterStyleSet()
{
//...
 StyleSet->Set("MarsEditor.WindowPickup", new IMAGE_
BRUSH("WindowPickup", Icon40x40));
 StyleSet->Set("MarsEditor.WindowPickup.Small", new IMAGE_
BRUSH("WindowPickup", Icon20x20));
//...
}
```

Now the window is done, time to launch the editor, open the pickup window we just created and create some pickups Blueprints that inherit from `AMarsPickup`. Now as you place the pickups in the level you will see them appear in our window and deleting an actor will remove them. You can also select the actors in our window. The window we have created provides a nice overview of all pickups.

SPAWNER WINDOW

For this window we will re-use the spawner class, `AMarsSpawner`, we made for the editor mode tool. If we take a look at that class, we see that we have a `Class` and `Team` variable, so it would be useful to display both of these in our window. It would also be nice to sort on both of them. This means we want to have some sort of columns we display the data in and be able to sort each column. A tree view list like last time will be a bad fit for this, we are going to use a list view for this window. The list view and the tree view widget basically function the same way, meaning that the widget and the data structure are completely separated from each other. Their interface is also very similar, but there will be some minor differences.

This time we will add support for editing the `Class` and `Team` data directly in our window. Since we create our own widget for each row, we can extend it quite a bit more than we did last time.

It could also be useful to be able to filter the data by only showing spawners for one team, so we will add some controls for this also. Finally, we will add a custom right click menu and add a way to select all spawner of same class.

First thing we will do is add our new window to our `FMarsEditorWindows` helper class. Since we already have the class, this will be very easy, in the MarsEditorWindows.h file add

```
  TSharedRef<SDockTab> OnSpawnSpawnerTab(const FSpawnTabArgs&
_tabArgs);
  static const FName SpawnerWindowName;
```

And in MarsEditorWindows.cpp file add the following lines, following the same patterns as for the pickup window.

```
#include "Windows/Spawner/MarsSpawnerListViewWidget.h"

const FName FMarsEditorWindows::SpawnerWindowName =
TEXT("MarsSpawnerWindow");
void FMarsEditorWindows::Init()
{
  //...
  FGlobalTabmanager::Get()->RegisterNomadTabSpawner(Spawner
WindowName, FOnSpawnTab::CreateRaw(this, &FMarsEditorWindows::
OnSpawnSpawnerTab))
     .SetDisplayName(FText::FromString("Mars Spawner Window"))
     .SetGroup(marsGroup)
     .SetIcon(FSlateIcon(FMarsEditorModule::GetStyleSetName(),
"MarsEditor.WindowSpawner"));
}

void FMarsEditorWindows::Shutdown()
{
  //...
  FGlobalTabmanager::Get()->UnregisterNomadTabSpawner(Spawner
WindowName);
}

TSharedRef<SDockTab> FMarsEditorWindows::OnSpawnSpawnerTab
(const FSpawnTabArgs& _tabArgs)
{
  return SNew(SDockTab)
     .TabRole(ETabRole::NomadTab)
     [
       SNew(SMarsSpawnerListViewWidget)
     ];
}
```

Since we have already hooked up `FMarsEditorWindow` in `FMarsEditorModule`, we do not need to do that again. However we must add the icon for our new window in MarsEditor.cpp.

```
void FMarsEditorModule::RegisterStyleSet()
{
  //...
  StyleSet->Set("MarsEditor.WindowSpawner", new IMAGE_
BRUSH("WindowSpawner", Icon40x40));
  StyleSet->Set("MarsEditor.WindowSpawner.Small", new IMAGE_
BRUSH("WindowSpawner", Icon20x20));
  //...
}
```

Now we can start with our helper class. In /Plugins/MarsEditor/Source/MarsEditor/Public/Windows/Spawner/ create MarsSpawnerListViewWidget.h and add the following code.

```
#pragma once

#include "Widgets/Views/SHeaderRow.h"
#include "Widgets/Views/SListView.h"
#include "Widgets/Views/STableRow.h"

#include "Mars/MarsSpawner.h"

struct FSpawnerData : public TSharedFromThis<FSpawnerData>
{
  TWeakObjectPtr<AMarsSpawner> Spawner;
};
typedef TSharedPtr<FSpawnerData> FSpawnerDataPtr;

class SMarsSpawnerListViewWidget : public SCompoundWidget
{
public:
  SLATE_BEGIN_ARGS(SMarsSpawnerListViewWidget)
    {}
  SLATE_END_ARGS()

 //ListView
public:
  void Construct(const FArguments& _args);
  TSharedRef<ITableRow> OnGenerateRow(FSpawnerDataPtr _item,
const TSharedRef<STableViewBase>& _tableViewBase) const;
  void OnSelectionChanged(FSpawnerDataPtr _pickup,
ESelectInfo::Type _info);
private:
  void RegenerateList();
  void AddActor(AActor* _actor);
  TSharedPtr< SListView< FSpawnerDataPtr > > ListWidget;
  TArray<FSpawnerDataPtr> ListViewData;
  bool RequestSortingAndRefresh = false;
```

```
//TODO - Add Columns and sorting
//TODO - Add Delegates
//TODO - Add filter controls
//TODO - Add context menu
};
```

At first glance this is quite similar to our first window, but we also have a lot of TODOs for more functionality to add. Our data structure is even simpler than the tree view, since we just need a link to our actor, there's no tree structure to keep track of this time. The widget we create is a `SListView` instead of `STreeView`, they share the same inheritance, so they are very similar. Like the tree view implementation, we have our `OnSelectionChanged` and `AddActor` function. This time we also have a `RegenerateList` function though. This will rebuild our data structure completely; we will need to do this when we change filters later on. Let's start with the implementation of all what we have before we start filling in our TODOs. In /Plugins/MarsEditor/Source/MarsEditor/Private/Windows/Spawner/ create Mars SpawnerListViewWidget.cpp and add the following code.

```
#include "Windows/Spawner/MarsSpawnerListViewWidget.h"

#include "Kismet/GameplayStatics.h"
#include "Widgets/Input/SComboBox.h"

#include "Windows/Spawner/MarsSpawnerListViewTableRow.h"
#include "MarsSharedLibrary.h"

void SMarsSpawnerListViewWidget::Construct(const FArguments&
_args)
{
  RegenerateList();

  ChildSlot
  [
    SNew(SVerticalBox)
    //TODO Add filter controls here
    + SVerticalBox::Slot()
    .AutoHeight()
    [
      SAssignNew(ListWidget, SListView<
TSharedPtr<FSpawnerData> >)
        .ListItemsSource(&ListViewData)
        .OnGenerateRow(this, &SMarsSpawnerListViewWidget::
OnGenerateRow)
        .OnSelectionChanged(this, &SMarsSpawnerListViewWidget
::OnSelectionChanged)
        .SelectionMode(ESelectionMode::Multi)
        //TODO Column info goes here
    ]
  ];
}
```

The construction is almost identical to how we created the tree view. We point the list view to our data array, and we add some callbacks to generate a widget row and for if the selection changes. We also allow multi selection, so by holding down Ctrl or Shift we can select multiple items in our list. Let's move on.

```
void SMarsSpawnerListViewWidget::RegenerateList()
{
  TArray<AActor*> spawners;
  UGameplayStatics::GetAllActorsOfClass
(GEditor->GetEditorWorldContext().World(),
AMarsSpawner::StaticClass(), spawners);
  ListViewData.Empty(spawners.Num());
  for (AActor* actor : spawners)
  {
     AddActor(actor);
  }
}
```

Regenerate list simply clears all of our data, then we get all spawn actors and re-add them again. Not much finesse here, just a brute force approach. We will not be doing this very often so performance isn't super important, so I don't think it's worth the dev time and complexity of doing this smarter.

```
void SMarsSpawnerListViewWidget::AddActor(AActor* _actor)
{
  AMarsSpawner* spawnerActor = Cast<AMarsSpawner>(_actor);
  if (spawnerActor == nullptr)
  {
    return;
  }
  //TODO Filter logic will go here later
  FSpawnerDataPtr spawnerData = MakeShared<FSpawnerData>();
  spawnerData->Spawner = spawnerActor;
  ListViewData.Add(spawnerData);

  RequestSortingAndRefresh = true;
}
```

Right now the `AddActor` logic is quite simple, we make sure the actor is a spawner and then we add it to our data array. We will be adding some filtering here later though. Now instead of rebuilding the widget directly here like we did with the tree view we will just mark that we want to do a refresh. We will be covering how to do this refresh and sorting later when we add the columns.

Now we need to take a look at `OnSelectionChanged`.

```
void SMarsSpawnerListViewWidget::OnSelectionChanged
(FSpawnerDataPtr _spawner, ESelectInfo::Type _info)
{
  if (_info == ESelectInfo::Direct)
  {
```

```
    return;
  }
  FScopedTransaction transaction(FText::FromString("Select
spawner"));
  GEditor->SelectNone(false, false, false);
  TArray<FSpawnerDataPtr> selection = ListWidget->
GetSelectedItems();
  for(int i = 0; i < selection.Num(); ++i)
  {
    if (selection[i]->Spawner.IsValid())
    {
      GEditor->SelectActor(selection[i]->Spawner.Get(), true,
false);

      if (i == selection.Num() - 1)
      {
        GEditor->MoveViewportCamerasToActor
(*selection[i]->Spawner.Get(), false);

        const FLevelEditorModule& levelEditorModule =
FModuleManager::LoadModuleChecked< FLevelEditorModule
>("LevelEditor");
        const TSharedPtr< SDockTab > levelEditorTab =
levelEditorModule.GetLevelEditorInstanceTab().Pin();
        if (levelEditorTab.IsValid())
        {
          levelEditorTab->DrawAttention();
        }
      }
    }
  }
  GEditor->NoteSelectionChange();
}
```

In essence, we are doing the same thing we did with the pickup window. We create an undo buffer, select an actor, move the camera and give the level editor viewport focus. However, there are some differences this time around. First off, we ignore all this logic if the select info is direct. `Direct` means we set it directly from code and it did not come from a mouse/keyboard input event. Later on, we will be changing the selection through code, and we do not want to trigger this logic then.

Since we are allowing multi selection this time, we need to handle it a bit differently. Instead of using the `_spawner` variable passed into us, we will get the selection from the widget and loop through it. While we select all items in the level editor, we only move the camera on the last selection. Before we can look at `OnGenerateRow`, we need to look at how to set up the columns.

Columns and Sorting

We are going to add three columns, one for the team, one for the actor's name and one for the spawner class. We will also add support for sorting on two columns at once, one primary and one secondary. If the primary column values are equal, we will sort by the secondary values. Start with replacing "`//TODO - Add Columns and sorting`" in the header with the following code.

```
  //Columns
public:
  static const FName ColumnID_Team;
  static const FName ColumnID_Name;
  static const FName ColumnID_Class;

  EColumnSortMode::Type GetColumnSortMode(const FName
_columnID) const;
  EColumnSortPriority::Type GetColumnSortPriority(const FName
_columnID) const;
  void ChangeColumnSorting(const EColumnSortPriority::Type
_priority, const FName& _columnID, const EColumnSortMode::Type
_mode);

  virtual void Tick(const FGeometry& _geometry, const double
_currentTime, const float _dt) override;
private:
  EColumnSortMode::Type PrimarySortingMode =
EColumnSortMode::Ascending;
  EColumnSortMode::Type SecondarySortingMode =
EColumnSortMode::None;
  FName PrimarySortingColumn = ColumnID_Name;
  FName SecondarySortingColumn = NAME_None;
  void ApplySorting();
```

Quite a bit of functions and variables we need for this! Each column will need a unique name identifier, so we start with the variables for that. Then we have some functions related to the columns and their sorting and a tick function. Finally, we have some variables to keep track of the primary/secondary sorting mode and column. `ApplySorting` is our function where, as the name suggest, we will do the actual sorting of our data. Time to head to the .cpp file and start implementing these functions, first let's set up the column ID names.

```
const FName SMarsSpawnerListViewWidget::
ColumnID_Team(TEXT("Team"));
const FName SMarsSpawnerListViewWidget::
ColumnID_Name(TEXT("Name"));
const FName SMarsSpawnerListViewWidget::
ColumnID_Class(TEXT("Class"));
```

We will add the column info to the ListView widget, replace "`//TODO Column info goes here`" in the `Construct` function with the following code.

```
.HeaderRow
(
  SNew(SHeaderRow)
  + SHeaderRow::Column(ColumnID_Team)
```

```
    .FixedWidth(75)
    .SortMode(this, &SMarsSpawnerListViewWidget::
GetColumnSortMode, ColumnID_Team)
    .OnSort(this, &SMarsSpawnerListViewWidget::
ChangeColumnSorting)
    .SortPriority(this, &SMarsSpawnerListViewWidget::
GetColumnSortPriority, ColumnID_Team)
    .DefaultLabel(FText::FromString("Team"))
  + SHeaderRow::Column(ColumnID_Name)
    .SortMode(this, &SMarsSpawnerListViewWidget::
GetColumnSortMode, ColumnID_Name)
    .OnSort(this, &SMarsSpawnerListViewWidget::
ChangeColumnSorting)
    .SortPriority(this, &SMarsSpawnerListViewWidget::
GetColumnSortPriority, ColumnID_Name)
    .DefaultLabel(FText::FromString("Name"))
  + SHeaderRow::Column(ColumnID_Class)
    .SortMode(this, &SMarsSpawnerListViewWidget::
GetColumnSortMode, ColumnID_Class)
    .OnSort(this, &SMarsSpawnerListViewWidget::
ChangeColumnSorting)
    .SortPriority(this, &SMarsSpawnerListViewWidget::
GetColumnSortPriority, ColumnID_Class)
    .DefaultLabel(FText::FromString("Class"))
)
```

The list view has built-in support for a `SHeaderRow` slate widget, so let's add it and create our three columns in it, giving each one their correct ID and a display name. We also need to give each column a `SortMode`, `OnSort` and `SortPriority` function. In theory we can have completely different functions to each column if we want to, but it's usually more practical to have them share functions, it would have been nice to be able to set this once for the widget, instead of having to do it per slot, but it's not possible. By default, the column size will be split evenly between them all, but we want to Team column to be smaller so we give it a `FixedWidth` of 75, this does also mean we cannot resize it, but it's good enough for our purpose. Now let's look at the callbacks we hooked up.

```
EColumnSortMode::Type SMarsSpawnerListViewWidget::GetColumnSort
Mode(const FName _columnID) const
{
  if (PrimarySortingColumn == _columnID)
  {
    return PrimarySortingMode;
  }
  else if (SecondarySortingColumn == _columnID)
  {
    return SecondarySortingMode;
  }
  return EColumnSortMode::None;
```

```
}

EColumnSortPriority::Type SMarsSpawnerListViewWidget::GetColum
nSortPriority(const FName _columnID) const
{
  if (_columnID == PrimarySortingColumn)
  {
    return EColumnSortPriority::Primary;
  }
  else if (_columnID == SecondarySortingColumn)
  {
    return EColumnSortPriority::Secondary;
  }

  return EColumnSortPriority::Max; // No specific priority.
}
```

The getters are quite straightforward, we just return the mode and priority if it's a matching column, making sure we separate the primary and secondary variables. Now let's set the sorting variables.

```
void SMarsSpawnerListViewWidget::ChangeColumnSorting(const
EColumnSortPriority::Type _priority, const FName& _columnID,
const EColumnSortMode::Type _mode)
{
  if (_priority == EColumnSortPriority::Primary)
  {
    PrimarySortingColumn = _columnID;
    PrimarySortingMode = _mode;
    //We cannot be both primary and secondary
    if (PrimarySortingColumn == SecondarySortingColumn)
    {
      SecondarySortingColumn = NAME_None;
      SecondarySortingMode = EColumnSortMode::None;
    }
  }
  else
  {
    SecondarySortingColumn = _columnID;
    SecondarySortingMode = _mode;
  }

  RequestSortingAndRefresh = true;
}
```

We just set the primary and secondary variables here, making sure we reset the secondary variables if we set that column to primary, since it cannot be both primary and secondary at the same time. Then we set our bool for requesting a sorting and refresh. Next let's take a look at our tick function.

```
void SMarsSpawnerListViewWidget::Tick(const FGeometry&
_geometry, const double _currentTime, const float _dt)
{
  if (RequestSortingAndRefresh)
  {
    for (int i = ListViewData.Num() - 1; i >= 0; --i)
    {
      if (ListViewData[i]->Spawner.IsValid() == false)
      {
        ListViewData.RemoveAtSwap(i);
      }
    }
    ApplySorting();
    ListWidget->RebuildList();
    RequestSortingAndRefresh = false;
  }
}
```

First, we go through all items and check if one is invalid and remove it. In our pickup window we never solved that we don't get callbacks when actors are added/deleted from undo/redo operations. This time we are going to solve that by triggering a re-sort of our list when this happens. We will see later how we actually detect this. Then we apply our sorting and then we rebuild our list view widget. Now we are ready to take a look at how we do the sorting.

```
void SMarsSpawnerListViewWidget::ApplySorting()
{
  ListViewData.Sort([this](const FSpawnerDataPtr& _a, const
FSpawnerDataPtr& _b)
  {
    if (_a->Spawner.IsValid() == false || _b->Spawner.
IsValid() == false)
    {
      return false;
    }

    //Get compare results for all columns
    FString spawnerNameA = _a->Spawner->GetActorLabel();
    FString spawnerNameB = _b->Spawner->GetActorLabel();
    int nameCompareResult = spawnerNameA.Compare
(spawnerNameB);
    int classesCompareResult = _a->Spawner->Class <
_b->Spawner->Class ? 1 : -1;
    if (_a->Spawner->Class == _b->Spawner->Class)
    {

      classesCompareResult = 0;
    }
    int teamCompareResult = _a->Spawner->Team < _b->
Spawner->Team ? 1 : -1;
    if (_a->Spawner->Team == _b->Spawner->Team)
```

```
    {
      teamCompareResult = 0;
    }

    //Do primary sorting
    bool result = false;
    bool primaryCheckWasEqual = false;
    if (PrimarySortingColumn == ColumnID_Name)
    {

      result = nameCompareResult > 0;
      primaryCheckWasEqual = nameCompareResult == 0;
    }
    else if (PrimarySortingColumn == ColumnID_Class)
    {

      result = classesCompareResult > 0;
      primaryCheckWasEqual = classesCompareResult == 0;
    }
    else if (PrimarySortingColumn == ColumnID_Team)
    {
     result = teamCompareResult > 0;
     primaryCheckWasEqual = teamCompareResult == 0;
    }
     result = PrimarySortingMode == EColumnSortMode::Ascending
? result : !result;

    //Do secondary sorting if needed
    if (primaryCheckWasEqual && SecondarySortingMode !=
EColumnSortMode::None)
    {
     if (SecondarySortingColumn == ColumnID_Name)
     {
       result = nameCompareResult > 0;
     }
     else if (SecondarySortingColumn == ColumnID_Class)
     {
       result = classesCompareResult > 0;
     }
     else if (SecondarySortingColumn == ColumnID_Team)
     {
       result = teamCompareResult > 0;
     }
     result = SecondarySortingMode ==
EColumnSortMode::Ascending ? result : !result;
    }
    return result;
  });
}
```

Lots of code, but's it's not too complicated. First, we calculate the compare results for all columns, so we know if the item is "smaller", equal or "larger". Then we apply the primary sorting for our selected column, and if the primary values are equal, we apply the secondary sorting also. If the sorting mode is not Ascending, we just invert the results.

WidgetRow

The widget for the tree view row was quite simple, it was just a text block. But now that we have columns it's a bit more complex. For every row, we will be creating one widget for each column cell we have. Unreal comes with support for all this, we will have to inherit from `SMultiColumnTableRow`, which the list view understands how to communicate with and this will automatically handle resizing of the columns and placement and that kind of stuff for us, so it will save us quite a bit of work. Let's start with taking a look at the `OnGenerateRow` function.

```
TSharedRef<ITableRow> SMarsSpawnerListViewWidget::OnGenerate
Row(FSpawnerDataPtr _item, const TSharedRef<STableViewBase>&
_tableViewBase) const
{
  return SNew(SMarsSpawnerListViewTableRow, _tableViewBase,
_item);
}
```

We return a new widget type here, where we pass in the table view base, which is the base class for `SListView`, in other words our list view widget and we also pass in the item this row is for.

Before we start with the creation of our widget for the row let's discuss what we want it to show and be able to do. We have three pieces of information we want to display on our row, our team, our actor label and our class. But we also want to be able to change the class on the spawner actor directly from this row. So instead of just showing what class it is, we will add a dropdown window so we can change the value if we want to. This means we can change this value directly from our window, we don't need to select the actor, find the correct place in the details panel and then change the value. It speeds up this process quite a bit.

In /Plugins/MarsEditor/Source/MarsEditor/Public/Windows/Spawner/ create MarsSpawnerListViewTableRow.h and add the following code.

```
#pragma once

#include "MarsSpawnerListViewWidget.h"

class SMarsSpawnerListViewTableRow : public SMultiColumnTable
Row<FSpawnerDataPtr>
{
public:
  SLATE_BEGIN_ARGS(SMarsSpawnerListViewTableRow) { }
  SLATE_END_ARGS()

  void Construct(const FArguments& _args, const
TSharedRef<STableViewBase>& _tableViewBase, const
FSpawnerDataPtr _spawner);
```

```
  virtual TSharedRef<SWidget> GenerateWidgetForColumn(const
FName& _columnName) override;

  FSpawnerDataPtr Spawner;
  //Dropdown display widget
  TSharedPtr<STextBlock> CollapsedDropdownWidget;
  //Dropdown data
  TArray< TSharedPtr< FName > > ClassNameItems;
  //enum<->name converter data
  TMap<FName, EClasses> NameToEnumConverter;
};
```

The multi column widget take our data type as a template argument and then we have to implement the `GenerateWidgetForColumn` function. This is where we will create a new widget for the requested column on this row, it will be called once for each column cell on each row. Then we have a bunch of variables we are going to need, we have our item data and then some variables we will need for our dropdown widget. Time to create the .cpp file, in /Plugins/MarsEditor/Source/MarsEditor/Private/Windows/Spawner/ create MarsSpawnerListViewTableRow.cpp and start adding the following code.

```
#include "Windows/Spawner/MarsSpawnerListViewTableRow.h"

void SMarsSpawnerListViewTableRow::Construct(const FArguments&
_args, const TSharedRef<STableViewBase>& _tableViewBase, const
FSpawnerDataPtr _spawner)
{
  Spawner = _spawner;
  for (int i = 0; i < static_cast<int>(EClasses::Max); ++i)
  {
    EClasses classType = static_cast<EClasses>(i);
    FName name = UEnum::GetValueAsName(classType);
    NameToEnumConverter.Add(name, classType);
    ClassNameItems.Add(MakeShareable(new FName(name)));
  }

  SMultiColumnTableRow<FSpawnerDataPtr>::Construct
(FSuperRowType::FArguments(), _tableViewBase);
}
```

Here we dig out the FNames from our enum and create a shared pointer to those FNames, this is so we can make use of them in our dropdown and easily read the result back from the dropdown. Once we are done with our setup, we call our parents `Construct` function. Now let's start generating the widgets for each column cell.

```
TSharedRef<SWidget> SMarsSpawnerListViewTableRow::
GenerateWidgetForColumn(const FName& _columnName)
{
  if (_columnName == SMarsSpawnerListViewWidget::
ColumnID_Name)
  {
```

```
    //TODO name widget
  }
  else if (_columnName == SMarsSpawnerListViewWidget::
ColumnID_Team)
  {
    //TODO team widget
  }
  else if (_columnName == SMarsSpawnerListViewWidget::
ColumnID_Class)
  {
    //TODO class dropdown widget
  }
  return SNullWidget::NullWidget;
}
```

This is the skeleton needed for our function, for each column we will be returning a widget. This means that each individual column cell can have completely different widgets and indeed that is exactly what we are going to do. Let's start with the name column. Replace "`//TODO name widget`" with the following code.

```
FString name = Spawner->Spawner->GetActorLabel();
return SNew(STextBlock).Text(FText::FromString(name));
```

Just a simple textblock with the actor label in, that's all we need for this first cell. Now replace "`//TODO team widget`" with the following code.

```
FLinearColor color(FLinearColor::White);
if (Spawner->Spawner.IsValid())
{
  if (Spawner->Spawner->Team == ETeams::Red)
  {
    color = FLinearColor::Red;
  }
  else
  {
    color = FLinearColor::Blue;
  }
 }
return SNew(SBorder)
    .BorderImage(FAppStyle::GetBrush(TEXT("Menu.Background")))
    .BorderBackgroundColor(color);
```

There's a bit more happening here, but not much. Instead of writing the name of the team, we draw a box with the colour of the team. We could also add an icon here if we have a special icon for each team. Now it's time for the dropdown, which will be a bit more complicated. Replace "`//TODO class dropdown widget`" with the following code.

```
FString currentClassName("Invalid");
if (Spawner->Spawner.IsValid())
```

```
{
  currentClassName = UEnum::GetValueAsString(Spawner->
Spawner->Class);
}
return SNew(SComboBox<TSharedPtr<FName> >)
 .OptionsSource(&ClassNameItems)
 .OnGenerateWidget_Lambda([](TSharedPtr<FName> _item)
 {
  return SNew(STextBlock).Text(FText::FromName(*_item));
 })
 .OnSelectionChanged_Lambda([this](TSharedPtr<FName> _selection,
ESelectInfo::Type _selectInfo)
 {
  if (Spawner->Spawner.IsValid() && _selection.IsValid() &&
CollapsedDropdownWidget.IsValid())
  {
   EClasses* classPtr = NameToEnumConverter.Find(*_selection);
   if (classPtr != nullptr)
   {
    FScopedTransaction transaction(FText::FromString
("Change spawner class"));
    Spawner->Spawner->Modify();
    Spawner->Spawner->Class = *classPtr;
    CollapsedDropdownWidget->SetText(FText::FromName
    (*_selection));
   }
  }
 })
 [
  SAssignNew(CollapsedDropdownWidget,
STextBlock).Text(FText::FromString(currentClassName))
 ];
```

There's a bit more to go through here. First thing we do is dig out the FName from the spawner for the current selected class. We do this to display the correct starting value. Next up we set up a `SComboBox`, this is the dropdown widget, another very useful slate widget that can be a bit intimidating the first time you use it. But once you understand it, it's easy to use. An important thing to know about it is that it has one widget for when it's collapsed, and then when the dropdown is extended, we have a different widget for every row.

The first thing it needs is our data type as a template argument. We are going with FName as our data type, but the data type can be anything you want it to be. Next, we give it our array of options in `OptionsSource`, this is all the options we want in the dropdown menu, we give it all class names that we generated earlier in the `Construct` function. In `OnGenerateWidget_Lambda` we create a widget for each row in the dropdown. We could also give it a function in `OnGenerateWidget`, this is a common pattern in slate, to have both a _Lambda version and an ordinary function callback. Here we just do a simple text block, but if you want to you could add an icon also for example.

After this we have the selection changed lambda (again, you could set up a function in `OnSelectionChanged` instead if you want to). Before we change our data, we set up a scoped transaction and call modify on our actor (again, this must be done before we do any changes on it) so we can undo/redo our changes if needed. Then we have to manually set the text in our collapsed widget (`CollapsedDropdownWidget`). After the selection changed lambda, we set up our collapsed widget. We go with just simple textblock here and it's usually enough I think, but you can add an icon or something to make the selected values more readable.

That's it for our multi-column table row widget, quite a bit more to set up then when we just had a single column, but we also have a lot more information and sorting capabilities, so we do get a lot for that extra code. We now have enough to start using our window, but we are not done improving it yet.

Undo/Redo of Actor Deletion/Creation

I mentioned earlier that we would handle actors being added/deleted from undo/redo a bit better (or well, at all). In the pickup window we relied on the `OnLevelActorAdded` delegate and as we discovered, it does not trigger when we undo a deletion, this time we are going to rely on a different delegate to get around this shortcoming. In MarsSpawnListViewWidget.h replace "`//TODO - Add Delegates`" with the following code.

```
  //Delegates
  void OnLevelActorRemoved(AActor* _actor);
  void OnPostPropertyChanged(UObject* _object,
FPropertyChangedEvent& _property);
public:
  ~SMarsSpawnerListViewWidget();
```

Then we can hook them up in the `Construct` function in the .cpp file.

```
  GEditor->OnLevelActorDeleted().AddRaw(this, &SMarsSpawnerLis
tViewWidget::OnLevelActorRemoved);
  FCoreUObjectDelegates::OnObjectPropertyChanged.AddRaw(this,
&SMarsSpawnerListViewWidget::OnPostPropertyChanged);
```

So instead of the actor added delegate, we will use the `OnObjectPropertyChange` delegate. This is called whenever a property is changed on any actor, so it will be called a lot more, so we need to be mindful of this and not add too expensive code in it. But it will be called after an actor is created due to an undo/redo operation. Of course we must also remove our delegates when our window is closed, so let's add the destructor.

```
SMarsSpawnerListViewWidget::~SMarsSpawnerListViewWidget()
{
  GEditor->OnLevelActorDeleted().RemoveAll(this);
  FCoreUObjectDelegates::OnObjectPropertyChanged.
RemoveAll(this);
}
```

Now let's take a look at these two functions.

```
void SMarsSpawnerListViewWidget::OnLevelActorRemoved(AActor*
_actor)
{
  if (Cast<AMarsSpawner>(_actor))
  {
    int index = ListViewData.IndexOfByPredicate([_actor](const
FSpawnerDataPtr& _other)
      { return _actor == _other->Spawner; }
    );
    if (index != INDEX_NONE)
    {
      ListViewData.RemoveAt(index);
    }
    ListWidget->RequestListRefresh();
  }
}
```

The remove function check if the deleted actor is a spawner, finds the index, deletes it and then requests the list to refresh itself.

```
void SMarsSpawnerListViewWidget::OnPostPropertyChanged
(UObject* _object, FPropertyChangedEvent& _property)
{
  if (AMarsSpawner* newSpawner = Cast<AMarsSpawner>(_object))
  {
    bool foundSpawner = ListViewData.ContainsByPredicate
([newSpawner](const FSpawnerDataPtr& _other)
      {
        return newSpawner == _other->Spawner;
      });

    if( foundSpawner == false)
    {
      AddActor(newSpawner);
    }
    else
    {
      RequestSortingAndRefresh = true;
    }
  }
}
```

Whenever we receive this callback, we check if this actor is a spawner and we already have it in our list, if so a refresh and resort is good enough. But if it's not in our list we add it, this means it was just recreated from a redo operation. This function is also one of the reasons why we do not refresh and sort directly but set a bool for it and do it once per frame. This function can be called multiple times per frames, so we need to be mindful what we do in here.

Filter Controls

Now our window is starting to work pretty well, but we can add some additional controls to it to make it easier to use. To improve how we work with different teams, we will add a way to filter out one team and also a button to switch teams on our current selection. We will add a button and two checkboxes above the listview. In MarsSpawnListViewWidget.h replace "`//TODO - Add filter controls`" with the following code.

```
FReply OnSwapTeamClicked();
bool DisplayRedTeam = true;
bool DisplayBlueTeam = true;
```

First, we have a function for the button we will add, then some bools we will use to control what we should filter out or not. Now let's look at the implementation of this. In `SMarsSpawnerListViewWidget::Construct` we left a "`//TODO Add filter controls here`" we will replace now. We are going to add another vertical slot which we will fill with a horizontal box with several horizontal slots with the controls we want. Quite often our slate code is going to be nested vertical/horizontal boxes like this, so it's a good pattern to get used to.

```
+ SVerticalBox::Slot()
.AutoHeight()
.Padding(5.0f, 5.0f, 5.0f, 5.0f)
[
  SNew(SHorizontalBox)
    + SHorizontalBox::Slot()
    .AutoWidth()
    .Padding(5)
    .VAlign(VAlign_Center)
    [
      SNew(SButton)
      .OnClicked(this, &SMarsSpawnerListViewWidget::OnSwapTeam
Clicked)
      [
        SNew(STextBlock)
        .Text(FText::FromString("Swap Team"))
      ]
    ]
    + SHorizontalBox::Slot()
    .AutoWidth()
    .Padding(5)
    .VAlign(VAlign_Center)
    [
      SNew(SCheckBox)
      .IsChecked(DisplayRedTeam ? ECheckBoxState::Checked :
ECheckBoxState::Unchecked)
      .OnCheckStateChanged_Lambda([this](ECheckBoxState
_newState)
      {
```

```
        DisplayRedTeam = _newState == ECheckBoxState::Checked;
        RegenerateList();
      })
    ]
    + SHorizontalBox::Slot()
    .AutoWidth()
    .Padding(5)
    .VAlign(VAlign_Center)
    [
      SNew(STextBlock)
      .Text(FText::FromString("Red Team"))
    ]
    + SHorizontalBox::Slot()
    .AutoWidth()
    .Padding(5)
    .VAlign(VAlign_Center)
    [
      SNew(SCheckBox)
      .IsChecked(DisplayBlueTeam ? ECheckBoxState::Checked :
ECheckBoxState::Unchecked)
      .OnCheckStateChanged_Lambda([this](ECheckBoxState
_newState)
      {
        DisplayBlueTeam = _newState ==
ECheckBoxState::Checked;
        RegenerateList();
      })
    ]
    + SHorizontalBox::Slot()
    .AutoWidth()
    .Padding(5)
    .VAlign(VAlign_Center)
    [
      SNew(STextBlock)
      .Text(FText::FromString("Blue Team"))
    ]
]
```

We start with a vertical slot that we place our horizontal box in, then we create a new horizontal slot which we place our button in, we will look into the function for when we click the button later. Inside the button we just place a simple text block. The we have four more horizontal slots. One with a checkbox followed by a text block for the red team, and then the same things for the blue team. The checkbox widgets will simply change our bool and request our list to regenerate itself. By default checkboxes display a small, well, checkbox. But you can also change them to display a radio button instead.

```
.Style(FAppStyle::Get(), "RadioButton")
```

As I mentioned in the last chapter, Unreal has a standard for when to use which one, you should use the normal checkbox if you can have multiple options checked, like we will allow here. But if your options are mutually exclusive you should use a radio button. So, if checking your option unchecks some other options, they should all use the radio button style. Now let's look into the function to swap team.

```
FReply SMarsSpawnerListViewWidget::OnSwapTeamClicked()
{
  TArray<FSpawnerDataPtr> selection =
ListWidget->GetSelectedItems();
  if (selection.IsEmpty() == false)
  {
    FScopedTransaction transaction(FText::FromString("Change
spawner team"));
    int spawnersChanged = 0;
    for (FSpawnerDataPtr& spawner : selection)
    {
      spawner->Spawner->Modify();
      spawner->Spawner->Team = spawner->Spawner->Team ==
ETeams::Blue ? ETeams::Red : ETeams::Blue;
      ++spawnersChanged;
    }
    RequestSortingAndRefresh = true;
    if (spawnersChanged > 0)
    {
      UMarsSharedLibrary::AddNotification("Swap team",
FString::Printf(TEXT("%i spawners changed team"),
spawnersChanged), EMarsNotificationType::Success);
    }
    else
    {
      UMarsSharedLibrary::AddNotification("Swap team", "No
spawners in selection!", EMarsNotificationType::Fail);
    }
  }
  else
  {
    UMarsSharedLibrary::AddNotification("Swap team", "No
spawners in selection!", EMarsNotificationType::Fail);
  }
  return FReply::Handled();
}
```

We start with getting our selection from the widget. If it's empty, we display a notification with an error message, but if it's not empty, we set up a scoped transaction buffer again, we want to be able to undo/redo this action. Then we loop through our selection, call modify on the actor then we switch the team (again, order is important here, modify needs to be called before our changes for the system to properly detect them). Finally, we set our bool for requesting a refresh and sort and then we post a notification about how many spawners we changed team on. Note that while this function requires us to return a `Handled/Unhandled` reply, it makes no difference. Unreal will automatically convert any unhandled replies to buttons to handled. But in case this changes in the future we return Handled, since we did handle the input. We have one list thing we need to do before the filtering is working. In the AddActor function we need to replace "//TODO `Filter logic will go here later`" with the following code.

```
if (spawnerActor->Team == ETeams::Red && !DisplayRedTeam)
{
 return;
}
if (spawnerActor->Team == ETeams::Blue && !DisplayBlueTeam)
{
 return;
}
```

This is what will actually do the filtering, if a spawner doesn't match our filter, we just return so we don't add it to our list.

Right Click Menu

Now let's look at adding a right click menu to a list/tree view. As usual, we are going to have to supply our own widget for it, but we can use the `FMenuBuilder` again like we did in the Toolbar chapter to make generating this widget easy. In the right click menu we are going to add an option to select all spawner of the class type we clicked on. In MarsSpawnerListViewWidget.h replace "//TODO – Add context menu" with the following code.

```
TSharedPtr<SWidget> OnGetContextMenuContent() const;
void OnSelectAll();
```

We need to add the callback to generate the context menu to our listview. In the `Construction` function, update the creation of the list view widget to look like this.

```
SAssignNew(ListWidget, SListView< TSharedPtr<FSpawnerData> >)
  //...
  .SelectionMode(ESelectionMode::Multi)
  .OnContextMenuOpening(this, &SMarsSpawnerListViewWidget::
OnGetContextMenuContent)
```

Now let's look at the implementation of the function.

```
TSharedPtr<SWidget> SMarsSpawnerListViewWidget::OnGetContext
MenuContent() const
{
    FMenuBuilder menuBuilder(true, NULL);
```

```
    menuBuilder.BeginSection("SpawnerContextMenu", FText::From
String("Spawner"));
  {
    FUIAction selectAllAction = FUIAction(FExecuteAction::
CreateRaw(const_cast<SMarsSpawnerListViewWidget*>(this),
&SMarsSpawnerListViewWidget::OnSelectAll));
    menuBuilder.AddMenuEntry(FText::FromString("Select
all"), FText::FromString("Select all"), FSlateIcon(),
selectAllAction);
  }
  menuBuilder.EndSection();
  return menuBuilder.MakeWidget();
}
```

Just like we did for the settings menu in the toolbar, the big difference is that when we create the menu builder, we pass in true as the first parameter. This says we want to menu to close after we have made our selection. Just like we did in the toolbar chapter we can create sections, submenus, toggles and we can also insert our own widget into the menu builder if we want to. So, it's quite flexible in what it can do, but also really straightforward to use.

Lastly, we need to take a look at the `OnSelectAll` function.

```
void SMarsSpawnerListViewWidget::OnSelectAll()
{
  const TArray<FSpawnerDataPtr> selection =
ListWidget->GetSelectedItems();
  if (selection.IsEmpty() == false)
  {
   if (selection[0]->Spawner.IsValid())
   {
      FScopedTransaction transaction(FText::FromString("Select
all spawners with same class"));
      EClasses selectClass = selection[0]->Spawner->Class;
      GEditor->SelectNone(false, false, false);
      TArray< FSpawnerDataPtr> newListSelection;
      for (FSpawnerDataPtr& spawner: ListViewData)
      {
        if (spawner->Spawner.IsValid())
        {
          AMarsSpawner* spawnerActor = spawner->Spawner.Get();
          if (spawnerActor->Class == selectClass)
          {
            spawnerActor->Modify();
            GEditor->SelectActor(spawnerActor, true, false);
            newListSelection.Add(spawner);
          }
        }
      }

      ListWidget->SetItemSelection(newListSelection, true);
```

```
        GEditor->NoteSelectionChange();
      }
   }
}
```

For our right click menu, we do not get what item we clicked on as a parameter, so instead we have to dig out the current selection from our list view widget. Right clicking on an item selects it first, then calls our callback. Since we want to be able to undo this operation, we start with creating a scoped transaction variable. We will have two selections we have to update, the editor selection and the list view widget selection. There's no Unreal logic connecting these two so it's up to us to set them both to the right values in this case.

We start with clearing the editor selection, then as we loop through all the items in our list view, whenever one is of the correct class we select it in the editor (without notification) and also add the item to the `newListSelection` array we created. Once we have looped though all the items, this is what we use to tell the list view widget what items should be selected.

And that is it, our spawner window is now complete. With the spawner and pickup windows, we now have quite a bit of different functionality we can use to build more windows quite easily. What window you choose to build will depend on your project of course, but they can save a lot of time for people using it so take some time and think about what windows you could add to your project and talk with people about what window they would like to have. The windows can also be used while you are playing in the editor, maybe you want to add a window that logs all decisions the AI takes where you can click on each decision to get more information why it was taken. Or a window that controls time of day and weather to let artists preview things in different conditions more easily.

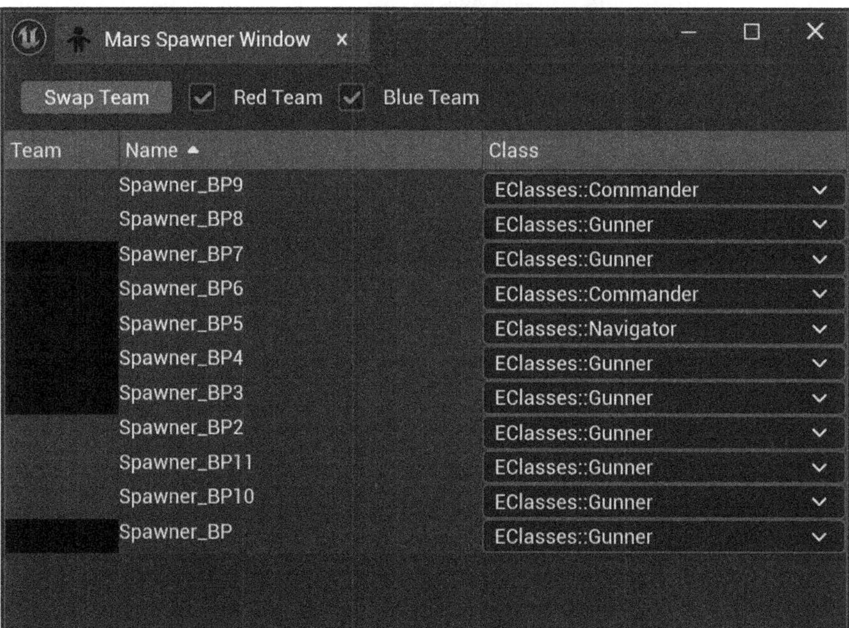

4 Data Visualization

Presenting our data in a good way is a topic that often gets ignored, when we create our tool or expose our variables or functions, it's often obvious to us what everything does and mean. This is natural since we are currently implementing the functionality so we have good context about it, in fact the moment we create the functionality is when we will have the best knowledge and context about it. When we revisit it a few months later, we might have forgotten why we did certain things the way we did. For people using the tools or tweaking the variables it can be even worse, since they usually cannot look at the code to understand it, nor should they need to.

We should always strive to present the data in clear and readable way. It should always be clear what a variable is, for example this means people should always know what unit a variable is in. For example, if you have a velocity variable, people should know if it is in m/s or km/h (or something weird like mph). Let us say you have a percentage related variable with a default value of 0. If I enter a value of 1.5 will that be 150% or 1.5%? Programmers will tend to answer 150% but for other people 1.5% can be the natural answer. This might seem like a small issue, but whenever people can misunderstand something, it is bound to happen and then they will have to figure it out by trial and error or ask you. This interrupts the flow and just wastes time for everyone, so obviously we want to avoid it.

Another issue to consider is if the data is in an array, it can be quite hard to get a good overview of it, you will have to expand the array and the elements to see the values, so we have a lot of UI real estate dedicated to things other than the information we are after. And depending on the data, you might have to expand element after element to find what you are after, again not just wasting time but also the patience of people working with the system. Frustrated people do not make good games; we want to remove as much friction from creating the game as possible and this is an important aspect of it.

The good news is that Unreal has several good systems we can work with, from just telling it what the data is, to creating our own slate widgets to display the data. In this chapter I will go through several off the methods we have available, and in my opinion, you should *always* be using one of them for *any* variable/function that is exposed to Blueprints.

META FLAGS

When it comes to variables the most important thing to give us the context we need, is of course the variable name and category, but we can also give more context on the actual data on the variables. We will do this by just adding the correct `UPROPERTY` flags to our variables. The first thing we will do is add the correct unit. This will only work for int and float variables. To add a unit, we simply need to add a meta flag with either the `Unit` or `ForceUnit` keyword followed by the unit we want. If we use

DOI: 10.1201/9781003511748-5

`ForceUnit` we do not allow Unreal to convert our unit, if we use `Units` we do allow Unreal to change how the unit is displayed.

Here's an example.

```
UPROPERTY(EditAnywhere, meta = (Units = "kg"))
float Mass = 75.0f;
```

As we can see we now get a small unit suffix on our data, which is nice. Now our designers know we wanted the mass in kilograms and not in tons or grams. The context *might* have been obvious from the naming, especially for us when creating it. But now we have removed any potential for confusion about the unit of the variable. Also, since we used `Units` instead of `ForceUnits` Unreal will convert this unit to users' preference and can even convert between different size of the same unit (gram to kilogram or ton for example). This is set up in Edit > Project Settings… > Editor > Appearance and under advanced. Here you can choose what units you prefer and to Length/Mass/Time you can add multiple units, then Unreal will convert between them. Even if Unreal converts a unit, for example you specified you wanted kilograms, but the user has set up using pounds, the value you will see in code and Blueprint is kilograms, correctly converted.

If possible, you should *always* have the proper unit on a variable. Here some examples on the more useful unit types.

- Degrees – "deg"
- Radians – "rad"
- Centimetres – "cm"
- Seconds – "sec"
- Percent – "%"
- Multiplier – "x"

You can find a list of all 64 unit types here
\Engine\Source\Runtime\Core\Private\Math\UnitConversion.cpp

Next thing we can give more context about is the expected (or allowed) size of the variable, again, this only works for floats and integers. We can clamp the value of our parameter with the `ClampMin` and `ClampMax` meta keyword like this.

```
  UPROPERTY(EditAnywhere, meta = (Units = "cm", ClampMin =
"0", ClampMax = "250.0"))
  float Length = 180.0f;
```

Now we cannot enter values outside our valid range, so we can trust the value in our parameter more. Now you will also notice that our variable got a slider for editing in the editor, which is quite nice and also helps with giving us a better overview. There are some meta keywords to help us control the behaviour of this slider. The first thing we can do is remove it if we don't want it with NoSpinbox.

```
  UPROPERTY(EditAnywhere, meta = (Units = "cm", ClampMin =
"0", ClampMax = "250.0", NoSpinbox))
  float Length = 180.0f;
```

We can also have some control over how much we increase/decrease when we use the slider. I say some, because this is a hint, not a guarantee. If we try to force really small values it will not work and Unreal will pick a value that it thinks makes sense depending on the clamp range and the screen size of the slider widget. But in most cases, it works really well. We control this with the Delta keyword. This only controls the behaviour of the slider, you can still manually type in any value you want (it will still be clamped of course).

```
  UPROPERTY(EditAnywhere,meta = (Units = "cm", ClampMin = "0",
ClampMax = "250.0", Delta = "5"))
  float Length = 180.0f;
```

Finally, we can also control the min/max of the slider but still allow data to manually be entered manually outside the range. We do this with the UIMin and UIMax meta keyword. This only controls the values where the slider starts and ends. If we enter data manually, we can go outside the range. We can combine both ClampMin/Max and UIMin/Max together or just use one of them. We can choose to only have a min value of either without any max value specified, or the other way around.

```
  UPROPERTY(EditAnywhere, meta = (Units = "cm", UIMin = "0",
UIMax = "250.0"))
  float Length = 180.0f;
```

Sometimes we have dependencies between variables, we have one variable to enable a functionality and then several variables for tweaking the values to it. It's a quite common mistake to try and tweak the values to something you have missed to enable and then to not understand why your tweaks are not working properly. I'm sure this has happened to us all and we have wasted time and then felt stupid when we release our mistake. With the EditCondition meta keyword we can visualize this dependency between variable, making it impossible to make this mistake. Let's take a look at an example.

```
  UPROPERTY(EditAnywhere, meta = (InlineEditConditionToggle))
  bool OverrideHealth;
  UPROPERTY(EditAnywhere, meta = (EditCondition =
"OverrideHealth"))
  int Health;
```

The `InlineEditConditionToggle` keyword turns the bool into a little checkbox placed infront of the variable (or variables) that has it as an `EditCondition`. Without this it would just be placed on its own row like any other variable. So, when the edit condition is false our variable it greyed out, we can choose to instead hide it completely with the `EditConditionsHides` meta keyword.

```
  UPROPERTY(EditAnywhere, meta = (EditCondition =
"OverrideHealth", EditConditionHides))
  int Health;
```

Now we will not see `Health` at all if the edit condition is false, be aware that this will hide the entire row. So, if you are using `InlineEditConditionToggle` on `OverrideHealth` it will also be hidden.

As an edit condition we can also use functions, as long as it's an `UFUNCTION` we can use it. We can even use a Blueprint function if we want to.

```
  UFUNCTION()
  bool CanHaveArmor();
  UPROPERTY(EditAnywhere, meta = (EditCondition =
"CanHaveArmor"))
  int Armor;
```

In fact, we can check multiple values against each other, we can even do simple math in the edit condition. We can use any integer or float type of data, bools and even UENUMs

```
  UFUNCTION(BlueprintImplementableEvent)
  bool CanHaveMagicalArmor();
  UPROPERTY(EditAnywhere, meta = (EditCondition =
"CanHaveArmor && CanHaveMagicalArmor", EditConditionHides))
  int MagicArmor;
```

Here's a list of all operators we can use in the edit condition.

- ==
- !=
- <
- <=
- >
- >=
- ||
- &&
- !

- +
- -
- *
- /

So far, we have focused on the look of a single variable at a time, but when we start using arrays, we can really use some help with getting a better overview. Everything we have done so far will of course work on data in an array. But we have to expand the array and the element in the array to see the data. That's quite a lot of clicks and screen space needed to find the data we are after, and we might have to expand quite a lot of elements before we find the one element we are looking for.

The first thing we can do to improve this is for static arrays, if we know the size of the array we can display an enum name instead of the `Index[0]` part.

```
UENUM(BlueprintType)
enum class ETeams : uint8
{
  Red,
  Blue,
  Max UMETA(Hidden),
};
USTRUCT(BlueprintType)
struct FMarsTeamInfo
{
  GENERATED_BODY()

  UPROPERTY(EditAnywhere)
  FString TeamName;
};

UPROPERTY(EditAnywhere)
FMarsTeamInfo Teams[(uint8)ETeams::Max];
```

Note that we must do the enum cast with (uint8), anything else and we will not get the enum names showing up. The result is better, it's now easier to find the correct entry, but we have no information about the entry, we must still expand the element to see that.

Of course, quite often we do not have static array, thus we don't know the name of the element. But we can still dig out a little bit of information and display with the `TitleProperty` meta keyword. It will allow us to display one variable in the struct without having to expand the full element.

```
UPROPERTY(EditAnywhere, meta = (TitleProperty = "TeamName"))
TArray<FMarsTeamInfo> Teams;
```

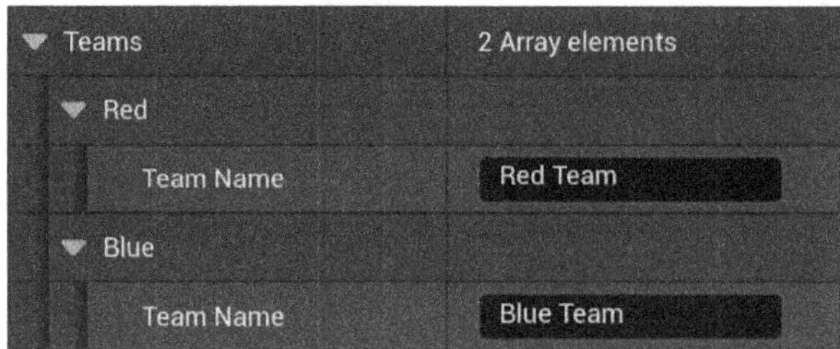

This will also help us find the element we are after more quickly, but we still need to expand it to see the rest of the data of course. Both of these methods are nice but limited. They also don't work together. But they are very easy to add, so this is the bare minimum you should do if you have arrays with your own data structures.

CUSTOM SLATE WIDGETS FOR CODE STRUCTS

We can however do a lot better; we can get full control of how we want our data to be displayed. We can do this by creating our own slate widget and connecting our own struct to our slate widget. It's a bit more work needed then just specifying some `UPROPERTY` flags, but the result is also a lot more powerful.

The way we will do all this is by inheriting from `IPropertyTypeCustomization`, with this class we can register our structs and specify how we want our data to look. The class itself is quite simple; with just two functions we need to implement.

One for creating the slate widget for the header, which is the row for the struct that can be expanded to show all the variables in it. And one for the children, which is for each variable in the struct.

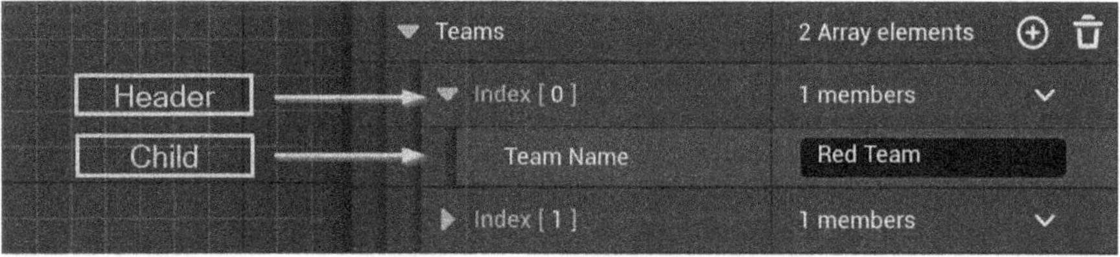

In most cases, we will not be interested in changing the look of the children at all, the default behaviour is perfectly fine for them. What we are after is improving the header with more information, so we get a better overview. We will be creating our own base class that gives the children a default look (we can always override it if we want to) and that handles refreshing of the header row whenever we change any child data. Let us take a look at the base class first. In /Plugins/MarsEditor/Source/MarsEditor/Public/DetailsCustomization/ create MarsBaseDetails.h and add the following code.

```
#pragma once

#include "CoreMinimal.h"
#include "IPropertyTypeCustomization.h"

class IPropertyHandle;

class FMarsBaseDetails : public IPropertyTypeCustomization
{
public:
  // IPropertyTypeCustomization interface
  virtual void CustomizeHeader(TSharedRef< class
IPropertyHandle > _structPropertyHandle, class
FDetailWidgetRow& _widgetRow,
    IPropertyTypeCustomizationUtils&
_structCustomizationUtils) override;
  virtual void CustomizeChildren(TSharedRef< class
IPropertyHandle > _structPropertyHandle, class
IDetailChildrenBuilder& _structBuilder,
    IPropertyTypeCustomizationUtils&
_structCustomizationUtils) override;

protected:
  void CustomDetailsDelegateOnAllChildPropertyChanged
(FSimpleDelegate& _delegate, TSharedRef< IPropertyHandle >
_structPropertyHandle);
  void OnDataChanged();
  TSharedPtr< IPropertyUtilities > PropertyUtilities;
  FSimpleDelegate OnDataChangedDelegate;
};
```

From the interface we have two functions we will be implementing; the first one is to create the widget for the header of the property. The second one is for the child or children of it. Then we have our own functions and delegate we will use to refresh our header widget if any data from a child changes. Let's look at the implementation next, in /Plugins/MarsEditor/Source/MarsEditor/Private/DetailsCustomization/ create MarsBaseDetails.cpp and add the following code.

```
#include "DetailsCustomization/MarsBaseDetails.h"

#include "IDetailChildrenBuilder.h"
#include "IPropertyUtilities.h"

void FMarsBaseDetails::CustomizeHeader(TSharedRef<
IPropertyHandle > _structPropertyHandle, FDetailWidgetRow&
_widgetRow,
  IPropertyTypeCustomizationUtils& _structCustomizationUtils)
```

```
{
  PropertyUtilities = _structCustomizationUtils.
GetPropertyUtilities();
  OnDataChangedDelegate = FSimpleDelegate::CreateSP(this,
&FMarsBaseDetails::OnDataChanged);

  CustomDetailsDelegateOnAllChildPropertyChanged(OnDataChanged
Delegate, _structPropertyHandle);
}
```

For our header we don't create a default widget here, since we will always be implementing a custom one it doesn't really serve any purpose. Instead, we create a delegate we will call to force a refresh of our widget, this is why we save `PropertyUtilities`. This delegate we assign to each child property handle. Meaning for every variable in our struct, we will connect a delegate to the property widget of that member variable. Whenever the variable changes value we will refresh our own widget, this is so we can update the header widget if the user changes a variable in our struct.

```
void FMarsBaseDetails::CustomDetailsDelegateOnAllChild
PropertyChanged(FSimpleDelegate& _delegate, TSharedRef<
IPropertyHandle > _structPropertyHandle)
{
  uint32 numChildren = 0;
  _structPropertyHandle->GetNumChildren(numChildren);
  for (uint32 i = 0; i < numChildren; ++i)
  {
    _structPropertyHandle->GetChildHandle(i)->
SetOnPropertyValueChanged(_delegate);
    CustomDetailsDelegateOnAllChildPropertyChanged(_delegate,
_structPropertyHandle->GetChildHandle(i).ToSharedRef());
  }
}
```

This recursive function simple goes through all variables in our struct and assign our delegate for when their value changes.

```
void FMarsBaseDetails::OnDataChanged()
{
  if ( PropertyUtilities.IsValid() )
  {
    PropertyUtilities->ForceRefresh();
  }
}
```

Our function for when any data changes simple calls a force refresh, this will refresh our header (and child) widgets, keeping them up to date with the actual data. This might sound very heavy handed but remember this is only active when our widget is visible, meaning when we have an actor selected with this data. If we are not looking at anything with this data, this code is never running. Ideally, we would only update our header widget if any data we are using changes, but then we have to implement that manually for every single custom detail class we make and our goal here is to make creating them easier, because we want to have a lot of them. We will just refresh ourselves if any child change data while we are looking at it.

```
void FMarsBaseDetails::CustomizeChildren(TSharedRef<
IPropertyHandle > _structPropertyHandle,
IDetailChildrenBuilder& _structBuilder,
  IPropertyTypeCustomizationUtils& _structCustomizationUtils)
{
  uint32 numChildren = 0;
  _structPropertyHandle->GetNumChildren(numChildren);
  for (uint32 i = 0; i < numChildren; ++i)
  {
    TSharedPtr< IPropertyHandle > childHandle =
_structPropertyHandle->GetChildHandle(i);
    if (childHandle->GetProperty())
    {
      _structBuilder.AddProperty(childHandle.ToSharedRef());
    }
  }
}
```

We just go through all our children and have them build their own default widgets. In other words, we do not change anything, we keep the default widgets for them. Since we are after improving the header, this is perfectly fine. But if you want to do something more advanced in presenting or editing the data here, this would be the place to do it.

And that is it for our base class, we now handle refreshing and a default behaviour for our children. This is going to cover most, if not all, use cases for the custom data visualization classes we will make.

Before we create our first real details customization, we need some test data to work with. In your game project (/Mars/Source/ for me) create MarsStructs.h and add the following code.

```
#pragma once

#include "CoreMinimal.h"

#include "MarsStructs.generated.h"

USTRUCT(BlueprintType)
struct FMarsActorInfo
{
  GENERATED_BODY()

  UPROPERTY(EditAnywhere)
  FString Name;
```

```
  UPROPERTY(EditAnywhere, meta = (ForceUnits = "yr", ClampMin
= "0", ClampMax = "150"))
  int Age = 40;

  UPROPERTY(EditAnywhere)
  bool OverrideMesh = false;

  UPROPERTY(EditAnywhere, meta = (EditCondition =
"OverrideMesh"))
  UStaticMesh* Mesh = nullptr
};
```

The usage of this struct is not important, we will just use it to see how we can improve its visualization in the editor.

For our first custom data visualization we will improve `FMarsActorInfo`. In /Plugins/MarsEditor/Source/MarsEditor/Public/DetailsCustomization/ create Mars ActorInfoDetails.h and add the following code.

```
#pragma once

#include "CoreMinimal.h"
#include "IPropertyTypeCustomization.h"

#include "DetailsCustomization/MarsBaseDetails.h"

class FMarsActorInfoDetails : public FMarsBaseDetails
{
public:
  static TSharedRef< IPropertyTypeCustomization
> MakeInstance() { return MakeShareable( new
FMarsActorInfoDetails ); }

  // IPropertyTypeCustomization interface
  virtual void CustomizeHeader( TSharedRef< class
IPropertyHandle > _structPropertyHandle, class
FDetailWidgetRow& _widgetRow,
    IPropertyTypeCustomizationUtils& _structCustomizationUtils )
override;
};
```

We override the function for customizing the header, but we also added a `MakeInstance` function, this is the function we wall call later to actually create an instance of this class and hook it up. Time to look at the implementation of this, in /Plugins/MarsEditor/Source/MarsEditor/Private/DetailsCustomization/ create Mars ActorInfoDetails.cpp and add the following code.

```
#include "DetailsCustomization/MarsActorInfoDetails.h"

#include "DetailWidgetRow.h"
#include "Widgets/Text/STextBlock.h"
#include "Mars/MarsStructs.h"
```

```
void FMarsActorInfoDetails::CustomizeHeader( TSharedRef<
IPropertyHandle > _structPropertyHandle, FDetailWidgetRow&
_widgetRow,
  IPropertyTypeCustomizationUtils& _structCustomizationUtils )
{
  FMarsBaseDetails::CustomizeHeader(_structPropertyHandle,
_widgetRow, _structCustomizationUtils);

  TSharedPtr< IPropertyHandle > nameHandle=
_structPropertyHandle->GetChildHandle(GET_MEMBER_NAME
_CHECKED(FMarsActorInfo, Name));
  TSharedPtr< IPropertyHandle > ageHandle =
_structPropertyHandle->GetChildHandle(GET_MEMBER_NAME
_CHECKED(FMarsActorInfo, Age));
  TSharedPtr< IPropertyHandle > overrideMeshHandle=
_structPropertyHandle->GetChildHandle(GET_MEMBER_NAME
_CHECKED(FMarsActorInfo, OverrideMesh));
  TSharedPtr< IPropertyHandle > meshHandle =
_structPropertyHandle->GetChildHandle(GET_MEMBER_NAME
_CHECKED(FMarsActorInfo, Mesh));

  FString name;
  nameHandle->GetValue(name);

  int age;
  ageHandle->GetValue(age);

  FString headerString = FString::Printf(TEXT( "Name: %s" ),
*name);
  FString dataString = FString::Printf(TEXT("Age: %i"), age);

  //TODO insert widget code here
}
```

After calling our parent class, we start digging out the property handles to all variables in our struct, we do this through the property handle to our struct. This way we can get any data that Unreal's reflection system knows about. In other words, all variables that are marked with `UPROPERTY`.

If our data structure is still being iterated on a lot, it's probably not worth doing a visualiser for it yet since we must also change any details customization connected to it. This is something to keep in mind, the visualisers are best suited for data structures that are more stable, so we have less places to update when we change things. On the other hands, updating the visualizer is quite quick also and because we are using `GET_MEMBER_NAME_CHECKED` we will get a compile error if the variable we are using is no longer there. I have *never* regretted creating a visualiser for a struct. Once we have our property handles, we get the actual data to our name and our age and then place it in the string we will actually display. Now let's replace the "`//TODO insert widget code here`" with the following code.

```
  _widgetRow
  .NameContent()
```

```
    [
      SNew( STextBlock )
      .Text( FText::FromString( headerString ))
    ]
    .ValueContent()
    [
      SNew(SVerticalBox)
      + SVerticalBox::Slot()
      .AutoHeight()
      .Padding(FMargin(2.0f))
      [
        SNew( STextBlock )
        .Text( FText::FromString( dataString ) )
      ]
      + SVerticalBox::Slot()
      .AutoHeight()
      .Padding(FMargin(2.0f))
      [
        SNew(SHorizontalBox)
        + SHorizontalBox::Slot()
        .AutoWidth()
        [
          overrideMeshHandle->CreatePropertyValueWidget()
        ]
        + SHorizontalBox::Slot()
        .AutoWidth()
        [
          meshHandle->CreatePropertyValueWidget()
        ]
      ]
];
```

We get the widget passed in as a parameter, we just have to fill it out. We must fill in the name part (the data on the left side in the widget) and the value part (the data on the right side in the widget). For the name part we keep it simple, we just display the name variable. For the value part we do a lot more though. Not only do we display the value of the age variable, but we also add the normal widget from the property handle. This default widget is what is normally used, which means it handles editing of the value. In other words, we have now enabled the editing of a variable in our struct, without the need to expand the struct.

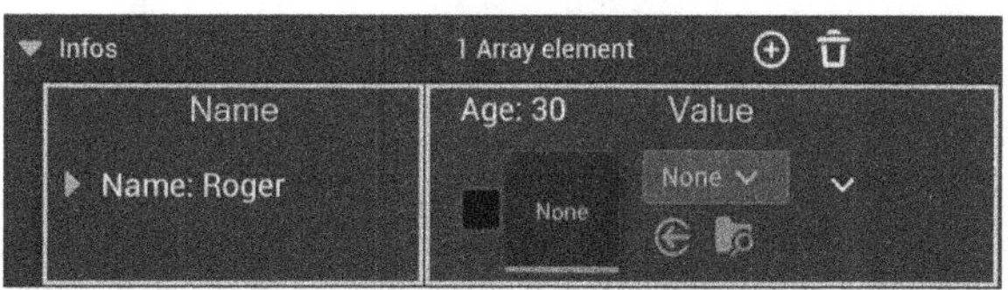

Alright, we are almost done with our first custom visualiser. The only thing missing now is to register it. We will do this from our module, `FMarsEditorModule`. Add the following code to the header.

```
  void RegisterCustomDetails();
  void UnregisterCustomDetails();
```

Next add the following code to the .cpp file.

```
void FMarsEditorModule::StartupModule()
{
  //...
  RegisterCustomDetails();
}
void FMarsEditorModule::ShutdownModule()
{
  //...
  UnregisterCustomDetails();
}

void FMarsEditorModule::RegisterCustomDetails()
{
  if (FModuleManager::Get().IsModuleLoaded("PropertyEditor"))
  {
    FPropertyEditorModule& pm = FModuleManager::
GetModuleChecked< FPropertyEditorModule >("PropertyEditor");
    pm.RegisterCustomPropertyTypeLayout(FMarsActorInfo::
StaticStruct()->GetFName(), FOnGetPropertyTypeCustomizationIns
tance::CreateStatic(&FMarsActorInfoDetails::MakeInstance));
  }
}
void FMarsEditorModule::UnregisterCustomDetails()
{
  if (FModuleManager::Get().IsModuleLoaded("PropertyEditor"))
  {
    FPropertyEditorModule& pm = FModuleManager::
GetModuleChecked< FPropertyEditorModule >("PropertyEditor");
    pm.UnregisterCustomPropertyTypeLayout(FMarsActorInfo::
StaticStruct()->GetFName());
  }
}
```

Here we just register our struct to our custom data visualizer. That's it! Now you can compile and take a look at it. Create an array with our struct and fill in some data, thanks to our own slate widgets for this we get a very good overview of the elements in the array without needing to expand them, making it a lot easier to find the element we are after.

This example simple displayed all the information in the struct in a better way, but we can of course also summarize the data in other interesting way. Add the following struct to MarsStructs.h in your game project.

```
USTRUCT(BlueprintType)
struct FMarsTeamInfo
{
```

```
  GENERATED_BODY()

  UPROPERTY(EditAnywhere)
  FString TeamName;

  UPROPERTY(EditAnywhere)
  TArray<FMarsActorInfo> TeamMembers;
};
```

This struct has an array of the struct we just implemented a visualizer for, so that variable will already be displayed in a nice way. What we are going to do here is go through the entire TeamMember array and summarize it for the widget of `FMarsTeamInfo`. In /Plugins/MarsEditor/Source/MarsEditor/Public/Details Customization/ create MarsTeamInfoDetails.h and add the following code.

```
#pragma once

#include "CoreMinimal.h"
#include "IPropertyTypeCustomization.h"

#include "DetailsCustomization/MarsBaseDetails.h"

class FMarsTeamInfoDetails : public FMarsBaseDetails
{
public:
  static TSharedRef< IPropertyTypeCustomization
> MakeInstance() { return MakeShareable( new
FMarsTeamInfoDetails); }

  // IPropertyTypeCustomization interface
  virtual void CustomizeHeader( TSharedRef< class
IPropertyHandle > _structPropertyHandle, class
FDetailWidgetRow& _widgetRow,
IPropertyTypeCustomizationUtils& _structCustomizationUtils )
override;
};
```

It's almost exactly like our first visualizer. The only that has really changes is the class name. The implementation will be different though, in /Plugins/MarsEditor/Source/MarsEditor/Private/DetailsCustomization/ create MarsTeamInfoDetails.cpp and add the following code.

```
#include "DetailsCustomization/MarsTeamInfoDetails.h"

#include "DetailWidgetRow.h"
#include "Widgets/Text/STextBlock.h"

#include "Mars/MarsStructs.h"

void FMarsTeamInfoDetails::CustomizeHeader( TSharedRef<
IPropertyHandle > _structPropertyHandle, FDetailWidgetRow&
_widgetRow, IPropertyTypeCustomizationUtils&
_structCustomizationUtils )
```

```
{
  FMarsBaseDetails::CustomizeHeader(_structPropertyHandle,
_widgetRow, _structCustomizationUtils);

  FString headerString;
  FString dataString;

  TSharedPtr< IPropertyHandle > nameHandle =
_structPropertyHandle->GetChildHandle(GET_MEMBER_NAME
_CHECKED(FMarsTeamInfo, TeamName));
  TSharedPtr< IPropertyHandle > membersHandle =
_structPropertyHandle->GetChildHandle(GET_MEMBER_NAME
_CHECKED(FMarsTeamInfo, TeamMembers));

  FString name;
  nameHandle->GetValue(name);

  void* dataPtr;
  membersHandle->GetValueData( dataPtr );
  TArray<FMarsActorInfo>* membersPtr = reinterpret_cast<TArray
<FMarsActorInfo>*>(dataPtr);

  if (membersPtr != nullptr )
  {
    headerString = FString::Printf( TEXT( "Team: %s" ),
*name);
    if (membersPtr->IsEmpty() == false)
    {

      int sumAge = 0;
      for (int i = 0; i < membersPtr->Num(); ++i)
      {
        sumAge += (*membersPtr)[i].Age;
      }
      dataString += FString::Printf(TEXT("Num players:
%i\nAvg age: %.2f"), membersPtr->Num(), sumAge /
float(membersPtr->Num()));
    }
    else
    {
      dataString = FString("No members yet");
    }
  }

  _widgetRow
  .NameContent()
  [
    SNew( STextBlock )
    .Text( FText::FromString( headerString ))
  ]
  .ValueContent()
  [
    SNew( SHorizontalBox )
    + SHorizontalBox::Slot()
```

```
        .AutoWidth()
        .HAlign( HAlign_Center )
        .VAlign( VAlign_Center)
        [
          SNew( STextBlock )
          .Text( FText::FromString( dataString ) )
        ]
    ];
}
```

Just like the last visualizer, we get the property handles to the data we want to display. To get the TeamMembers data we will have to get the raw pointer to it and cast it manually, this of course means if we were to change the data type of that variable, this code will still compile but it will crash, so do keep this in mind, we now have a hidden dependency on the data struct. Again, this is why it's best to write the visualizer when the struct is stable and not being iterated on any longer. Displaying all the team members could get quite big, so that might not be the most useful thing we can do here. But we can display how many members are in the team and then also the average age.

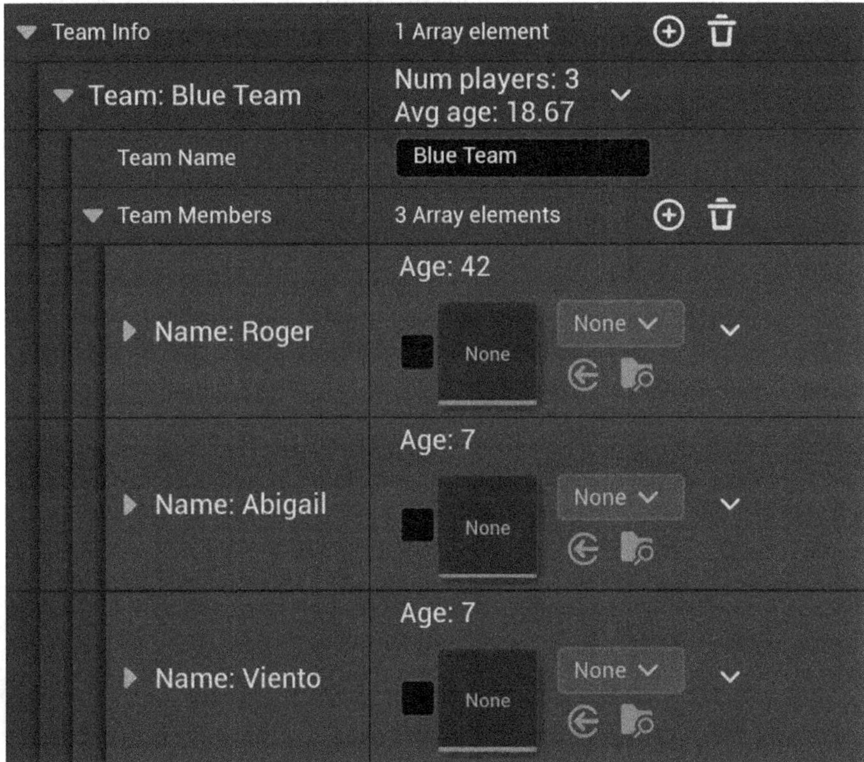

Now we just need to register our visualizer. Again, we will do this from our module, `FMarsEditorModule`. Add the following code in the .cpp file.

```
void FMarsEditorModule::RegisterCustomDetails()
{
  //...
  pm.RegisterCustomPropertyTypeLayout(FMarsTeamInfo::Static
Struct()->GetFName(), FOnGetPropertyTypeCustomizationInstance::
CreateStatic(&FMarsTeamInfoDetails::MakeInstance));
  }
}
void FMarsEditorModule::UnregisterCustomDetails()
{
   //...
   pm.UnregisterCustomPropertyTypeLayout(FMarsTeamInfo::
StaticStruct()->GetFName());
}
```

And that is all! Now you can create custom visualizers for any of our code structs in your project. So, are they worth for every single struct in your project? I don't think so, you should implement these for structs that are used in arrays only, since this is where they really make a big difference. Of course it's possible to do it for structs that are not used in arrays, but it's just not as useful.

CUSTOM SLATE WIDGETS FOR BLUEPRINT STRUCTS

Now, one big restriction with this is that it only works for struct we have defined in code, we cannot do it to Blueprint structs. But why is that? We access all the data through the reflection system, and it knows about all the data in Blueprint also. Thus, we should be able to make this work for Blueprint structs as well. In fact, with one small engine modification we can. Now doing this will come with some risk, if we remove a variable in our code struct, we will get a compile error. But if we start registering Blueprint struct, we cannot know about their actual data layout in compile time, so we need to be more careful in how we handle the data, but if we are it will be perfectly safe. It can be worth doing though, since some Blueprint structs can get quite big (and then they are painful to try to move to code) so this method can really help. Let's take a look at what is needed.

First off we will need to edit this function `FPropertyEditorModule::GetPropertyTypeCustomization` in /Engine/Source/Editor/PropertyEditor/Private/PropertyEditorModule.cpp. This is where all properties check if they have a custom visualiser connected. Currently all Blueprint created struct will have the same property type name, "`StructProperty`", this is no good for us since we need them to have a unique name. We will change the property type name to use the name of the Blueprint struct instead. At the end of the function, right before it returns the layout callback connected to the property name add this code.

```
//...
//#MARS ENGINE MOD START - Use the BP struct name, this allows
us to do details visuals on BP structs
if (PropertyTypeName == FName("StructProperty"))
{
  PropertyTypeName = StructProperty->Struct->GetFName();
}
//#MARS ENGINE MOD END

return FindPropertyTypeLayoutCallback(PropertyTypeName,
PropertyHandle, InstancedPropertyTypeLayoutMap);
```

Now when we have a Blueprint struct, instead of using the name `StructProperty` we will use the actual name of the Blueprint. Let's create a Blueprint struct and call it HealthInfo. Give it an integer variable called Health and a boolean variable called HasArmor.

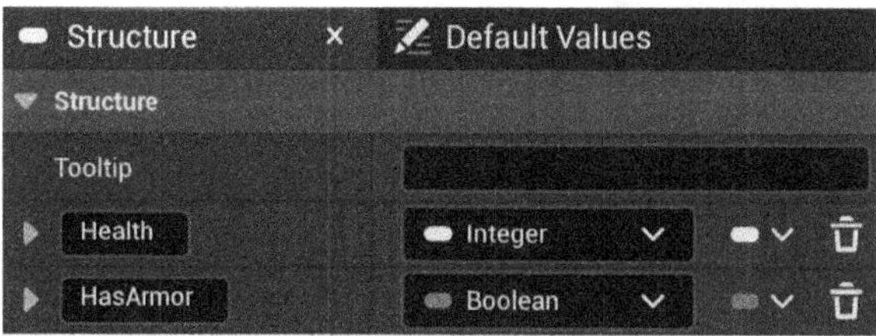

In /Plugins/MarsEditor/Source/MarsEditor/Public/DetailsCustomization/ create MarsHealthInfoDetails.h and add the following code.

```
#pragma once

#include "CoreMinimal.h"
#include "IPropertyTypeCustomization.h"

#include "DetailsCustomization/MarsBaseDetails.h"

class FMarsHealthInfoDetails : public FMarsBaseDetails
{
public:
  static TSharedRef< IPropertyTypeCustomization
> MakeInstance() { return MakeShareable( new
FMarsHealthInfoDetails); }

  virtual void CustomizeHeader( TSharedRef< class
IPropertyHandle > _structPropertyHandle, class
FDetailWidgetRow& _headerRow,
IPropertyTypeCustomizationUtils& _structCustomizationUtils )
override;
};
```

No surprise here, same as the other classes we made. In /Plugins/MarsEditor/Source/MarsEditor/Private/DetailsCustomization/ create MarsHealthInfoDetails.cpp and add the following code.

```
#include "DetailsCustomization/MarsHealthInfoDetails.h"
#include "DetailWidgetRow.h"
#include "Widgets/Text/STextBlock.h"

void FMarsHealthInfoDetails::CustomizeHeader( TSharedRef<
IPropertyHandle > _structPropertyHandle, FDetailWidgetRow&
_headerRow, IPropertyTypeCustomizationUtils&
_structCustomizationUtils )
{
  FMarsBaseDetails::CustomizeHeader(_structPropertyHandle,
_headerRow, _structCustomizationUtils);

  FString headerString;
  FString dataString;

  TSharedPtr< IPropertyHandle > healthHandle =
_structPropertyHandle->GetChildHandle(FName("Health_4_5BAAAF06
4A127D02835FDFB0CE2B3C35"));
  int health = 0;
  if (healthHandle != nullptr)
  {
    healthHandle->GetValue(health);
  }

  TSharedPtr< IPropertyHandle > armorHandle =
_structPropertyHandle->GetChildHandle(FName("HasArmor
_7_F34250DB4FBEEFD1323583852852A34B"));
  bool hasArmor = false;
  if (armorHandle != nullptr)
  {
    armorHandle->GetValue(hasArmor);
  }

  headerString = FString::Printf(TEXT( "Health: %i" ),
health);
  dataString = FString::Printf(TEXT("HasArmor: %s"), hasArmor
? TEXT("Yes") : TEXT("No"));

  _headerRow
  .NameContent()
  [
    SNew( STextBlock )
    .Text( FText::FromString( headerString ))
  ]
  .ValueContent()
  [
    SNew( STextBlock )
```

```
        .Text( FText::FromString( dataString ) )
    ];
}
```

This implementation is mostly the same, but we do get the property handles in a slightly different way. Before we used the `GET_MEMBER_NAME_CHECKED` macro which verified that the variable exists and if not caused a compile error. We cannot use that anymore, there's no way for the compiler to know about the layout of our Blueprint structs. We will have to find our handle through its name directly instead. This is not the display name of the variable, but the unique id name for the variable. This name has a hash value in it and also a counter that increases for every change done do it. This means that for any change at all to a variable in a Blueprint struct, a new name will be generated. At first this can sound bad, since we will have to update the code to find the new name if that happens, but it means we can be sure that the data type matches what we expect it to be, otherwise we would have a new name. In other words, we can be sure that our code doesn't crash, as long as we check if our property handle isn't null.

In order to find the name of the property handle, we need to put a breakpoint in our new `CustomizeHeader` function that we have registered. Then as soon as we select an actor with our struct in it, our breakpoint will hit. In the `_structPropertyHandle` parameter we will have the data we need; this is the handle to struct and all variables in that struct are in here. In `_structPropertyHandle`, you will find a variable called `PropertyNode`, and here you will find an array of all children in `ChildNodes`. This array has the property handles to all variables in the struct, each one of them has a variable called `PropertyPath`, this is the name we are after. In my test Blueprint struct I have a variable called "Health"; it gets the name "Health_4_5BAAAF064A127D02835FDFB0CE2B3C35".

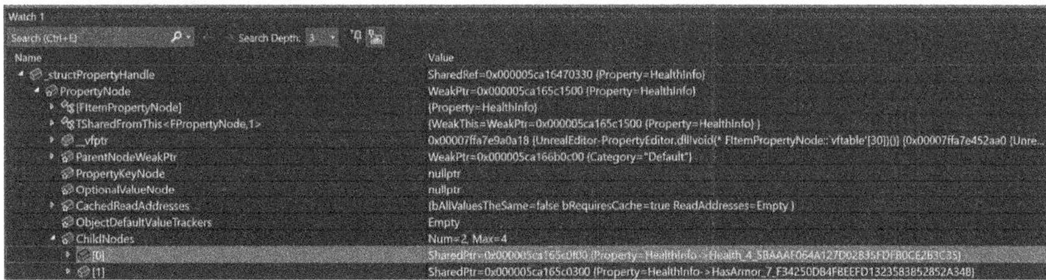

Now we just need to register our visualizer. Again, we will do this from our module, `FMarsEditorModule`. Add the following code in the .cpp file.

```
void FMarsEditorModule::RegisterCustomDetails()
{
    //...
    pm.RegisterCustomPropertyTypeLayout(FName("HealthInfo"),
FOnGetPropertyTypeCustomizationInstance::CreateStatic
(&FMarsHealthInfoDetails::MakeInstance));
```

```
    }
}
void FMarsEditorModule::UnregisterCustomDetails()
{
    //...
    pm.UnregisterCustomPropertyTypeLayout(FName
("HealthInfo"));
}
```

Of course, if we were to change the name of our Blueprint class, this will still compile but our details class will never get created since the names doesn't match. Now changing the name of the struct isn't something that is done very often, so this is fine and even if we do change it, it will not crash, it will just not work.

And that is it, now we can display the data however we want like before. Now we can customize both our code struct and Blueprint structs. We have both displayed the data better and allowed the user to edit the data directly from our new slate widgets. This can of course be expanded a lot; you can insert whatever slate widget you feel like here. You can add buttons, dropdown, popups, and so on. Anything you can do in slate widgets can be done here.

5 Commandlets

Commandlets are small programs that you can run from a command line. This makes them easy to launch from a build machine, or like we did with the compile all Blueprints commandlet earlier, where we created a button in the editor that launched the commandlet and then presented the output back in a more useful format. In this chapter we will be creating two new commandlets, one for checking all our assets for broken physics and one for checking a world partitioned map for incorrect static meshes usage.

COLLISION CHECKER

This commandlet will scan through all static mesh assets and verify their collision so it's valid. If a static mesh with broken collision is used in game, it can be quite hard to track down so it's a good idea to validate them. One way to do this is with a commandlet that scans through, loads and verifies all static meshes. We will also extend the content browser right click menu so we can launch the commandlet directly from it, allowing us to right click a folder and run it on all assets in that folder instead of all assets in the entire game. Then we will also add functionality for checking if a mesh is cutting nav when it shouldn't, since cutting nav can be expensive it's a good idea to verify its usage. The way we will do it here might not be correct for your game, since it will depend on what you consider to be "correct" nav mesh cutting. But you will get the knowledge you need to apply your own rules easily.

Before we start looking at the code, we need to talk a bit about how we launch a commandlet and how we pass data to it. In order to start a commandlet we have to pass in `"-run=CommandletName"` when we start the editor, then followed by any parameters we want. The parameters should always start with "-", for example `"-checkForBrokenMeshes"`. We can also pass in values with the parameters by using "=", for example `"-includeFolders=/Game/"`. We can have multiple values also by separating them with a "," for example `"-includeFolders=/Game/,/Engine/"`. We pass these into the command line version of the editor, depending on what config you are building the name will vary, but it will have the same name as the ordinary unreal editor exe, but with -Cmd added to it. For example, `Engine\Binaries\Win64\UnrealEditor-Win64-DebugGame-Cmd.exe`. The first parameter needs to be to our project name (the name of our uproject file), then our module name followed by the commandlet name and after that any parameters we want to pass in. So, if you have a command window open in your project base folder this line will launch the commandlet.

```
Engine\Binaries\Win64\UnrealEditor-Win64-DebugGame-Cmd.
exe Mars -run=MarsEditor.MarsCollisionCheckerCommandlet
-checkBrokenMeshes -includeFolders=/Game/
```

DOI: 10.1201/9781003511748-6

If you are launching the game through Visual Studio, you can add the parameters by right clicking on your project in the solution explorer, selecting properties, going to Debugging and the add the parameters in Command Arguments. For example, `Mars -run= MarsEditor.MarsCollisionCheckerCommandlet -checkBrokenMeshes -includeFolders=/Game/`

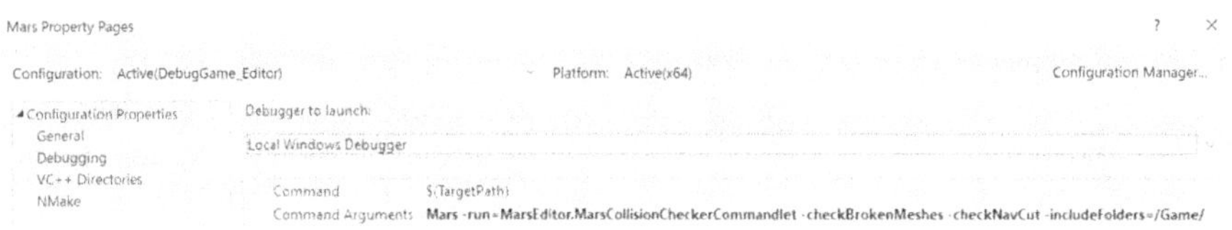

I specify my commandlet with ModuleName.CommandletName. Technically just specifying the commandlet name is enough *if* the module has been loaded. We haven't changed where our commandlet is loaded currently so we don't need to specify the module name. However, we will be changing the loading phase later in this book. I think it's a good practice to always specify the module name also, it will be automatically loaded by Unreal if it fails to find the module. In other words, even if our module has a later loading phase it will be loaded so our commandlet can be used if we specify the module name.

Before we start looking at the actual commandlets, we will create a new debug log channel for our commandlet. Creating our own log channels to use in any `UE_LOG` calls is very easy. In MarsEditor.h we are going to add

```
DECLARE_LOG_CATEGORY_EXTERN(LogMarsCommandlet, Log, All);
```

And in MarsEditor.cpp we add the following line.

```
DEFINE_LOG_CATEGORY(LogMarsCommandlet);
```

This creates a new debug output channel we can use in other files; we say the name of it, followed by the default log level followed by the maximum compile time log level. Any log levels that are more verbose than our default level will be ignored unless we manually increase the log level of it with the log console command, like this.

```
Log LogMarsCommandlet VeryVerbose
```

Entering that in the console will increase the log level and show everything up to and including the `VeryVerbose` category. Of course, we can also just edit the default value locally when we are debugging. While you can use any default Unreal log channels, it's quite easy to set up your own to control how much spam your own system generates, so it's a good idea to do. Now let's get started with our first commandlet.

In /Plugins/MarsEditor/Source/MarsEditor/Public/Commandlets/ create Mars CollisionCheckerCommandlet.h and add the following code.

```
#pragma once

#include "CoreMinimal.h"

#include "Commandlets/Commandlet.h"

#include "MarsCollisionCheckerCommandlet.generated.h"

class FAssetRegistryModule;
struct FAssetData;

UCLASS()
class UMarsCollisionCheckerCommandlet : public UCommandlet
{
  GENERATED_BODY()
public:
  virtual int32 Main(const FString& _params) override;
private:
  bool IsAssetInIncludeFolder(const FAssetData& _asset) const;
  void CheckForBrokenMeshes(FAssetRegistryModule&
_assetRegistry);
  void CheckForIncorrectNavCutting(FAssetRegistryModule&
_assetRegistry);
  TArray<FString> IncludeFolders;

};
```

As you can see, commandlets are quite simple in their structure. All we need to override is the `Main` function. Then we have our own functions we will implement. Let's take a look at the .cpp file. In /Plugins/MarsEditor/Source/MarsEditor/Private/Commandlets/ create MarsCollisionCheckerCommandlet.cpp and add the following code.

```
#include "Commandlets/MarsCollisionCheckerCommandlet.h"

#include "Modules/ModuleManager.h"
#include "AssetRegistry/AssetRegistryModule.h"
#include "Engine/StaticMesh.h"
#include "PhysicsEngine/BodySetup.h"
#include "StaticMeshCompiler.h"

#include "MarsSharedLibrary.h"
#include "MarsEditor.h"

int32 UMarsCollisionCheckerCommandlet::Main(const FString&
_params)
{
  bool checkForBrokenMeshes = FParse::Param(FCommandLine::
Get(), TEXT("checkBrokenMeshes"));
  bool checkNavCutting = FParse::Param(FCommandLine::Get(),
TEXT("checkNavCut"));
  FString folders;
  if (FParse::Value(FCommandLine::Get(),
TEXT("includeFolders="), folders))
```

```
  {
    folders.ParseIntoArray(IncludeFolders, TEXT(","));
  }
  if (IncludeFolders.IsEmpty())
  {
    UE_LOG(LogMarsCommandlet, Error, TEXT("UMarsCollision
CheckerCommandlet didn't have any include folders"));
    return 1;
  }

  FAssetRegistryModule& assetRegistryModule = FModuleManager::
LoadModuleChecked<FAssetRegistryModule>(AssetRegistryConstants
::ModuleName);
  assetRegistryModule.Get().SearchAllAssets(true);
  if (checkForBrokenMeshes)
  {
    CheckForBrokenMeshes(assetRegistryModule);
  }
  if(checkNavCutting)
  {
    CheckForIncorrectNavCutting(assetRegistryModule);
  }
  return 0;
}
```

The `UCommandlet` base class has some functions for handling the param line (the `ParseCommandLine` function) but I find the `FParse` class easier to use, it has more helper functions, and you need to write less code to get what you want so we will be using it instead. Here we check if we should check for broken collision on meshes and if we should check for incorrect nav cutting settings. We also dig out all folders we should check this on. While we could certainly hardcode this to check all of our game content (the /Game/ folder), we want to be able to run this by right clicking on a folder in the content browser, so it has to be a parameter to our commandlet. If we failed finding any include folders, we return 1, any non-negative return value is considered an error.

Then we get (and if it's not loaded, this call will load it for us) the asset registry module. This is what we will use to scan for all the data assets we need and the first thing we will do with it is to search for all assets, so everything will be ready for us when we start to iterate through assets to find what we are after.

Next up is our function for checking all static meshes for valid collision.

```
void UMarsCollisionCheckerCommandlet::CheckForBrokenMeshes
(FAssetRegistryModule& _assetRegistry)
{
  TArray<FAssetData> staticMeshAssetList;
  _assetRegistry.Get().GetAssetsByClass(UStaticMesh::Static
Class()->GetClassPathName(), staticMeshAssetList, true);
  UE_LOG(LogMarsCommandlet, Display, TEXT("Static meshes to
scan: %i"), staticMeshAssetList.Num());
```

```
  for (FAssetData& assetData : staticMeshAssetList)
  {
    if (IsAssetInIncludeFolder(assetData) )
    {
      UStaticMesh* mesh = Cast<UStaticMesh>(assetData.
GetAsset());
      if (mesh != nullptr && mesh->GetBodySetup() != nullptr)
      {
        mesh->GetBodySetup()->CreatePhysicsMeshes();
        FKAggregateGeom* geometry = &mesh->
GetBodySetup()->AggGeom;
        for (int32 i = 0; i < geometry->ConvexElems.Num();
++i)
        {
          FBox box = geometry->ConvexElems[i].ElemBox;
          if (box.ContainsNaN() || box.GetSize().Length() >
100000.0f)
          {
            UE_LOG(LogMarsCommandlet, Error, TEXT("Asset with
broken physics: %s"), *assetData.GetObjectPathString());
          }
        }
      }
    }
    UE_LOG(LogMarsCommandlet, Display, TEXT("Done scanning
static mesh %s"), *assetData.GetObjectPathString());
  }
}
```

We start with getting all `UStaticMesh` assets from the asset registry. This will give us all static mesh assets, but not any Blueprints that has static meshes in them, which is exactly what we want in this case. Then we loop through the list and for every asset, we check if it's part of our included folders.

If it is part of our include folders, we check that it has a body setup, make sure it creates its physics state and then we go through all the convex elements in the geometry and check that the values are sane. There are more types of geometry data here (sphere, box, capsules and so on) but in my experience they are always good, but the convex elements can have incorrect values. This will of course depend on your content pipeline and how you get the static meshes into the engine. So, this check will not be for every project, but it still serves as a good example of what is possible to do. Anytime you get bad/corrupt content into your game that causes issues you should think about how you can automate a check for validating it and commandlets like this is one possible tool for it.

We also make use of our new log channel to output how many meshes we will scan and when we are done with every mesh and of course, every error. These log messages we can use later when we run this commandlet from the editor, just like we did with the compile all Blueprint commandlet.

Now let us take a look at how we can check navcutting on our assets.

```
void
UMarsCollisionCheckerCommandlet::CheckForIncorrectNavCutting
(FAssetRegistryModule& _assetRegistry)
{
  TArray<FAssetData> blueprintAssetList;
  _assetRegistry.Get().GetAssetsByClass(UBlueprint::Static
Class()->GetClassPathName(), blueprintAssetList, true);

  UE_LOG(LogMarsCommandlet, Display, TEXT("BPs to scan: %i"),
blueprintAssetList.Num());

  for (const FAssetData& asset : blueprintAssetList)
  {
    UE_LOG(LogMarsCommandlet, Display, TEXT("scanning asset
%s"), *asset.GetObjectPathString());
    if (IsAssetInIncludeFolder(asset) == false)
    {
      continue;
    }
    const UBlueprint* blueprint = Cast<UBlueprint>(asset.
GetAsset());
    if (blueprint == nullptr || blueprint->
GeneratedClass == nullptr)
    {
      continue;
    }
    AActor* cdo = Cast<AActor>(blueprint->GeneratedClass->
GetDefaultObject());
    if (cdo == nullptr)
    {
      continue;
    }
    TArray<UActorComponent*> allComponents =
UMarsSharedLibrary::GetComponentsCDOFromActorClass(UStaticMesh
Component::StaticClass(), cdo->GetClass());
    for (UActorComponent* component : allComponents)
    {
      UStaticMeshComponent* staticMeshComponent =
Cast<UStaticMeshComponent>(component);
      if (staticMeshComponent == nullptr)
      {
        continue;
      }
      if (staticMeshComponent->Mobility ==
EComponentMobility::Movable )
      {
        if (const UStaticMesh* mesh =
staticMeshComponent->GetStaticMesh())
        {
```

```
        if (mesh->IsCompiling())
        {
          FStaticMeshCompilingManager::Get().
FinishAllCompilation();
        }
        if (staticMeshComponent->IsNavigationRelevant())
        {
          UE_LOG(LogMarsCommandlet, Error, TEXT("Blueprint
%s has a movable Static Mesh Component %s that can cut nav"),
*asset.AssetName.ToString(), *staticMeshComponent->GetName());
        }
      }
    }
  }
 }
}
```

Same basic pattern here, instead of getting all static mesh assets, we get all Blueprint assets. From this `UBlueprint` we can get our class type. However, we need an actual object of this class type, and more specific we need the actor components of this object. If we just need the actor object, we could get the CDO (ClassDefaultObject) of the class. Every `UCLASS` has an CDO object which holds the default values for that class type (of all the data types the reflection system knows about, so all `UPROPERTY` members). But unfortunately, Unreal doesn't have a way of getting the components from the CDO (not entirely true, we can get all components that are created through code, but we also want components that are added from Blueprint), so we instead call our own function that will get this for us, `GetComponentsCDOFromActorClass`. We will take a look at this soon but first let's continue with the above code.

After getting the components we go through them and check if they are movable and navigation relevant and then produce an error. Navigation relevant means that they are blocking the nav and also have nav cutting on. However, in order to see if they are blocking the nav the mesh asset need to be fully loaded, we check if it's still being loaded with `IsCompiling` on the asset. If it is, we just flush all static mesh compilation.

Since cutting nav is expensive it's an operation we want to avoid if possible and static meshes default to cutting nav. This means a lot of small static meshes that characters might be using (say a cigarette) will default to cutting nav, which we do not want. In your project you might have cases where you want movable static meshes to cut nav, so maybe you need to check the size of the bounding box or if you have a good naming convention, the path of the asset to figure out if it should cut nav or not and then check if the value is correct. Validating your assets like this every night is a good idea, you will catch errors when they happen, so they are easy to fix.

Now let's take a look at `GetComponentsCDOFromActorClass`, in MarsSharedLibrary.h add this function.

```
  UFUNCTION(BlueprintCallable, Category = "Util")
  static TArray< UActorComponent* >
GetComponentsCDOFromActorClass (const TSubclassOf<
UActorComponent > _componentClass,
const TSubclassOf< AActor > _actorClass);
```

Then in the .cpp file the implementation.

```
#include "Engine/BlueprintGeneratedClass.h"
#include "Engine/SCS_Node.h"

TArray< UActorComponent* > UMarsSharedLibrary::GetCompone
ntsCDOFromActorClass(const TSubclassOf< UActorComponent >
_componentClass,
const TSubclassOf< AActor > _actorClass)
{
  TArray< UActorComponent* > results;
  if (_actorClass == nullptr)
  {
    return results;
  }

  UBlueprintGeneratedClass* blueprintGenerateClass = Cast<
UBlueprintGeneratedClass >(_actorClass);

  //Get all BP added components
  //This does not include timelines and other components that
comes from nodes in the graph
  TSubclassOf< AActor > actorClass = _actorClass;
  while (actorClass != AActor::StaticClass())
  {
    UBlueprintGeneratedClass* actorBlueprintGeneratedClass =
Cast< UBlueprintGeneratedClass >(actorClass);
    if (!actorBlueprintGeneratedClass)
    {
      break;
    }
    if (actorBlueprintGeneratedClass->SimpleConstructionScript
== nullptr)
    {
      break;
    }

    const TArray< USCS_Node* >& nodes =
actorBlueprintGeneratedClass->SimpleConstructionScript->
GetAllNodes();
    for (USCS_Node* node : nodes)
    {
      if (node->ComponentClass != nullptr &&
node->ComponentClass->IsChildOf(_componentClass))
      {
        //We need to dig out the template from our original
actor CDOs BP class, not the current level in the hierarchy we
are on
```

```
        UActorComponent* actualComponentTemplate = node->
GetActualComponentTemplate(blueprintGenerateClass);
        if (actualComponentTemplate != nullptr)
        {
          results.Emplace(actualComponentTemplate);
        }
      }
    }

    actorClass = Cast< UClass >(actorClass->GetSuperStruct());
  }

  //Get all code generated components
  AActor* actorCDO = _actorClass->GetDefaultObject< AActor
>();
  if (actorCDO != nullptr)
  {
    TArray< UActorComponent*, TInlineAllocator< 16 > >
allComponents;
    actorCDO->GetComponents(_componentClass, allComponents);
    results.Append(allComponents);
  }
  return results;
}
```

This function is a bit complex, turns out it's not easy to just get all the components from just the class type. From our class type, we must traverse the inheritance hierarchy, getting the components we are after from each level in the hierarchy. We do this through a `UBlueprintGeneratedClass` object, this is the class where the compiled Blueprint bytecode is stored. Each `UBlueprintGeneratedClass` only contains the components that were added in that Blueprint, it does not contain the components from its parent Blueprint. This is why we need to go through each level in the hierarchy and get all components at each level. Note that this will not give us components that are created in the graph, which makes sense since we haven't executed anything in the graph.

Once we have gotten all the components that have been added through Blueprints, we finish with getting the components from the CDO, in other words the components that are added through code. Ok back to our commandlet, we only have one function left.

```
bool UMarsCollisionCheckerCommandlet::IsAssetInIncludeFolder
(const FAssetData& _asset) const
{
  for (const FString& folder : IncludeFolders)
  {
    if (_asset.PackagePath.ToString().StartsWith(folder))
    {
      return true;
    }
  }
  return false;
}
```

This function is rather easy, we just compare the asset package path to our include folders, if we find a match we return true.

Now we have a fully functional commandlet we can run from the command line, so it's perfect to use from a buildmachine to help us catch errors early. We can also add a button for running it from the editor, exactly like we did with the compile all Blueprint commandlet. Since we have already covered that in this book, we will not be doing that again. We did make sure to add debug logs so that we can make a progress bar. What we will do however is add this to the context menu in the content browser, in other words when right clicking a folder in the content browser

Content Browser Integration

As usual, we will create a small helper class that we will use from MarsEditorModule. In /Plugins/MarsEditor/Source/MarsEditor/Public/ContentBrowserExtension/ create MarsEditorCollisionChecker.h and add the following code.

```
#pragma once

struct FToolMenuContext;

class FMarsEditorCollisionChecker
{
public:
  void RegisterMenus();
private:
  void CheckFolders(const FToolMenuContext& _context);
};
```

Quite simple, one function where we will register ourselves to the right click menu in the content browser and one function where we will launch our commandlet. Let's look at the implementation of this. In /Plugins/MarsEditor/Source/MarsEditor/Private/ContentBrowserExtension/ create MarsEditorCollisionChecker.cpp and add the following code.

```
#include "ContentBrowserExtension/
MarsEditorCollisionChecker.h"

#include "ContentBrowserMenuContexts.h"

void FMarsEditorCollisionChecker::RegisterMenus()
{
  UToolMenu* menu = UToolMenus::Get()->ExtendMenu
("ContentBrowser.FolderContextMenu");
  FToolMenuSection& section = menu->FindOrAddSection
("MarsEditor", FText::FromString("Mars Editor"));
  section.AddMenuEntry(
    "CollsionChecker",
    FText::FromString("Check for broken physics"),
```

```
    FText::FromString("Checks all static meshes in this folder
for broken physics"),
    FSlateIcon(FAppStyle::GetAppStyleSetName(), "Icons.
Validate"),
    FToolMenuExecuteAction::CreateRaw(this, &FMarsEditorCollis
ionChecker::CheckFolders)
  );
}
```

We start with digging out the menu object for `ContentBrowser.FolderContextMenu`, in other words the right click menu in the content browser. This is the same way we added ourselves to the toolbar and the tools menu. Once we have the menu, we create a new section in it with `FindOrAddSection`, it's always best to use this function rather than `AddSection` in case we in the future want to add more things, this way we don't have to worry about which things get called first if we have multiple things we are adding to the menu. Then we add out menu entry, we provide a key name for it, a display name, a hover description text, an icon (we are re-using an engine icon here, you can provide your own or skip it completely) and then our function to call when we get executed. Let's take a look at that function next.

```
void FMarsEditorCollisionChecker::CheckFolders(const
FToolMenuContext& _context)
{
  if (const UContentBrowserFolderContext* context = _context.
FindContext<UContentBrowserFolderContext>())
  {
    const TArray<FString>& paths = context->
GetSelectedPackagePaths();
    FString projFilePath = FPaths::GetProjectFilePath();
    FString unrealEditor = FPlatformProcess::ExecutablePath();
    FString params = projFilePath + " -run=
MarsCollisionCheckerCommandlet -checkBrokenMeshes
-includeFolders=";
    for (const FString& path : paths)
    {
      params += path + ",";
    }
    void* pipeRead = nullptr;
    void* pipeWrite = nullptr;
    if (!FPlatformProcess::CreatePipe(pipeRead, pipeWrite))
    {
      return;
    }

    FProcHandle proc = FPlatformProcess::CreateProc
(*unrealEditor, *params, true, true, true, nullptr, 0,
nullptr, pipeWrite);
    FString stringOutput;
    if (proc.IsValid())
```

```
    {
      FScopedSlowTask slowTask(50.0f, FText::FromString
("Checking static meshes… patience please"));
      slowTask.MakeDialog(true, false);

      do
      {
        FString thisRead = FPlatformProcess::ReadPipe
(pipeRead);
        stringOutput += thisRead;
        if (slowTask.ShouldCancel())
        {
          FPlatformProcess::TerminateProc(proc, true);
        }
        FPlatformProcess::Sleep(0.5f);
      } while (FPlatformProcess::IsProcRunning(proc));
    }
    FPlatformProcess::ClosePipe(pipeRead, pipeWrite);
    FPlatformProcess::CloseProc(proc);

    TArray< FString > arr;
    stringOutput.ParseIntoArrayLines(arr);

    TArray< TSharedRef< FTokenizedMessage > > errorMessages;
    for (const FString& s : arr)
    {
      if(s.Contains(TEXT("LogMarsCommandlet: Error:"),
ESearchCase::IgnoreCase))
      {

        TSharedRef< FTokenizedMessage > message = FTokenized
Message::Create(EMessageSeverity::Error);
        FString assetPart;
        if (s.Split(TEXT("Asset with broken physics: "),
nullptr, &assetPart))
        {
          message->AddToken(FAssetNameToken::Create(asset
Part));
          message->AddToken(FTextToken::Create(FText::
FromString("Invalid collision detected")));
          // Do not add duplicate messages
          if (!errorMessages.ContainsByPredicate(
            [&](const TSharedRef< FTokenizedMessage >&
_candidate)
            {

              return _candidate->ToText().CompareTo
(message->ToText()) == 0;
            }))
          {
            errorMessages.Add(message);
          }
```

```
            }
        }
    }
    FMessageLog messageLog = FMessageLog("CollisionChecker");
    messageLog.NewPage(FText::FromString("Check all
collision"));
    messageLog.AddMessages(errorMessages);
    messageLog.Open(EMessageSeverity::Error, true);
  }
}
```

This should look familiar; this is how we did the compile all Blueprints button we added earlier. The first big difference is that we get our selection from the content browser, through its context object. We then add these folders as our include folders. This time we did not add any logic for updating the progress bar since it usually executes pretty fast, but it's easily extended to correctly update the progress bar with what we learned from the compile all Blueprints button. Of course, we add our broken assets, with a link to the asset, to the message log. Exactly like we did with the compile all Blueprint button. We are almost done, now we just need to add our little helper class to our plugin module. Start with adding the following code to MarsEditor.h

```
#include "ContentBrowserExtension/
MarsEditorCollisionChecker.h"

class FMarsEditorModule : public IModuleInterface

{
  //...
  FMarsEditorCollisionChecker CollisionChecker;
};
```

And then the following code in the .cpp file.

```
void FMarsEditorModule::RegisterMenus()
{
  //...
  CollisionChecker.RegisterMenus();
}
```

Validate Assets in Folder
MARS EDITOR
Check for broken physics

Finally we just need to add "ContentBrowser" in PrivateDependencyModuleNames in MarsEditor.Build.cs, you can now launch the editor and try it out, right clicking on a folder in the content browser and you will see our new menu entry there.

STATIC MESH REPLACER

Our next commandlet we will create will go through a level and look for any static meshes placed in it that have a Blueprint class using the same mesh and if so, then replace it with the Blueprint class instead. For example, if an artist placed a health kit model in a level, but we have a health kit pickup class, we want to replace the static mesh that the player cannot interact with, but expects to be able to, with the proper Blueprint class. This means we are first going to need to scan through all Blueprints and keep track of what static meshes they have and then load a level scan through all static meshes in it, remove them if we find a match and spawn a new actor in its place and save the level. We will also be doing this on world partitioned levels, which means we will use the `WorldPartitionBuilderCommandlet` and send in our own builder to it. You could say we are sending in a commandlet to a commandlet for it to run. The good thing with this is that we don't have to care about loading and unloading the world partition cells in the map, we only have to worry about what to do with each cell.

In /Plugins/MarsEditor/Source/MarsEditor/Public/Commandlets/ create MarsStaticMeshCheckerCommandlet.h and add the following code.

```
#pragma once

#include "WorldPartition/WorldPartitionBuilder.h"
#include "MarsStaticMeshCheckerCommandlet.generated.h"

UCLASS()
class UMarsStaticMeshCheckerWorldPartitionBuilder : public
UWorldPartitionBuilder
{
  GENERATED_BODY()

public:
  virtual bool RequiresCommandletRendering() const override
{ return false; }
  virtual ELoadingMode GetLoadingMode() const override
{ return ELoadingMode:: IterativeCells; }
  virtual bool PreRun(UWorld* _world,
FPackageSourceControlHelper& _packageHelper) override;
  virtual bool RunInternal(UWorld* _world, const FCellInfo&
_cellInfo, FPackageSourceControlHelper& _packageHelper)
override;

private:
  UPROPERTY()
  TMap<UStaticMesh*, UClass*> StaticMeshToBPClass;
};
```

As mentioned, we will be using the `WorldPartitionBuilderCommandlet` to launch our builder commandlet, so we need to inherit from `UWorld PartitionBuilder` instead of `UCommandlet`. First of we need to specify if we need rendering or not, we will not need any, and what kind of loading we need, we will go with iterating over the cells one by one, we could load the entire map here (but depending on your project that could be quite big!) or we can also do a custom loading, then we have to handle the loading ourselves. Then we also need to implement the `RunInternal` function, which is what will be called for each cell if we are iterating, or once if we are loading the entire world. Finally, we also override `PreRun` since we need to do some prep work to figure out which static meshes we need to check for. Finally, we have a map variable for all the static meshes we should look for and to what classes they should be replaced with, make sure you mark this with `UPROPERTY()` so the garbage collector is aware of your pointers. Time to look at the .cpp file. In /Plugins/MarsEditor/Source/MarsEditor/Private/Commandlets/ create MarsStaticMeshCheckerCommandlet.cpp and add the following code.

```
#include "Commandlets/MarsStaticMeshCheckerCommandlet.h"

#include "AssetRegistry/AssetRegistryModule.h"
#include "Components/StaticMeshComponent.h"
#include "CoreMinimal.h"
#include "Engine/Blueprint.h"
#include "Engine/StaticMesh.h"
#include "Engine/StaticMeshActor.h"
#include "WorldPartition/WorldPartition.h"
#include "WorldPartition/WorldPartitionHelpers.h"

#include "MarsSharedLibrary.h"

bool UMarsStaticMeshCheckerWorldPartitionBuilder::PreRun
(UWorld* _world, FPackageSourceControlHelper& _packageHelper)
{
  FAssetRegistryModule& assetRegistryModule = FModuleManager::
LoadModuleChecked<FAssetRegistryModule>(AssetRegistryConstants
::ModuleName);
  assetRegistryModule.Get().SearchAllAssets(true);
  TArray<FAssetData> blueprintAssetList;
  assetRegistryModule.Get().GetAssetsByClass(UBlueprint::
StaticClass()->GetClassPathName(), blueprintAssetList, true);
  for (const FAssetData& asset : blueprintAssetList)
  {
    const UBlueprint* blueprint = Cast<UBlueprint>(asset.
GetAsset());
    if (!blueprint || !blueprint->GeneratedClass)
    {
      continue;
    }
    AActor* cdo = Cast<AActor>(blueprint->
GeneratedClass->GetDefaultObject());
    if (!cdo)
    {
      continue;
    }
```

```
    TArray<UActorComponent*> allComponents = UMarsSharedLibrary
::GetComponentsCDOFromActorClass(UStaticMeshComponent::StaticC
lass(), cdo->GetClass());
    if(allComponents.Num() == 1)
    {
      UStaticMeshComponent* staticMeshComponent = Cast<UStatic
MeshComponent>(allComponents[0]);
      if (staticMeshComponent && staticMeshComponent->
GetStaticMesh())
      {
        StaticMeshToBPClass.Add(staticMeshComponent->
GetStaticMesh(), cdo->GetClass());
      }
    }
  }

  return true;
}
```

It's very similar to what we did with the nav cut checker. We go through all Blueprint assets and get their static mesh components. However, we only want to do the replacement if we have one static mesh component, if there are multiple components, we will probably replace them wrong, so we ignore those cases. Now we have a map of all static meshes we should replace and the class they should be replaced with. Time to look at the actual replacement logic.

```
bool UMarsStaticMeshCheckerWorldPartitionBuilder::Run
Internal(UWorld* _world, const FCellInfo& _cellInfo,
FPackageSourceControlHelper& _packageHelper)
{
  UWorldPartition* worldPartition = _world->
GetWorldPartition();
  if (!worldPartition)
  {
    UE_LOG(LogMarsCommandlet, Error, TEXT("Failed to retrieve
WorldPartition."));
    return false;
  }
  TArray<FString> packagesToDelete;
  TArray<UPackage*> packagesToSave;
  FWorldPartitionHelpers::FForEachActorWithLoadingParams
forEachActorWithLoadingParams;
  FWorldPartitionHelpers::ForEachActorWithLoading(worldPartit
ion, [this, _world, &packagesToDelete, &packagesToSave] (const
FWorldPartitionActorDescInstance* _actorDescInstance)
    {
      AStaticMeshActor* actor = Cast<AStaticMeshActor>
(_actorDescInstance->GetActor());
      if (actor != nullptr)
      {
```

```
        UClass** bpToReplaceWith = StaticMeshToBPClass.
Find(actor->GetStaticMeshComponent()->GetStaticMesh());
        if (bpToReplaceWith != nullptr)
        {
          AActor* newActor = _world->SpawnActor<AActor>
(*bpToReplaceWith, actor->GetActorTransform());
          if (newActor != nullptr)
          {
            actor->Destroy();
            packagesToSave.Add(newActor->GetPackage());
            packagesToDelete.Add(_actorDescInstance->
GetActorPackage().ToString());
          }
        }
      }

      return true;
    }, forEachActorWithLoadingParams);
  DeletePackages(packagesToDelete, _packageHelper, false);
  SavePackages(packagesToSave, _packageHelper);
  return true;
}
```

In order to loop through all the actors, we make use of the `FWorldPartitonHelpers` functions. This helper library has a bunch of different useful functions for looping through actors in a world partition level. We want to loop through all the actors and make sure they are fully loaded, so we make use of the `ForEachActorWithLoading` function. Then for each actor we check if it is a `AStaticMeshActor` and if the mesh is one that we should replace. If it is, we spawn a new actor of the right class with the transform from the static mesh actor we are going to delete. Then we delete the old actors and keep track of what packages we want to delete and what packages we want to add. `UWorldPartitionBuilder` has some helper functions for adding and deleting actors we make use of here.

That's it, we now have a commandlet that can replace static meshes with a Blueprint that you can launch with the following command line arguments.

```
Mars "/Game/MarsBasicMap_WP" -run=WorldPartitionBuilderCommand
let -builder=MarsStaticMeshCheckerWorldPartitionBuilder
```

Again, Mars is my game project name so replace this with whatever your project name is. After the project name is the map we want to run this on, then we specify the commandlet and finally our builder we want to use.

6 Extending Editor Debugging

In this chapter we will look into various ways of improving iteration speed for gameplay scripting. Iteration speed for gameplay scripting is often determined by the need to actually play the game to test the changes, this can be as quickly as just playing the combat scenario directly in the editor or requiring cooking a new build and progressing through a mission the test the flow. So, in order to improve this our goal is to move as much useful information as possible into edit time and not gameplay time. When selecting a gameplay actor, we want to see the information we need to know if anything is wrong with the actor and in some cases, it makes sense to add support to edit the setting directly in the viewport and not through the details window.

COMPONENT VISUALIZER

The first system we will look into is component visualizers. They are great for extending components with more contextual information and they are quite easy to extend so we can edit the data directly in the viewport. For our example we will look into a component that handles setting up and editing a patrol route for an AI. We want to be able to add new points, move around the existing points and delete points. We will also display some information about the patrol route, first of showing the actual path in the world and also how many points and the total length of the patrol route.

For this example, we will have an actor component that is responsible for the patrol route an AI will take, we will not do any game functionality implementation of course, it just serves as an example for the tool we will create. In /Source/Mars/AI/ create MarsPatrolRouteComponent.h and add the following code, we do not need a .cpp file for it.

```
#pragma once

#include "CoreMinimal.h"
#include "Components/SceneComponent.h"

#include "MarsPatrolRouteComponent.generated.h"

UCLASS( meta = (BlueprintSpawnableComponent))
class MARS_API UMarsPatrolRouteComponent : public
USceneComponent
{
  GENERATED_BODY()
public:
  UPROPERTY( EditInstanceOnly )
  TArray<FVector> PatrolLocations;
};
```

 DOI: 10.1201/9781003511748-7

For our patrol route component, we will create a new visualizer component that will be responsible for all the debug drawing and input handling. This component will only exist and be registered in the editor so it will have zero runtime cost. Let's start with creating our component visualizer, in /Plugins/MarsEditor/Source/MarsEditor/Public/ComponentVisualizers/ create MarsPatrolRouteComponentVisualizer.h and add the following code.

```
#pragma once

#include "CoreMinimal.h"
#include "ComponentVisualizer.h"
#include "Framework/Commands/Commands.h"
#include "Framework/Commands/UICommandList.h"

class FPrimitiveDrawInterface;
class FSceneView;
class UActorComponent;
class UMarsPatrolRouteComponent;

class FMarsPatrolRouteComponentVisualizer : public
FComponentVisualizer
{
public:
};
```

We will be adding a lot more code here, but we will be doing it step by step this time. For now, we will leave it completely empty, although we did add a lot of includes and forward declarations we are going to need later. Now we can register the visualizer in `FMarsEditorModule`, in MarsEditor.h add the following function definitions.

```
class FMarsEditorModule : public IModuleInterface
{
  //...
  void RegisterComponentVisualizers();
  void UnregisterComponentVisualizers();
};
```

And then the implementation in the cpp file.

```
void FMarsEditorModule::RegisterComponentVisualizers()
{
  if (GUnrealEd != nullptr)
  {
    TSharedPtr<FComponentVisualizer> patrolRouteVisualiser =
MakeShareable(new FMarsPatrolRouteComponentVisualizer);
    GUnrealEd->RegisterComponentVisualizer
(UMarsPatrolRouteComponent::StaticClass()->GetFName(),
patrolRouteVisualiser);
    patrolRouteVisualiser->OnRegister();
  }
```

```
}
void FMarsEditorModule::UnregisterComponentVisualizers()
{
  if (GUnrealEd != nullptr)
  {
    GUnrealEd->UnregisterComponentVisualizer
(UMarsPatrolRouteComponent::StaticClass()->GetFName());
  }
}
```

Call these functions in StartupModule and ShutdownModule.

```
void FMarsEditorModule::StartupModule()
{
  //...
  RegisterComponentVisualizers();
};
void FMarsEditorModule::ShutdownModule ()
{
  //...
  UnregisterComponentVisualizers();
};
```

We also need to add some includes.

```
#include "Editor/UnrealEdEngine.h"
#include "UnrealEdGlobals.h"
#include "ComponentVisualizers/MarsPatrolRouteComponent
Visualizer.h"
#include "Mars/AI/MarsPatrolRouteComponent.h"
```

There's one problem with this code however, we need access to `GUnrealEd` in order to register our newly created visualizer. But the engine is in the process of initializing when our plugin is loading. We need to change when our plugin is initialized so that we have access to the engine. We control this in MarsEditor.uplugin, we need to change the LoadingPhase of MarsEditor to be PostEngineInit instead of default, like this.

```
{
  "Name": "MarsEditor",
  "Type": "Editor",
  "LoadingPhase": "PostEngineInit"
},
```

You can find a list off all possible loading phases, with a description of when they are in /Engine/Source/Programs/UnrealBuildTool/System/ModuleDescriptor.cs. We can still let our MarsShared load during the default phase. Even though we switched our loading phase, we still need to make sure we null check `GEditor`, as it will still be null in some cases, for example during cooking. While we are in here, we should also change CanContainContent to be true since we will soon add a texture we will use.

```
"CanContainContent": true,
```

Now we are ready to start adding the functionality to our visualizer, we will start with adding a button to add a new point to the patrol route. The button will be shown on the actor when we have it selected and have a simple sprite we will draw, and in order to get a callback for when then the user clicks our sprite, we will use the hit proxy system. This system allows us to mark everything we render so we can get a callback when clicked. This will work on whatever we draw from when we set the hit proxy, including debug lines. We will start with adding a hit proxy for adding a new patrol route location, in MarsPatrolRouteComponentVisualizer.h add the following.

```
struct HMarsPatrolRouteNewPointVisProxy : public
HComponentVisProxy
{
  DECLARE_HIT_PROXY();

  HMarsPatrolRouteNewPointVisProxy(const UActorComponent*
_component )
    : HComponentVisProxy(_component)
  {}
};
```

Then we are going to need to add some new function definitions and variables.

```
class FMarsPatrolRouteComponentVisualizer : public
FComponentVisualizer
{
public:
  FMarsPatrolRouteComponentVisualizer();
  virtual void DrawVisualization(const UActorComponent*
_component, const FSceneView* _view, FPrimitiveDrawInterface*
_pdi) override;
  virtual bool VisProxyHandleClick(FEditorViewportClient*
_viewportClient, HComponentVisProxy* _visProxy, const
FViewportClick& _click) override;

private:
  TWeakObjectPtr<UMarsPatrolRouteComponent> PatrolComponent;
  int SelectedPoint = INDEX_NONE;
  TObjectPtr<UTexture2D> AddLocationTexture;
};
```

Now let's take a look at the implementation of these functions and go through what they are used for, /Plugins/MarsEditor/Source/MarsEditor/Private/Component Visualizers/ create MarsPatrolRouteComponentVisualizer.cpp and add the following code.

```
#include "ComponentVisualizers/MarsPatrolRouteComponentVisual
izer.h"

#include "Components/ActorComponent.h"
#include "Engine/Canvas.h"
#include "SceneView.h"
#include "NavigationSystem.h"
#include "NavigationPath.h"

#include "Mars/AI/MarsPatrolRouteComponent.h"
IMPLEMENT_HIT_PROXY(HMarsPatrolRouteNewPointVisProxy,
HComponentVisProxy);

FMarsPatrolRouteComponentVisualizer::FMarsPatrolRoute
ComponentVisualizer()
  : AddLocationTexture(LoadObject<UTexture2D>(NULL, TEXT
("/MarsEditor/AddLocation.AddLocation")))
{
}
```

First, we have all of the includes we will be needing, although we are not using them all of them yet. Then we have the macro to set up the vis proxy we added, just the struct name and its parent. Then in the constructor we load the texture we will use for the new point button. This texture needs to be placed in /Plugins/MarsEditor/Content/. Next up let's take a look at the `DrawVisualization` implementation.

```
void FMarsPatrolRouteComponentVisualizer::DrawVisualization
(const UActorComponent* _component, const FSceneView* _view,
FPrimitiveDrawInterface* _pdi)
{
  PatrolComponent = Cast<UMarsPatrolRouteComponent>
(const_cast<UActorComponent*>(_component));
  if (PatrolComponent == nullptr)
  {
    return;
  }

  if (AddLocationTexture != nullptr)
  {
    _pdi->SetHitProxy(new
HMarsPatrolRouteNewPointVisProxy(_component));
    _pdi->DrawSprite(PatrolComponent->GetOwner()->
GetActorLocation() + FVector(0, 0, 50), 10.0f, 10.0f,
AddLocationTexture->GetResource(), FLinearColor::White, SDPG_
World, 0.0f, 0.0f, 0.0f, 0.0f);
    _pdi->SetHitProxy(nullptr);
  }
}
```

First thing we do is store what component we are working with. We need to do this since our visualizer component will be re-used when we select a new actor with another instance of the component and unfortunately there is no OnSelectionChanged function or similar. After that we set a new instance of our hit proxy on the Primitive Draw Interface, render our sprite and then we clear the hit proxy. Everything we draw with the PDI until we reset the hit proxy will generate a callback for us. It does this by keeping a big lookup table for each pixel on the screen, that's how it can generate a callback for debug things that don't have a physical representation, like a debug line or in this case a sprite with our texture on it. Now let's take a look at the callback we get.

```
bool FMarsPatrolRouteComponentVisualizer::VisProxyHandleClick
(FEditorViewportClient* _viewportClient, HComponentVisProxy*
_visProxy, const FViewportClick& _click)
{
  if (_visProxy == nullptr)
  {
    return false;
  }
  if (IsValid(PatrolComponent.Get()) == false)
  {
    return false;
  }
  if (_visProxy->IsA(HMarsPatrolRouteNewPointVisProxy::
StaticGetType()))
  {
    GEngine->Exec(PatrolComponent->GetWorld(), TEXT("Editor.
ComponentVisualizer.AutoSelectComponent false"));
    FScopedTransaction transaction(FText::FromString("Added
new patrol point"));
    PatrolComponent->GetOwner()->Modify();
    SelectedPoint = PatrolComponent->PatrolLocations.
Add(PatrolComponent->GetOwner()->GetActorLocation());
    return true;
  }
  return false;
}
```

If the proxy is of our new point type, we set up an undo/redo buffer and mark our actor as being modified so we can undo this operation easily. We then add a new point and default the location to our actors position, we also keep track of the index of this newly created in SelectedPoint, this is so we can place a translation widget on the correct position (more on this soon).

We also set Editor.ComponentVisualizer.AutoSelectComponent to false through a console command execution. This is to stop the FComponentVisualizerManager from clearing our active component visualizer due to a selection notify change, this will lead to us not being able to place a translation widget directly on our point, but the user must select the point first before we get the translation widget. The console command fixes this so we can get the translation widget directly. It's not a big difference but it makes working with this component nicer and small usability details like these matters and will add up over time.

Ok, now we are able to add new points, so the next step is to be able to edit their location directly through a widget. In order to handle the translation and the widget, we only need to add two new functions.

```
class FMarsPatrolRouteComponentVisualizer : public FComponent
Visualizer
{
public:
  //…
  virtual bool HandleInputDelta(FEditorViewportClient*
_viewportClient, FViewport* _viewport, FVector&
_deltaTranslate, FRotator& _deltaRotate, FVector& _deltaScale)
override;
  virtual bool GetWidgetLocation(const FEditorViewportClient*
_viewportClient, FVector& _location) const override;
  //…
};
```

One function for handling the widget location and one for handling the input for the widget, let's take a look at the declarations.

```
bool FMarsPatrolRouteComponentVisualizer::GetWidgetLocation
(const FEditorViewportClient* _viewportClient, FVector&
_location) const
{
  if ( IsValid(PatrolComponent.Get()) &&
PatrolComponent->PatrolLocations.IsValidIndex(SelectedPoint))
  {
    _location = PatrolComponent->PatrolLocations
[SelectedPoint];
    return true;
  }
  return false;
}
```

For the widget location we simple return the position of our patrol point in the route that we have selected, by returning true we let the system know that we want to display a transform widget. This widget will support translation, rotation and scale. Just like any other transformation widget in Unreal. Now let's take a look at how we handle the input.

```
bool FMarsPatrolRouteComponentVisualizer::HandleInputDelta
(FEditorViewportClient* _viewportClient, FViewport* _viewport,
FVector& _deltaTranslate, FRotator& _deltaRotate, FVector&
_deltaScale)
{
```

```
  if ( IsValid(PatrolComponent.Get()) && PatrolComponent->
PatrolLocations.IsValidIndex(SelectedPoint))
  {
    FScopedTransaction transaction(FText::FromString("Delete
patrol point"));
    PatrolComponent->GetOwner()->Modify();
    PatrolComponent->PatrolLocations[SelectedPoint] +=
_deltaTranslate;
    return true;
  }
  return false;
}
```

We simply add on the translation value we are getting, if we were interested in rotation and scale, we would just have to handle those values also. Of course we also add a scoped transition so we can undo this. So now we can create a new point and move it around, but we have no way to select the points. For this we will need to add a new hit proxy. In the .h file add this.

```
struct HMarsPatrolRoutePointVisProxy : public
HComponentVisProxy
{
  DECLARE_HIT_PROXY();

  HMarsPatrolRoutePointVisProxy(const UActorComponent*
_component, int _index)
    : HComponentVisProxy(_component),
    Index(_index)
  {}
  int Index = INDEX_NONE;
};
```

In this hit proxy we also keep track of an index, this will be the index into our patrol route point array and is what we will use to identify the different points from each other. Now in MarsPatrolRouteComponentVisualizer.cpp we must also add the macro implementation.

```
IMPLEMENT_HIT_PROXY(HMarsPatrolRoutePointVisProxy,
HComponentVisProxy);
```

Then in `DrawVisualization` we need to add the following code.

```
void FMarsPatrolRouteComponentVisualizer::DrawVisualization
(const UActorComponent* _component, const FSceneView* _view,
FPrimitiveDrawInterface* _pdi)
{
  //...
  for(int i = 0; i < PatrolComponent->PatrolLocations.Num();
++i)
```

```
  {
    _pdi->SetHitProxy(new HMarsPatrolRoutePointVisProxy
(_component, i));
    _pdi->DrawPoint(PatrolComponent->PatrolLocations[i],
FLinearColor::Blue, 50.0f, SDPG_World);
    _pdi->SetHitProxy(nullptr);
  }
};
```

We draw one blue point for each patrol route point with our new hit proxy, making sure we give each hit proxy the index to the array so we can tell them apart when we receive input from them. To handle the input we need to add the following code in `VisProxyHandleClick()`.

```
bool FMarsPatrolRouteComponentVisualizer::VisProxyHandleClick
(FEditorViewportClient* _viewportClient, HComponentVisProxy*
 _visProxy, const FViewportClick& _click)
{
  //...
  if (_visProxy->IsA(HMarsPatrolRoutePointVisProxy::StaticGet
Type()))
  {
    GEngine->Exec(PatrolComponent->GetWorld(), TEXT("Editor.
ComponentVisualizer.AutoSelectComponent false"));

    HMarsPatrolRoutePointVisProxy* pointProxy = static_cast
<HMarsPatrolRoutePointVisProxy*>(_visProxy);
    SelectedPoint = pointProxy->Index;
    return true;
  }
  return false;
}
```

Same as the input for our add point button, we first make sure we disable `Editor.ComponentVisualizer.AutoSelectComponent` so it doesn't notify about the selection change. Without this, the first click would be ignored requiring the user to click the first point twice before the click registers. Again, not a big difference but also not a nice experience. However, we are changing the value of this variable so we should set it back when we are done with, to do this we need to add the following function to our class.

```
class FMarsPatrolRouteComponentVisualizer : public
FComponentVisualizer
{
public:
  //...
  virtual void EndEditing() override;
  //...
};
```

And the implementation.

```
void FMarsPatrolRouteComponentVisualizer::EndEditing()
{
  if (PatrolComponent != nullptr)
  {
    GEngine->Exec(PatrolComponent->GetWorld(), TEXT("Editor.
ComponentVisualizer.AutoSelectComponent true"));
  }
}
```

EndEditing will trigger when we are done moving our widget. We set back Editor.ComponentVisualizer.AutoSelectComponent to its default value. Now we can add points and select and edit them, but we don't actually render the path yet, so let's extend DrawVisualization with some logic for it.

```
void FMarsPatrolRouteComponentVisualizer::DrawVisualization
(const UActorComponent* _component, const FSceneView* _view,
FPrimitiveDrawInterface* _pdi)
{
  //...
  UNavigationSystemV1* navSystem = UNavigationSystemV1::
GetCurrent(PatrolComponent->GetOwner());
  for(int i = 0; i < PatrolComponent->PatrolLocations.Num();
++i)
  {
    bool pointIsValid = true;
    int nextIndex = (i + 1) % PatrolComponent->
PatrolLocations.Num();
    if (nextIndex != i)
    {
      bool renderedPath = false;
      if (IsValid(navSystem))
      {
        UNavigationPath* result = navSystem->FindPath
ToLocationSynchronously(PatrolComponent->GetOwner(),
PatrolComponent->PatrolLocations[i],
PatrolComponent->PatrolLocations[nextIndex]);
        if (result != nullptr)
        {
          for (int indexPath = 0; indexPath <
result->PathPoints.Num() - 1; ++indexPath)
          {
            FVector startPos = result->PathPoints[indexPath]
+ FVector::UpVector * 10.0f;
            FVector endPos = result->PathPoints[indexPath + 1]
+ FVector::UpVector * 10.0f;
```

```
            _pdi->DrawLine(startPos, endPos, FLinearColor::
Blue, SDPG_World);
            renderedPath = true;
          }
        }
      }
      if (renderedPath == false)
      {
        pointIsValid = false;
        _pdi->DrawLine(PatrolComponent->PatrolLocations[i],
PatrolComponent->PatrolLocations[nextIndex], FLinearColor::
Red, SDPG_World);
      }
    }
    bool isPointValid = false;
    if (IsValid(navSystem))
    {
      FNavLocation outPos;
      const ANavigationData* navdata = navSystem->MainNavData;
      if (IsValid(navdata) && navSystem->ProjectPointToNavigation
(PatrolComponent->PatrolLocations[i], outPos))
      {
        isPointValid = (PatrolComponent->PatrolLocations[i] -
outPos.Location).Length() < 50.0f;
      }
    }
    _pdi->SetHitProxy(new HMarsPatrolRoutePointVisProxy
(_component, i));
    _pdi->DrawPoint(PatrolComponent->PatrolLocations[i],
isPointValid ? FLinearColor::Blue : FLinearColor::Red, 50.0f,
SDPG_World);
    _pdi->SetHitProxy(nullptr);
  }
}
```

Instead of simple drawing a straight line between our points, we can use the navigation system to find a path between the points for us and then render this path instead. If we fail finding a path, we fall back to a straight line but render it in red instead. After we have rendered the path for this point, we project our point to the nav and check if our point is too far away, we also render that point in red. Here I'm hardcoding this distance to 50cm, but it really should be a setting somewhere instead. This way we can preview the patrol route for the AI and see if the path is going where we expect it to or if it fails completely, making this tool a lot more useful and saving on iteration time since we longer need to start a PIE session, wait on the AI to take the patrol route and then walk through it to make sure it works completely, instead we directly see the result of the path finder. Now we need to add "`NavigationSystem`" in `PrivateDependencyModuleNames` in MarsEditor.Build.cs.

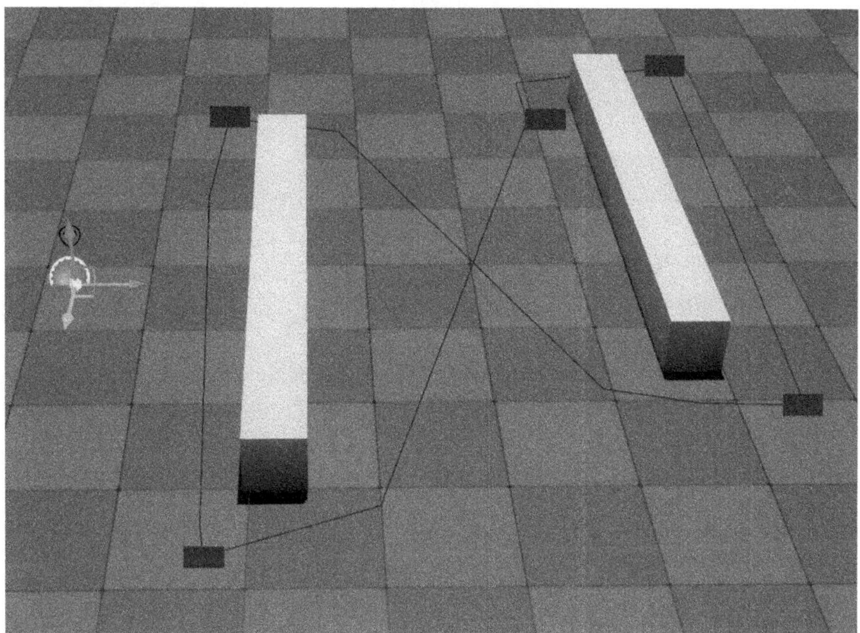

Our tool is improving, but there is one thing we still cannot do. Delete points. In order to do this, we are going to add our own right click menu on each point. So back to MarsPatrolRouteComponentVisualizer.h file and add the following code.

```
class FMarsPatrolRouteComponentVisualizer : public
FComponentVisualizer
{
public:
  //...
  virtual void OnRegister() override;
  virtual TSharedPtr<SWidget> GenerateContextMenu() const
override;
 private:
  void OnDeletePoint();
  TSharedPtr<FUICommandList> PointCommandList;
  //...
};
```

The support for context menus (right click menus) are built into the component visualizers, so there's not much we need. We will need our own `FUICommandInfo` and our own `FUICommandList`. This should be familiar from the other context menus we created. Let's first add our command. In MarsEditorCommands.h add the following code.

```
class FMarsEditorCommands : public TCommands<FMarsEditor
Commands>
```

```
{
public:
  //...
  TSharedPtr< FUICommandInfo > DeletePoint;
};
```

And then the following code in MarsEditorCommands.cpp.

```
void FMarsEditorCommands::RegisterCommands()
{
  //...
  UI_COMMAND(DeletePoint, "Delete Patrol Point", "Delete the
currently selected patrol point.", EUserInterfaceActionType::
Button, FInputChord());
}
```

We have created commands like this before and registered them, so back to the implementation in the component visualizer, where we will create our command list and register our callback in it.

```
#include "MarsEditorCommands.h"

void FMarsPatrolRouteComponentVisualizer::OnRegister()
{
  const FMarsEditorCommands& commands =
FMarsEditorCommands::Get();

  PointCommandList = MakeShareable(new FUICommandList);
  PointCommandList->MapAction(
    commands.DeletePoint,
    FExecuteAction::CreateSP(this, &FMarsPatrolRouteComponent
Visualizer::OnDeletePoint),
    FCanExecuteAction());
}
```

Let's take a look at the callback function for deleting the point first.

```
void FMarsPatrolRouteComponentVisualizer::OnDeletePoint()
{
  if ( IsValid(PatrolComponent.Get()) && PatrolComponent->
PatrolLocations.IsValidIndex(SelectedPoint))
  {
    FScopedTransaction transaction(FText::FromString("Delete
patrol point"));
    PatrolComponent->GetOwner()->Modify();
    PatrolComponent->PatrolLocations.RemoveAt(SelectedPoint);
    SelectedPoint = INDEX_NONE;
  }
}
```

We just remove the point, and we also deselect the point by setting `SelectPoint` to an invalid value, otherwise we would select the next point automatically (or go out of bounds on the array). As always, we also add a scoped transaction so we can undo this operation. The final step is to generate the right click menu widget.

```
TSharedPtr<SWidget> FMarsPatrolRouteComponentVisualizer::
GenerateContextMenu() const
{
  FMenuBuilder menuBuilder(true, PointCommandList);
  menuBuilder.BeginSection("PatrolRouteEdit",
FText::FromString("Patrol Route Point"));
  menuBuilder.AddMenuEntry(FMarsEditorCommands::Get().
DeletePoint);
  TSharedPtr<SWidget> menuWidget = menuBuilder.MakeWidget();
  return menuWidget;
}
```

As in earlier chapters, we use the menu builder to add our command. We have already seen how we can extend things with the menubuilder, so we are keeping it simple this time.

We have one last thing to go through with the component visualizer and that is how to draw HUD elements. In MarsPatrolRouteComponentVisualizer.h file add the following code.

```
class FMarsPatrolRouteComponentVisualizer : public
FComponentVisualizer
{
public:
  //...
  virtual void DrawVisualizationHUD(const UActorComponent*
_component, const FViewport* _viewport, const FSceneView*
_view, FCanvas *_canvas) override;
  //...
};
```

And the following code in MarsPatrolRouteComponentVisualizer.cpp.

```
void FMarsPatrolRouteComponentVisualizer::DrawVisualizationHUD
(const UActorComponent* _component, const FViewport*
_viewport, const FSceneView* _view, FCanvas* _canvas)
{
  if (IsValid(PatrolComponent.Get()) == false)
  {
    return;
  }
  const FIntRect canvasRect = _canvas->GetViewRect();
  _canvas->DrawTile(canvasRect.Width() * 0.79f, canvasRect.
Height() * 0.19f, 200.0f, 75.0f, 0.0f, 0.0f, 1.0f, 1.0f,
FLinearColor::Black);
```

```
  FString routeInfo = FString::Printf(TEXT("Number of points:
%i"), PatrolComponent->PatrolLocations.Num());
  _canvas->DrawShadowedString(canvasRect.Width() * 0.8f,
canvasRect.Height() * 0.2f, *routeInfo, GEngine->
GetSmallFont(), FLinearColor::White);

  float distance = 0.0f;
  for (int i = 1; i < PatrolComponent->PatrolLocations.Num();
++i)
  {
    distance += (PatrolComponent->PatrolLocations[i] -
PatrolComponent->PatrolLocations[i - 1]).Length();
  }
  FString routeDistance = FString::Printf(TEXT("Distance:
%.2fm"), distance * 0.01);
  _canvas->DrawShadowedString(canvasRect.Width() * 0.8f,
canvasRect.Height() * 0.22f, *routeDistance, GEngine->
GetSmallFont(), FLinearColor::White);
}
```

This function gives us access to a `FCanvas` which we can use to render some information about the selected component. Here we draw a background tile and then some information about how many patrol points are in the route and how long the route is (ideally, we should pathfind here also to get the true length). This way we can get some useful information on the screen, but honestly the `FCanvas` isn't the greatest tool to draw more complicated things so the usefulness of this is limited. The canvas can also be used to project positions onto the screen, so we can draw text at a 3D position, but more on that later this chapter.

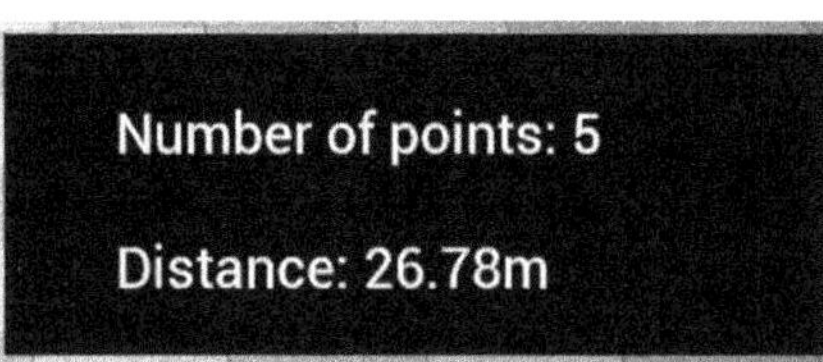

That is it for the component visualizer system. It does require a bit of setup for every new component type, and it has some quirks/issues if you have multiple components selected at the same time, but it has an easy and powerful to make use of the transformation widget in whatever way you prefer.

DEBUG INTERFACE

Sometimes setting up a completely new component visualizer is too much work for what we want, or we just don't have a component to connect our logic to since the logic is in the actor itself and refactoring it into its own component is just too much work, or just a bad idea. We just want to draw some debug information about the actor we have selected. There are several ways we could do this on.

First, we could tick the actor in the editor. In order to do this, we must specify that we want it to tick in the editor even when the game is not running by overriding the following function

```
virtual bool ShouldTickIfViewportsOnly() const override
{ return true; }
```

Of course, we must also enable tick on the actor by adding these lines in the constructor.

```
PrimaryActorTick.bStartWithTickEnabled = false;
PrimaryActorTick.bCanEverTick = true;
```

Now we will get calls to `OnTick` and we can debug render things or do other logic we might want. For certain types of objects this might be the right approach. Usually this is a bad idea however. Enabling ticks on object for editor reason can quickly make the editor sluggish once we start getting many actors in our level. Also, by having the same tick function being used for both gameplay and editor debug we can introduce new bugs where we rely on the behaviour in the editor and once we play the game standalone we see different behaviour due to this. This solution scales badly and potentially introduces new bugs.

Another method is to sign up to the selection delegates `USelection::SelectionChangedEvent`, `USelection::SelectObjectEvent` or `USelection::SelectNoneEvent`. This way we will get notified about any selection changes and can detect if this instance of the actor is selected or deselected. We could use this to register a new tick function like this.

```
FTSTicker::GetCoreTicker().AddTicker(FTickerDelegate::
CreateRaw(this, &AMarsOurActor::EditorTick));
```

This means we will not have a lot of ticking actors at once, which will be better for performance. However, once we start having a lot of actors in our levels, selection will start becoming sluggish due to the number of actors signed up to the delegate. Thus, this solution also scales badly.

Now we could improve this by just having a manager call the tick function manually only on our selection, all we would need then is an interface that the manager can work with. This way we can also limit the amount of actors we call tick on to preserve performance, which is very important for us since no one likes to work in a sluggish editor. Even better, we can make this interface Blueprint accessible so we can easily add it to any Blueprint we want. It does mean we must add an extra interface to the actors we want to use this on, but that cost is very minor, and we get a lot of flexibility in where we can implement editor ticking, so it is quite worth it. So, this solution will scale well, is fast and easy and even usable in Blueprints. We will need this interface to be placed in `MarsShared`, since we will obviously need to access it from the game. But `MarsShared` is a runtime module, it will not have access to some of the editor functions we will need. The actual editor code that makes use of the interface will be placed in the MarsEditor module. We always need to be mindful of which module we will place code in our plugin, otherwise we might end up with editor code in the runtime module, which will work fine as long we are building the editor, but as soon as we try to compile the game it will fail.

Let us start with creating the interface, In /Plugins/MarsEditor/Source/MarsShared/Public/ add MarsEditorDebugInterface.h and add the following code.

```
#pragma once

#include "MarsEditorDebugInterface.generated.h"

UINTERFACE(Blueprintable)
class MARSSHARED_API UMarsEditorDebugInterface : public
UInterface
{
  GENERATED_BODY()
};

class MARSSHARED_API IMarsEditorDebugInterface
{
  GENERATED_BODY()

public:
  UFUNCTION(BlueprintNativeEvent, BlueprintCallable,
CallInEditor, Category = "Debug", meta = (DevelopmentOnly))
  void EditorTick( float _deltaTime);
};
```

Our interface is quite simple, just one function. First, we make sure we make the interface Blueprintable since we want to be able to use it in Blueprints. Secondly, we make sure to add MARSSHARED_API so we can use it from other modules (like the game). Then, we make the actual function a BlueprintNativeEvent, so we can easily use it in either code or in Blueprints, CallInEditor is needed to specify that we should be able to call this function in the editor without a PIE session running, otherwise calling this function will silently fail. And finally, we add DevelopmentOnly so this node will not be included or called in our final shipping build of the game.

Even though we added the interface in MarsShared, we will do the actual ticking of it from MarsEditor, add the following in MarsEditor.h.

```
class FDelegateHandle;

class FMarsEditorModule: public IModuleInterface
{
  //...
  bool EditorTick(float _deltaTime);
private:
  FTSTicker::FDelegateHandle EditorTickHandle;
};
```

Since the `IModuleInterface` does not provide ticking support, we are going to have to sign up our tick function, so we need a delegate handle for that. Let's take a look at the registering in the cpp file.

```
void FMarsEditorModule::StartupModule()
{
  //...
  EditorTickHandle = FTSTicker::GetCoreTicker().AddTicker
(FTickerDelegate::CreateRaw(this, &FMarsEditorModule::
EditorTick));
}

void FMarsEditorModule::ShutdownModule()
{
  //...
  if (EditorTickHandle.IsValid())
  {
    FTSTicker::GetCoreTicker().RemoveTicker(EditorTickHandle);
    EditorTickHandle.Reset();
  }
}
```

The `FTSTicker` (ThreadSafeTicker) has a delegate we can use, we just need to sign up to it when starting up and remove ourselves when shutting down. Now let's take a look at the tick function itself.

```
#include "MarsEditorDebugInterface.h"

bool FMarsEditorModule::EditorTick(float _deltaTime)
{
  TArray<AActor*> selectedActors;
  UMarsSharedLibrary::GetSelectedActors(selectedActors);
  for (AActor* currentActor : selectedActors)
  {
    if (currentActor->GetClass()->ImplementsInterface(UMars
EditorDebugInterface::StaticClass()))
    {
      IMarsEditorDebugInterface::Execute_
EditorTick(currentActor, _deltaTime);
    }
    for (UActorComponent* currentComponent :
currentActor->GetComponents())
    {
      if (currentComponent->GetClass()->ImplementsInterface
(UMarsEditorDebugInterface::StaticClass()))
      {
        IMarsEditorDebugInterface::Execute_EditorTick
(currentComponent, _deltaTime);
```

```
            }
        }
    }
    return true;
}
```

We start with getting all our currently selected actors and then looping through them all, checking if they are implementing our debug interface and if so, we call it. Then we do the same for all the component on the selected actors. This makes our debug interface more flexible since we can add it to components also, the interface itself is not actor specific and works just as well on an actor component. Finally, we return true, which let the ticker class knows we want a tick the next frame also. Since we started using `USelection` we must also add an include for it.

Now this code has an obvious problem, it will not scale well. If we have a selection of several hundreds or thousands of actors, that will be a lot of debug rendering. We will need to limit how many times we call our tick function. We are going to make the number of calls into an user choice, since the ideal number can vary depending on context, if we are selecting several actors that are usually placed very close together maybe we want a very low number, or maybe even disable it completely. On the other hand, maybe we often work with selections that are larger, and we do want the debug rendering active. We have no way of knowing what is best for each user. So, we are going to make this number into an editor setting so each user can edit it locally to whatever they prefer. Luckily, we have already created a user setting file we can add this to. Edit MarsEditorUserSettings.h with the following code.

```
class UMarsEditorUserSettings: public UObject
{
  //...
  UPROPERTY(config, EditAnywhere, Category = "Debug
Interface")
  int MaxDebugTickAmount = 10;
};
```

We can now change this value in the editor preferences. You can find it here Edit > Editor Preferences > Mars Editor Settings.

We can edit our `EditorTick` function to the following.

```
bool FMarsEditorModule::EditorTick(float _deltaTime)
{
  //...
```

```
  const UMarsEditorUserSettings* editorSettings = GetDefault<
UMarsEditorUserSettings >();
  int maxTick = editorSettings->MaxDebugTickAmount;
  int currentTick = 0;
  for (AActor* currentActor : selectedActors)
  {
    if (currentActor->GetClass()->ImplementsInterface
(UMarsEditorDebugInterface::StaticClass()))
    {
      IMarsEditorDebugInterface::Execute_
EditorTick(currentActor,  _deltaTime);
      ++currentTick;
      if (currentTick >= maxTick)
      {
        break;
      }
    }
    for (UActorComponent* currentComponent :
currentActor->GetComponents())
    {
      if (currentComponent->GetClass()->ImplementsInterface
(UMarsEditorDebugInterface::StaticClass()))
      {
        IMarsEditorDebugInterface::Execute_
EditorTick(currentComponent, _deltaTime);
        ++currentTick;
        if (currentTick >= maxTick)
        {
          break;
        }
      }
    }
  }
  return true;
}
```

Now we have a working editor tick for any actor or component, accessible in both code and Blueprints that runs in a performant way. We can render debug lines/shapes when our is selected, which can be very useful.

3D TEXT IN EDITOR

Surprisingly, the editor doesn't have native support for rendering text at a 3D position (as of version 5.4.3) while not in a PIE session. When the game is running, we have this support, but it's implemented through the HUD class and accessed through the player controller, none of which we have in the editor. We are going to have to implement our own support for this. In order to do this, we will make use of `UDebugDrawService`. This system will allow us to get a callback with a `UCanvas` we can use for rendering, through the canvas we will be projecting and rendering our strings at a 3D world position. We will place this in our MarsShared module so we can use it both from MarsEditor, but also from the game (and any other plugin we might want to use it in). In /Plugins/MarsEditor/Source/MarsShared/Public/ edit MarsSharedModule.h and add the following code.

```
#pragma once

#include "CoreMinimal.h"
#include "Debug/DebugDrawService.h"
#include "Modules/ModuleManager.h"

class FMarsSharedModule : public IModuleInterface
{
public:
  virtual void StartupModule() override;
  virtual void ShutdownModule() override;

  bool EditorTick(float _deltaTime);

  void DrawDebugStringEditor(const FString& _string, const
FVector& _location, const FColor _color, float _duration,
float _scale);

private:
  void DebugDrawAllStrings(UCanvas* _canvas,
APlayerController* _controller);
  struct FMarsText3D
  {
    FMarsText3D(const FString& _string, const FVector&
_location, const FColor& _color, float _duration, float _scale)
      : String(_string)
      , Location(_location)
      , Color(_color)
      , Duration(_duration)
      , Scale(_scale)
    {
    }
    FString String;
    FVector Location;
    FColor Color;
    float Duration;
    float Scale;
  };
  TArray< FMarsText3D > DebugStringsWithDuration;

  FDebugDrawDelegate DebugDrawDelegate;
  FDelegateHandle DebugDrawDelegateHandle;

  FTSTicker::FDelegateHandle EditorTickHandle;
};
```

Just like in MarsEditorModule we have the Startup/ShutdownModule functions and the handle and EditorTick function which we are going to need in this module also. Then we have the actual function for adding a new string to be rendered, and one function to draw all strings, a new struct to store all information about every string we want to draw and some variables for the delegates we need. Let's start looking at the .cpp file next. In /Plugins/MarsEditor/Source/MarsShared/Private/ edit MarsSharedModule.cpp and add the following code.

```
#include "MarsSharedModule.h"

#include "Engine/Canvas.h"
#include "DebugRenderSceneProxy.h"
#include "Modules/ModuleManager.h"

#include "MarsEditorDebugInterface.h"

IMPLEMENT_MODULE(FMarsSharedModule, MarsShared)

void FMarsSharedModule::StartupModule()
{
  EditorTickHandle = FTSTicker::GetCoreTicker().AddTicker
(FTickerDelegate::CreateRaw(this, &FMarsSharedModule::EditorT
ick));
  FString viewFlagName(TEXT("EditorDebugText"));
  FEngineShowFlags::RegisterCustomShowFlag(*viewFlagName,
true, SFG_Normal, FText::FromString("3D Editor Text"));
  DebugDrawDelegate = FDebugDrawDelegate::CreateRaw(this,
&FMarsSharedModule::DebugDrawAllStrings);
  DebugDrawDelegateHandle = UDebugDrawService::Register
(*viewFlagName, DebugDrawDelegate);
}

void FMarsSharedModule::ShutdownModule()
{
  UDebugDrawService::Unregister(DebugDrawDelegateHandle);
  if (EditorTickHandle.IsValid())
  {
    FTSTicker::GetCoreTicker().RemoveTicker(EditorTickHandle);
    EditorTickHandle.Reset();
  }
}
```

Again, just like in MarsEditorModule we have the IMPLEMENT_MODULE macro, and then the EditorTick registering. But then we create a new show flag for our 3D strings. This is needed for the debug service, but it also means we can enable/disable the debug text rendering we are creating with the console command `ShowFlag.EditorDebugText 0/1` or through the Show menu in the viewport.

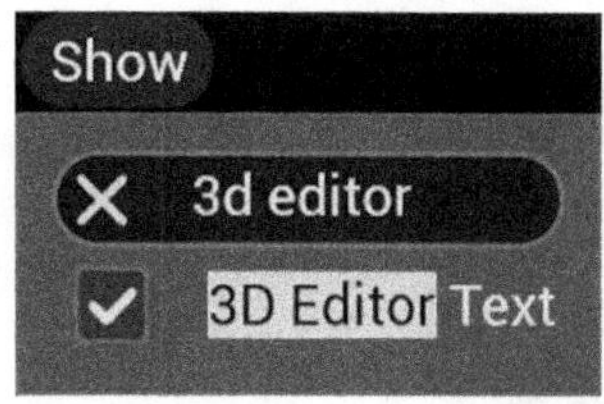

When we register ourselves to the debug service, we give it our show flag name and a delegate to our function that will render all the strings. Then for the unregistering we just give it the delegate handle. Next up is our function for adding strings to be drawn.

```
void FMarsSharedModule::DrawDebugStringEditor(const FString&
_string, const FVector& _location, const FColor _color, float
_duration, float _scale)
{
  DebugStringsWithDuration.Add(FMarsText3D(_string, _location,
_color, FMath::Max( 0.0f, _duration), _scale));
}
```

Very simple, we just add it to the array. We make sure we don't have a negative duration since that would cause the string to not render at all, we want it to render one frame at least even if someone passes in -1.0f for duration for some reason. Then our `EditorTick` function will look like.

```
bool FMarsSharedModule::EditorTick(float _deltaTime)
{
  for (int i = DebugStringsWithDuration.Num() - 1; i >= 0;
--i)
  {
    if (DebugStringsWithDuration[i].Duration >= 0.0f)
    {
      DebugStringsWithDuration[i].Duration -= _deltaTime;
    }
    else
    {
      DebugStringsWithDuration.RemoveAtSwap(i);
    }
  }
  return true;
}
```

We loop though the array backwards so we can safely delete any strings if they have expired. If the time is negative, we remove it, otherwise we just decrease the time. This is so we will always render each string at least for one frame. Now the important part, the actual rendering of the strings.

```
void FMarsSharedModule::DebugDrawAllStrings(UCanvas* _canvas,
APlayerController* _controller)
{
  const FFontRenderInfo fontRenderInfo = _canvas->
CreateFontRenderInfo(true, true);
  UFont* renderFont = GEngine->GetSmallFont();
  const FSceneView* view = _canvas->SceneView;

  for (const FMarsText3D& string : DebugStringsWithDuration)
```

```
    {
      if (FDebugRenderSceneProxy::PointInView(string.Location,
view))
      {
        const FVector screenLoc = _canvas->Project(string.
Location);
        _canvas->SetDrawColor(string.Color);
        _canvas->DrawText(renderFont, string.String,
screenLoc.X, screenLoc.Y, string.Scale, string.Scale,
fontRenderInfo);
      }
    }
}
```

We get a player controller as a parameter, but in the editor, it will always be null so let's ignore it. First, we get a font and create a render info for that font, saying we want to allow text clipping and shadows. We could also specify a glow here if we want, but that is not necessary for our purposes. Then we simple loop through all the strings we need to draw this frame, check if they are in view and then project their position to a screen location, set the draw colour we want to use and render it. The only thing missing now is an easier way to call `DrawDebugStringEditor` on our module, we will do this in MarsSharedLibrary. Add the following function definition in the .h file.

```
class MARSSHARED_API UMarsSharedLibrary : public
UBlueprintFunctionLibrary
{
  //...
  UFUNCTION(BlueprintCallable, Category = "Rendering|Debug")
  static void DrawDebugStringEditor(const FString& _string,
const FVector& _location, const FLinearColor _color =
FLinearColor::White, float _duration = 0.0f, float _scale =
1.0f);
};
```

We want this function to be Blueprint callable to make it more usable. Now, let's take a look at the implementation.

```
#include "MarsSharedModule.h"
//...
void UMarsSharedLibrary::DrawDebugStringEditor(const FString&
_string, const FVector& _location, const FLinearColor _color,
float _duration, float _scale)
{
  if (FMarsSharedModule* sharedModule = FModuleManager::
GetModulePtr< FMarsSharedModule >("MarsShared"))
  {
```

```
    sharedModule->DrawDebugStringEditor(_string, _location,
_color.ToFColorSRGB(), _duration, _scale);
  }
}
```

Not much to it, we just get our module and add it. Now we can very easily add useful information that is rendered from our selected actor (or its components), we can do it both from code and Blueprint. Being able to render 3D text in the editor is very useful, specially combined with our editor tick we just created. Personally I think this is more useful then the component visualizers, even though they have more powerful transformation widget handling which is nice. But getting helpful information about your current selection can be really helpful and speed up iteration and debugging quite a bit.

7 Google Sheet

In this chapter we will combining a lot of knowledge from earlier chapters, with some new things also, to create something a bit larger and more complex then we have so far. We will add support to upload or download a data table to a Google Sheets. This is a great way to allow designers to access data in a more friendly way and if you have designers that are comfortable with Google Sheets, they can make some advanced stuff in them to help them with tweaking various values in the game.

In order to do this, we have multiple things we need to implement. First off, we need to extend the right click menu for assets in the content browser, when we click on a data table, we want to inject a menu entry of our own. This should open up a completely new window that handles the upload/download process. In this window the user will choose which Google Sheet (and which page in that sheet) to upload/download from. We need to present this data and also allow the user to add/remove new sheets/pages. This is a lot more then we have done in slate so far, so I will show some good practices for handling larger slate windows. Then we need to do the actual upload/download which we will do in an external process and create a PowerShell script to handle the security and the actual upload/download. This part could also be done in Python if you are more comfortable with that. Of course, we must also set up the Google Sheet to allow us to do this and enable some Google API to allow this. We have quite a bit to go through in this chapter!

CONTENT BROWSER EXTENSION

We will start with looking at how we will add the entry to the right click menu in the content browser and how we control when our entry is added or not. In /Plugins/MarsEditor/Source/MarsEditor/Public/ContentBrowserExtension/ create MarsEditorDataTableExtension.h and add the following code.

```
#pragma once

#include "CoreMinimal.h"

class FMarsEditorDataTableExtension
{
public:
  TSharedRef< FExtender > AddMenuEntryForAssets(const TArray<
FAssetData >& _assetDataList);
  void AddMenuEntry(FMenuBuilder& _menuBuilder);
  void OpenWindow();
private:

  TWeakObjectPtr<UDataTable> SelectedDataTable;
};
```

DOI: 10.1201/9781003511748-8

We will be expanding this quite a bit soon, but this is a good start. In /Plugins/MarsEditor/Source/MarsEditor/Private/ContentBrowserExtension/ create MarsEditorDataTableExtension.cpp and add the following code.

```
#include "ContentBrowserExtension/MarsEditorDataTableExtension.h"
#include "Interfaces/IMainFrameModule.h"
#include "Widgets/Text/SMultiLineEditableText.h"

TSharedRef< FExtender > FMarsEditorDataTableExtension::AddMenu
EntryForAssets(const TArray< FAssetData >& _assetDataList)
{
  if (_assetDataList.Num() != 1 )
  {
    return MakeShareable(new FExtender());
  }
  if(_assetDataList[0].AssetClassPath.GetAssetName() !=
UDataTable::StaticClass()->GetFName())
  {
    return MakeShareable(new FExtender());
  }

  SelectedDataTable = Cast< UDataTable >(_assetDataList[0].
GetAsset());

  TSharedPtr< FExtender > menuExtender = MakeShareable(new
FExtender());

  menuExtender->AddMenuExtension("ImportedAssetActions",
EExtensionHook::Before, TSharedPtr< FUICommandList >(),
FMenuExtensionDelegate::CreateRaw(this,
&FMarsEditorDataTableExtension::AddMenuEntry));

  return menuExtender.ToSharedRef();
}
```

`AddMenuEntryForAssets` is our callback which we will hook up soon where we will receive the assets that was right clicked. If we do not want to add anything we just return an empty `FExtender` object. But if we have a single data table asset selected, we create a new menu extender and give it our function where we will add our menu entries. We also save which data table we clicked on, since we will need this to do the actual download/upload.

```
void FMarsEditorDataTableExtension::AddMenuEntry(FMenuBuilder&
_menuBuilder)
{
  _menuBuilder.AddMenuEntry(FText::FromString("Google Sheet
Upload/Download"), FText::FromString("Google Sheet Upload/
Download"), FSlateIcon(),
FUIAction(FExecuteAction::CreateRaw(this,
&FMarsEditorDataTableExtension::OpenWindow)));
}
```

When this function gets called, we will get a `FMenuBuilder`, which should be familiar by now since we have used it in earlier chapters. We add our entry with a callback to our `OpenWindow` function.

```
void FMarsEditorDataTableExtension::OpenWindow()
{
}
```

For now, I left this function empty, but this is where we will open a new window filled with our slate widgets, so there's going to be lots of code in here soon. Before we continue, let's hook up our helper class. Let's go to MarsEditor.h and add the following.

```
#include "ContentBrowserExtension/
MarsEditorDataTableExtension.h"


class FMarsEditorModule : public IModuleInterface
{
//...
public:
  void RegisterContentBrowserExtension();
  void UnregisterContentBrowserExtension();
private:
  FMarsEditorDataTableExtension DataTableExtender;
  FDelegateHandle DataTableExtenderHandle;
};
```

We follow the same pattern as before with our register/unregister functions here. But this time we also need a delegate handle to keep track of. Let's take a look at MarsEditor.cpp file to see why.

```
#include "ContentBrowserModule.h"
void FMarsEditorModule::StartupModule()
{
  //...
  RegisterContentBrowserExtension();
}

void FMarsEditorModule::ShutdownModule()
{
  //...
  UnregisterContentBrowserExtension();
}

void FMarsEditorModule::RegisterContentBrowserExtension()
{
  FContentBrowserModule& contentBrowserModule =
FModuleManager::LoadModuleChecked< FContentBrowserModule
>("ContentBrowser");
```

```
  TArray< FContentBrowserMenuExtender_SelectedAssets >&
assetExtenders =
contentBrowserModule.GetAllAssetViewContextMenuExtenders();

  int index = assetExtenders.Add(
FContentBrowserMenuExtender_SelectedAssets::CreateRaw
(&DataTableExtender, &FMarsEditorDataTableExtension::
AddMenuEntryForAssets));
  DataTableExtenderHandle = assetExtenders[index].GetHandle();
}

void FMarsEditorModule::UnregisterContentBrowserExtension()
{
  FContentBrowserModule& contentBrowserModule =
FModuleManager::LoadModuleChecked< FContentBrowserModule
>("ContentBrowser");
  TArray< FContentBrowserMenuExtender_SelectedAssets
>& assetExtenders = contentBrowserModule.
GetAllAssetViewContextMenuExtenders();

  assetExtenders.RemoveAll([this](const
FContentBrowserMenuExtender_SelectedAssets& _delegate)
    {
      return _delegate.GetHandle() == DataTableExtenderHandle;
    });

  DataTableExtenderHandle.Reset();
}
```

In order to register our data table helper class we have to get the `ContentBrowser` module, add ourselves to the array of all extenders and then save the handle so we can remove ourselves during shutdown of our module. When we register our extender, we give it the `AddMenuEntryForAssets` functions, which as we saw earlier is where we will do any filtering to check if we should inject anything in the right click menu. This function will get called every single time we right on anything in the content browser, so we should be mindful about what kind of checks we do in it, so that they are performant.

GOOGLE SHEET SETUP

We also need to set up a Google project and enable some APIs for it and create an account which will be what we use to download and upload to from a script, this account is what we need to share any sheet we want to use with. Start with going to the official Google Developers Console at https://console.cloud.google.com/apis/dashboard.

You are going to have to create a new project first, I'm calling my project UnrealBook. Then click Enable APIs and Services.

Now scroll down to the Google Workspace section and let's enable Google Drive API and Google Sheets API. Do the Google Drive API first and then the Google Sheets API.

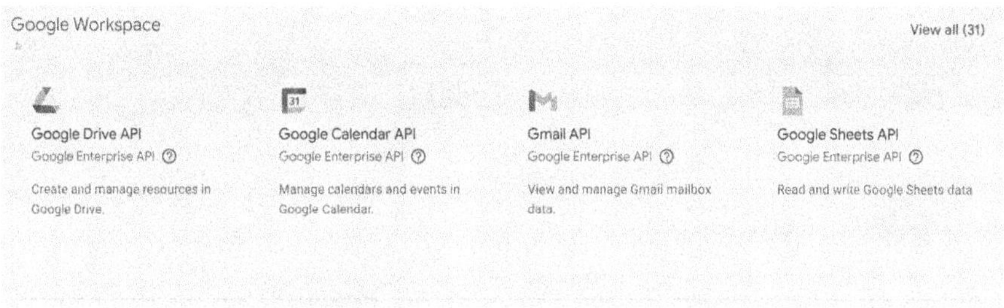

We will need these two APIs to handle the authorization and the communication with the Google Sheet. After enabling the Google Sheets API, go to the Credentials tab and click Create Credentials.

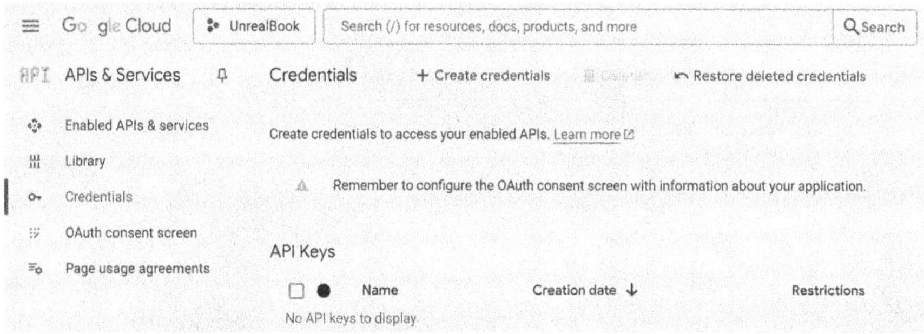

Choose a Service Account since this will allow us to use a certificate instead of username/password for the login validation.

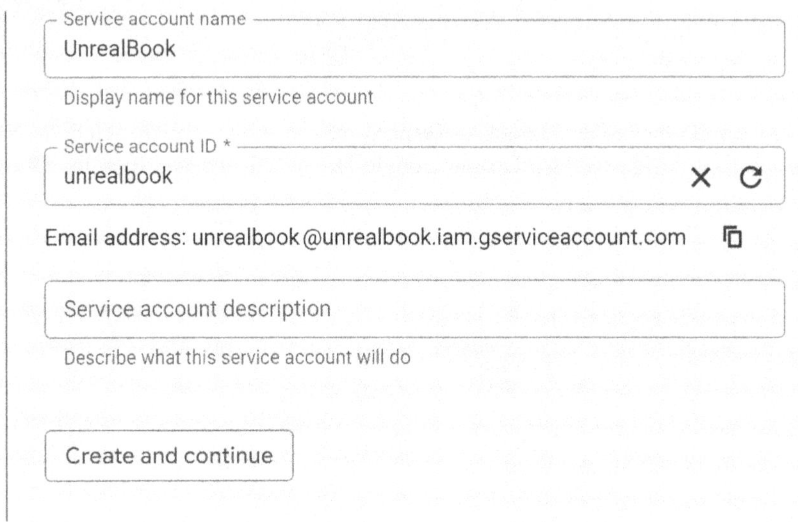

I'm naming my account UnrealBook. Write this account name and email address to it down, we will need it later. Then it's time set the access right for the account.

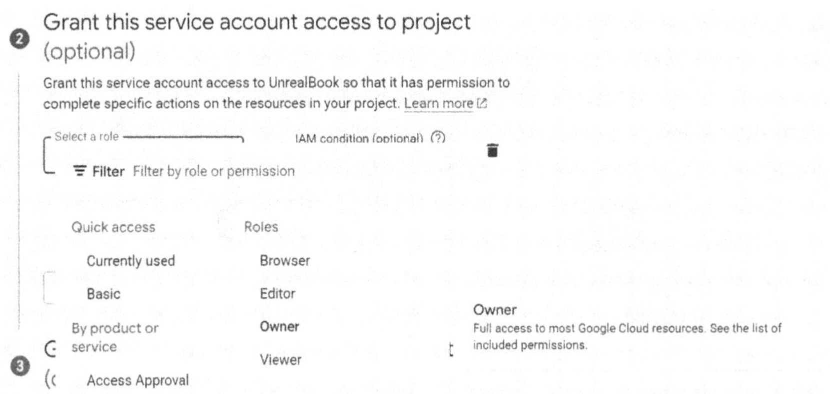

You will want Owner access. You can find it under Basic (or also under Project). Now click the newly created service account, then click the Keys tab and then choose Add Key and select Create New Key.

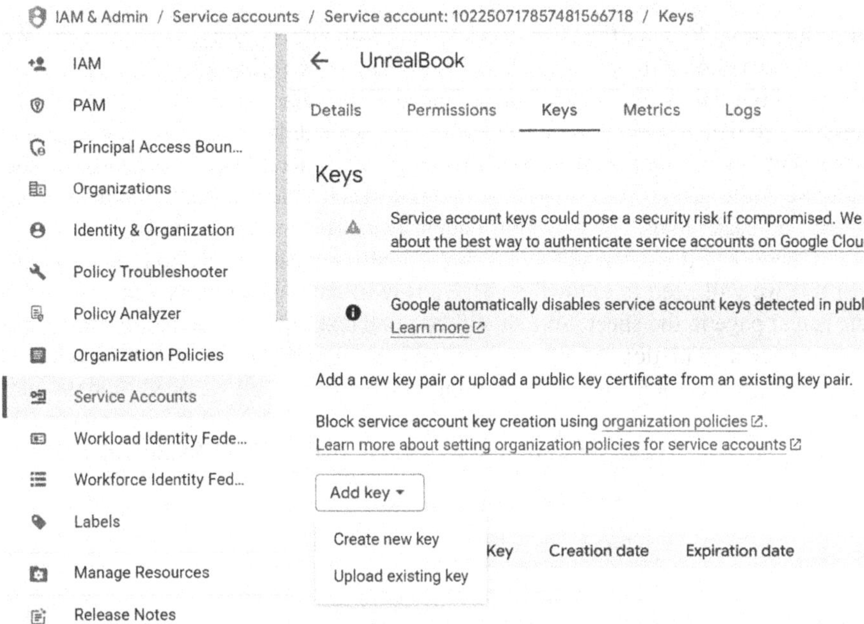

Select a P12 as key type and select Create, this will give you a private key file to download. Do *not* lose this file, you will not be able to get it again and you will have to create a new key if you lose it. Place it in /Plugins/MarsEditor/Scripts/.

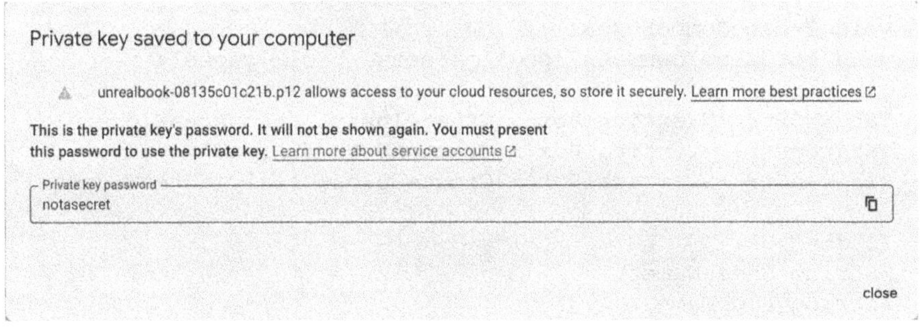

We will also need a password to the private key, but it's always "notasecret" so that is easy enough to keep track of, the private key file is the important thing. I check this file in with my scripts file in Perforce/GitHub in my projects, since access to this will be restricted for me, but how you handle this will of course depends on the security needs of your project. Now we have the Google setup part out of the way and can continue with some actual coding again.

SLATE WINDOW

Next up we will create the slate window, but without any actual functionality. We will add that soon. We have a bunch of requirements the window will need to fulfil. The most obvious is that we are going to need a download button and an upload button. But we will also need to select to where we upload/download to. Which Google Sheet and which page in the sheet. We are going to need two dropdowns for that. Now we could just let the user give us the URL each time, but the tool will be more useful and easier to us if we save this data instead. This means we will need a way to add a sheet (and if we can add things, we will also need to be able to remove them). For this we will need to know the URL, a way of naming the sheet and a name for the actual page in the sheet. So that will be three text fields and a button for the add and one for the deletion. Finally, we will also need to display some instructions on how to use it this tool, since we are going to use PowerShell we need to make sure the user has the correct version, and they are also going to need to install a Google module for PowerShell. We have quite a bit we need to do in Slate! Let's start in MarsEditorDataTableExtension.h and see what we need to add here.

```
class FMarsEditorDataTableExtension
{
//…
private:
  void UploadOrDownloadGoogleDoc(bool _upload);

  FReply AddNewSheet();
  FReply DownloadSheet();
  FReply UploadSheet();
  FReply DeleteSheet();
  FReply DeletePage();

  void CreateComboBoxes();
  void LoadDropdownData (bool _sheets, bool _pages);

  TSharedPtr< SVerticalBox > CreateInstallationAreaWidget();
  TSharedPtr< SVerticalBox > CreateAddSheetAreaWidget();
  TSharedPtr< SVerticalBox > CreateUploadDownloadAreaWidget();

  FString URL;
  FString SheetName;
  FString PageName;

  TArray< TSharedPtr< FString > > SheetsDropdownOptions;
  TArray< TSharedPtr< FString > > PagesDropdownOptions;

  TSharedPtr< SComboBox< TSharedPtr< FString > > >
SheetComboBox;
  TSharedPtr< SComboBox< TSharedPtr< FString > > >
PageComboBox;
```

```
  int SheetIndex = INDEX_NONE;
  int PageIndex = INDEX_NONE;

  bool InstructionsAreaCollapsed = true;
  bool AddNewSheetAreaCollapsed = true;
  bool UploadDownloadAreaCollapsed = false;
};
```

A bunch of functions for our button and variables to store things from the user text input we will need. We also need the arrays with data for the dropdown menus (`SheetsDropdownOptions` and `PagesDropdownOptions`), and to keep track of which we have selected (`SheetIndex` and `PageIndex`). We also have pointers to the actual dropdown widgets (`SheetComboBox` and `PageComboBox`), this is so we can force refresh after we add or delete a sheet/page. Finally, we have the *Collapsed bools, this is because we are going to split the window up in three parts and allow the user to collapse each part individually. You are only going to need the installation instructions once, so we can keep that collapsed most of the time. Same with adding new sheets/pages, you will not do that very often so it can also start collapsed and the user can expand it when needed. Then the actual upload/download area is probably always going to be used, so it might not really need to be collapsable, but we will follow the same pattern here so that the widget will look uniform and nice, but we will always start with it expanded.

Before we get started with the slate code, let's discuss it a bit. Doing small things in slate are quite manageable and you don't need to worry too much about how you structure your slate code, even if you tend to end up with more code than expected. This time we are going to be adding quite a few different slate widgets and since slate code is quite verbose things can quickly get out of hand. We can do this in one big block of course and quite a few places in the engine do it like this, but it gets very hard to get a good overview and very easy to make mistakes that become very time consuming to find and doing even very minor tweaks can become very time consuming because the code is so hard to navigate. Instead, we will be creating smaller segments of slate code and then combine these segments, we are also placing these different segments in different functions. The intent with his is not to re-use code, but to get a better overview and a more flexible code base for the slate window. Alright let's start with implementing to `OpenWindow()` function we left empty earlier.

```
void FMarsEditorDataTableExtension::OpenWindow()
{
  TSharedPtr< SVerticalBox > installationInstructionsWidget =
CreateInstallationAreaWidget();
  TSharedPtr< SVerticalBox > addSheetWidget =
CreateAddSheetAreaWidget();
  TSharedPtr< SVerticalBox > uploadDownloadAreaWidget =
CreateUploadDownloadAreaWidget();

  TSharedPtr< SExpandableArea >
installationInstructionsExpandableWidget;
```

```
  SAssignNew(installationInstructionsExpandableWidget,
SExpandableArea)
    .MinWidth(800)
    .InitiallyCollapsed(InstructionsAreaCollapsed)
    .OnAreaExpansionChanged_Lambda([this](const bool&
_isExpanded)
      {
        InstructionsAreaCollapsed =
!InstructionsAreaCollapsed;
      })
    .HeaderContent()
    [
      SNew(STextBlock)
        .Text(FText::FromString("Setup instructions"))
    ]
    .BodyContent()
    [
      installationInstructionsWidget.ToSharedRef()
    ];

  TSharedPtr< SExpandableArea > addSheetExpandableWidget;
  SAssignNew(addSheetExpandableWidget, SExpandableArea)
    .MinWidth(800)
    .InitiallyCollapsed(AddNewSheetAreaCollapsed)
    .OnAreaExpansionChanged_Lambda([this](const bool&
_isExpanded)
      {
        AddNewSheetAreaCollapsed = !AddNewSheetAreaCollapsed;
      })
    .HeaderContent()
    [
      SNew(STextBlock)
        .Text(FText::FromString("Add new sheet"))
    ]
    .BodyContent()
    [
      addSheetWidget.ToSharedRef()
    ];

  TSharedPtr< SExpandableArea >
uploadDownloadExpandableWidget;
  SAssignNew(uploadDownloadExpandableWidget, SExpandableArea)
    .MinWidth(800)
    .InitiallyCollapsed(UploadDownloadAreaCollapsed)
    .OnAreaExpansionChanged_Lambda([this](const bool&
_isExpanded)
      {
        UploadDownloadAreaCollapsed =
!UploadDownloadAreaCollapsed;
      })
```

```
    .HeaderContent()
    [
      SNew(STextBlock)
        .Text(FText::FromString("Upload/Download"))
    ]
    .BodyContent()
    [
     uploadDownloadAreaWidget.ToSharedRef()
    ];

  TSharedRef< SWindow > window = SNew(SWindow)
    .Title(FText::FromString("Upload or Download to a Google
Sheet"))
    .ClientSize(FVector2D(800, 900))
    .SupportsMaximize(false)
    .SupportsMinimize(false)
    [
      SNew(SVerticalBox)
        + SVerticalBox::Slot()
        .AutoHeight()
        .HAlign(HAlign_Center)
        .VAlign(VAlign_Top)
        [
          installationInstructionsExpandableWidget.
ToSharedRef()
        ]
        + SVerticalBox::Slot()
        .AutoHeight()
        .HAlign(HAlign_Center)
        .VAlign(VAlign_Top)
        [
          addSheetExpandableWidget.ToSharedRef()
        ]
        + SVerticalBox::Slot()
        .AutoHeight()
        .HAlign(HAlign_Center)
        .VAlign(VAlign_Top)
        [
          uploadDownloadExpandableWidget.ToSharedRef()
        ]
    ];

  IMainFrameModule& mainFrameModule = FModuleManager::
LoadModuleChecked< IMainFrameModule >(TEXT("MainFrame"));
  FSlateApplication::Get().AddWindowAsNativeChild(window,
mainFrameModule.GetParentWindow().ToSharedRef());
}
```

Since our window will be divided up in three parts, we have a function for generating the widget for each of those parts, we will be looking into these soon but for now we will just assume they are implemented. After that we create three

SExpendableArea, these will allow the user to collapse the entire widget which we want, it just needs a start state and then a lambda for when the user changes the expansion state. Then it has a small header part where we will just place a text widget, and it has a body part where we place our premade widgets. Then we place these expandable boxes in a SWindow widget, which is a widget for a free-floating window that the user can move around and resize. Even though we have these three premade widgets to save space and get an overview, this is still quite a bit of code, about 90 lines of it. As you can see when writing slate code, the lines really add up quickly and it's very easy to get lost fast. Anyway, finally we get the mainframe module and use this to open our slate widget as a new window. Now let's take a look at the installation instructions area widget function.

```
TSharedPtr< SVerticalBox > FMarsEditorDataTableExtension::
CreateInstallationAreaWidget()
{
  const FString installationInstructions = "Install latest
version of Powershell"
    "\nOpen a command prompt (Win + r and enter cmd) and
type\n"
    "winget install --id Microsoft.Powershell --source
winget\n"
    "Select yes to everyting\n\n"
    "Install Google powershell module\n"
    "Open a powershell command prompt, Win + R and enter
pwsh\n"
    "Type in\n"
    "Install - Module - Name UMN - Google - RequiredVersion
1.2.6\n"
    "Select yes to everything";

  TSharedPtr< SVerticalBox > installationInstructionsWidget;
  SAssignNew(installationInstructionsWidget, SVerticalBox)
    + SVerticalBox::Slot()
    .AutoHeight()
    .Padding(5.0f)
    .HAlign(HAlign_Center)
    [
      SNew(SHorizontalBox)
        + SHorizontalBox::Slot()
        .AutoWidth()
        .HAlign(HAlign_Left)
        [
          SNew(SMultiLineEditableText)
            .IsReadOnly(true)
            .Text(FText::FromString(installationInstructions))
        ]
    ];
  return installationInstructionsWidget;
}
```

As far as slate code goes, this is quite small and simple. Just a vertical box with a text widget in it. We are using the SMultiLineEditableText widget for two reasons. First, we have quite a bit of text that does requires multiple lines, so we need a widget that handles this well. But also, this widget allows the user to select text in it, and we can make it read only so it cannot be edited, even though the name of the widget implies it can. Since we have a couple of things in the installation instructions that require the user to write in text in a command prompt, it's nice if they can just copy paste the text required. Now you should also follow the installation instructions on your computer. We are going to need PowerShell installed and the Google PowerShell module also. Your computer probably already has PowerShell installed, but it might be an old version. Make sure you follow the instructions. If you do not have pwsh.exe on your computer but powershell.exe you have an old version and need to update. It's a bit confusing I know. Alright let's move on to the area that will allow the user to add new sheets/pages.

```
TSharedPtr< SVerticalBox > FMarsEditorDataTableExtension::
CreateAddSheetAreaWidget()
{
  const FString usageInstructions = "1. Create a new Google
Sheet\n"
    "2. Share it with unrealbook@unrealbook.iam.
gserviceaccount.com\n"
    "3. Copy adress into URL box\n"
    "4. Enter a display name for the sheet. This is the name
you will see in the dropdown\n"
    "5. Type in the page name you want to add, this must match
_exactly_\n"
    "6. Click Add Page\n"
    "7. Upload your datatable to make sure the row/column
format is correct.";

  //Installation instructions widget
  TSharedPtr< SHorizontalBox > usageInstructionWidget;
  SAssignNew(usageInstructionWidget, SHorizontalBox)
    + SHorizontalBox::Slot()
    .AutoWidth()
    .HAlign(HAlign_Left)
    [
      SNew(SMultiLineEditableText)
        .IsReadOnly(true)
        .Text(FText::FromString(usageInstructions))
    ];

  //URL text field
  TSharedPtr< SHorizontalBox > urlTextWidget;
  SAssignNew(urlTextWidget, SHorizontalBox)
    + SHorizontalBox::Slot()
    .AutoWidth()
    .HAlign(HAlign_Left)
```

```
    .VAlign(VAlign_Center)
    [
      SNew(STextBlock)
        .Text(FText::FromString(TEXT("URL ")))
    ]
    + SHorizontalBox::Slot()
    .HAlign(HAlign_Right)
    [
      SNew(SEditableTextBox)
        .MinDesiredWidth(300)
        .OnTextChanged_Lambda([this](const FText& _text)
          {
            URL = _text.ToString();
          })
    ];

  //Display name text field
  TSharedPtr< SHorizontalBox > nameTextWidget;
  SAssignNew(nameTextWidget, SHorizontalBox)
    + SHorizontalBox::Slot()
    .AutoWidth()
    .HAlign(HAlign_Left)
    .VAlign(VAlign_Center)
    [
      SNew(STextBlock)
        .Text(FText::FromString(TEXT("Display name")))
    ]
    + SHorizontalBox::Slot()
    .HAlign(HAlign_Right)
    [
      SNew(SEditableTextBox)
        .MinDesiredWidth(300)
        .OnTextChanged_Lambda([this](const FText& _text)
          {
            SheetName = _text.ToString();
          })
    ];

  //Page name text field
  TSharedPtr< SHorizontalBox > pageTextWidget;
  SAssignNew(pageTextWidget, SHorizontalBox)
    + SHorizontalBox::Slot()
    .AutoWidth()
    .HAlign(HAlign_Left)
    .VAlign(VAlign_Center)
    [
      SNew(STextBlock)
        .Text(FText::FromString(TEXT("Page name ")))
    ]
    + SHorizontalBox::Slot()
    .HAlign(HAlign_Right)
```

```
    [
      SNew(SEditableTextBox)
        .MinDesiredWidth(300)
        .OnTextChanged_Lambda([this](const FText& _text)
          {
            PageName = _text.ToString();
          })
    ];

  //Main vertical box
  TSharedPtr< SVerticalBox > addSheetWidget;
  SAssignNew(addSheetWidget, SVerticalBox)
    + SVerticalBox::Slot()
    .AutoHeight()
    .Padding(5.0f)
    .HAlign(HAlign_Center)
    [
      usageInstructionWidget.ToSharedRef()
    ]
    + SVerticalBox::Slot()
    .AutoHeight()
    .Padding(5.0f)
    .HAlign(HAlign_Center)
    [
      urlTextWidget.ToSharedRef()
    ]
    + SVerticalBox::Slot()
    .AutoHeight()
    .Padding(5.0f)
    .HAlign(HAlign_Center)
    [
      nameTextWidget.ToSharedRef()
    ]
    + SVerticalBox::Slot()
    .AutoHeight()
    .Padding(5.0f)
    .HAlign(HAlign_Center)
    [
      pageTextWidget.ToSharedRef()
    ]
    + SVerticalBox::Slot()
    .AutoHeight()
    .Padding(5.0f)
    .HAlign(HAlign_Center)
    [
      SNew(SButton)
        .Text(FText::FromString("Add Sheet"))
        .OnClicked_Raw(this, &FMarsEditorDataTableExtension::
AddNewSheet)
    ];
  return addSheetWidget;
}
```

Phew! Quite a bit of code! But it's not actually doing that much. Like before we use a read only `SMultiLineEditorableText` widget for the instructions since people will need to copy the email to share the document with. This is the email we created earlier so you will need to update `unrealbook@unrealbook.iam.gserviceaccount.com` to the account you created.

After this we create a bunch of vertical boxes with a text block and then an editable text box. These are where the user will enter the URL to the page they want to upload/download from and the display name we will show them when selecting this sheet in the future and finally what page in the sheet they want to upload and download from.

Finally, we add all this in a vertical box and also add a button that will call `AddNewSheet` for us if clicked. We will look at the implementation for this function in the next section, but first we will go through the rest of the slate setup. Next up is the upload/download area which has a bit more advanced slate widgets in it since it will have two dropdowns for choosing which sheet and which page to upload/download from. We will take a look at the combo boxes widget creation first.

```
void FMarsEditorDataTableExtension::CreateComboBoxes()
{
  LoadDropdownData(true, true);

  SheetComboBox = SNew(SComboBox<TSharedPtr<FString> >)
    .OptionsSource(&SheetsDropdownOptions)
    .OnGenerateWidget_Lambda([&](TSharedPtr<FString> _option)
-> TSharedRef<SWidget>
      {
        return SNew(STextBlock).Text(FText::
FromString(*_option));
      })
    .OnSelectionChanged_Lambda([this](TSharedPtr<FString>
_newChoice, ESelectInfo::Type _selectType)
      {
        SheetIndex = SheetsDropdownOptions.Find(_newChoice);
        LoadDropdownData(false, true);
      })
    .InitiallySelectedItem(nullptr)
    [
      SNew(STextBlock)
        .Text_Lambda([&]() -> FText
          {
            if (SheetsDropdownOptions.
IsValidIndex(SheetIndex))
            {
              return FText::FromString(*SheetsDropdownOptions
[SheetIndex]);
            }
            return FText::FromString(FString("Invalid"));
          })
    ];
```

```
  PageComboBox = SNew(SComboBox<TSharedPtr<FString> >)
    .OptionsSource(&PagesDropdownOptions)
    .OnGenerateWidget_Lambda([&](TSharedPtr<FString> _option)
-> TSharedRef<SWidget>
      {
       return SNew(STextBlock)
         .Text(FText::FromString(*_option));
      })
    .OnSelectionChanged_Lambda([this](TSharedPtr<FString>
_newChoice, ESelectInfo::Type _selectType)
      {
        PageIndex = PagesDropdownOptions.Find(_newChoice);
      })
    .InitiallySelectedItem(nullptr)
    [
      SNew(STextBlock)
        .Text_Lambda([&]() -> FText
          {
            if (PagesDropdownOptions.IsValidIndex(PageIndex))
            {
              return FText::FromString(*PagesDropdownOptions
[PageIndex]);
            }
            return FText::FromString(FString("Invalid"));
          })
    ];
}
```

We will look at implementation of `LoadDropdownData(true, true)` later, this function will load all our saved sheet and pages information and fill `SheetsDropdownOptions` and `PagesDropdownOptions` with proper data, we will look into how we save and load this information once we are done with all the slate setup. After that we created the two different dropdowns, one for our list of sheets and one for our list of pages. We need to save the pointers to this dropdown widgets since we will need to refresh them when add or delete data from them. The `SComboBox` slate widget is quite flexible and useful but also requires some setup. It has more options than we are using here, but let's go through the different options we are using. But first a note on the _Lamba option of the entries. These exist as function callback also, just drop the _Lambda from the name. For shorter implementation like these I prefer to use the lambda version, but if they get bigger, I would use the function callback version. I will select the option that makes the code more readable and easier to navigate.

- `OptionsSource` – This is our data we want to be in the dropdown list. All the sheet/page names for us.
- `OnGenerationWidget_Lamba` – This is where we create the widget for each option in the dropdown list, this is different from the widget for the

selected option though, these widgets are only visible when the dropdown is opened.
- `OnSelectionChanged_Lamda` – Here we save the index to our currently selected sheet or page. When we change sheet, we reload all the page data with `LoadDropdownData()`, this will also refresh the page combo box. This is because we only want to show the pages connected to the selected sheet and not all pages.
- `InitiallySelectedItem`, we don't start with selected item. But if we wanted to improve this window, we could start remembering which data table is connected to which sheet and then feed in that item here, thus always starting with the correct sheet selected.

After these options we have another block with another text block in it. This is where we create the widget for the currently selected option. In other words, it's entirely possible to have a different look on the slate widget for the dropdown options and for the selected option. Which could be nice in some cases, but usually they are the same as here and it would be nice if there was an option to not need to do this manually, but there isn't. Anyway, then we do the same thing again, but for the page combo box. Next up is the slate widget setup for the upload/download area of our window.

```
TSharedPtr< SVerticalBox > FMarsEditorDataTableExtension::
CreateUploadDownloadAreaWidget()
{
  CreateComboBoxes();

  //Sheet widgets
  TSharedPtr< SHorizontalBox > sheetWidgets;
  SAssignNew(sheetWidgets, SHorizontalBox)
    + SHorizontalBox::Slot()
    .AutoWidth()
    .HAlign(HAlign_Left)
    .VAlign(VAlign_Center)
    [
      SNew(STextBlock)
        .Text(FText::FromString(TEXT("Sheet ")))
    ]
    + SHorizontalBox::Slot()
    .AutoWidth()
    .HAlign(HAlign_Center)
    [
      SNew(SBox)
      .WidthOverride(300.0f)
      [
      SheetComboBox.ToSharedRef()
      ]
    ]
    + SHorizontalBox::Slot()
    .AutoWidth()
    .HAlign(HAlign_Right)
```

```
    [
      SNew(SButton)
        .OnClicked_Raw(this, &FMarsEditorDataTableExtension::
DeleteSheet)
        [
          SNew(SImage)
            .Image(FAppStyle::GetBrush("Icons.Delete"))
        ]
    ];

  //Page widgets
  TSharedPtr< SHorizontalBox > pageWidgets;
  SAssignNew(pageWidgets, SHorizontalBox)
    + SHorizontalBox::Slot()
    .AutoWidth()
    .HAlign(HAlign_Left)
    .VAlign(VAlign_Center)
    [
      SNew(STextBlock)
        .Text(FText::FromString(TEXT("Page ")))
    ]
    + SHorizontalBox::Slot()
    .AutoWidth()
    .HAlign(HAlign_Center)
    [
      SNew(SBox)
        .WidthOverride(300.0f)
        [
          PageComboBox.ToSharedRef()
        ]
    ]
    + SHorizontalBox::Slot()
    .AutoWidth()
    .HAlign(HAlign_Right)
    [
      SNew(SButton)
        .OnClicked_Raw(this, &FMarsEditorDataTableExtension::
DeletePage)
        [
          SNew(SImage)
            .Image(FAppStyle::GetBrush("Icons.Delete"))
        ]
    ];

  //Upload/download buttons
  TSharedPtr< SVerticalBox > uploadDownloadButtonsWidget;
  SAssignNew(uploadDownloadButtonsWidget, SVerticalBox)
    + SVerticalBox::Slot()
    .AutoHeight()
    .HAlign(HAlign_Center)
    [
```

```
      SNew(SHorizontalBox)
        + SHorizontalBox::Slot()
        .AutoWidth()
        [
          SNew(SButton)
            .Text(FText::FromString("Upload"))
            .OnClicked_Raw(this, &FMarsEditorData
TableExtension::UploadSheet)
        ]
        + SHorizontalBox::Slot()
        .AutoWidth()
        [
          SNew(SButton)
            .Text(FText::FromString("Download"))
            .OnClicked_Raw(this, &FMarsEditorData
TableExtension::DownloadSheet)
        ]
    ];

  //Main vertical box
  TSharedPtr< SVerticalBox > uploadDownloadAreaWidget;
  SAssignNew(uploadDownloadAreaWidget, SVerticalBox)
    + SVerticalBox::Slot()
    .HAlign(HAlign_Center)
    .AutoHeight()
    [
      sheetWidgets.ToSharedRef()
    ]
    + SVerticalBox::Slot()
    .HAlign(HAlign_Center)
    .AutoHeight()
    [
      pageWidgets.ToSharedRef()
    ]
    + SVerticalBox::Slot()
    .HAlign(HAlign_Center)
    .AutoHeight()
    [
      uploadDownloadButtonsWidget.ToSharedRef()
    ];

  return uploadDownloadAreaWidget;
}
```

Again, lots of code! But in reality, we are not actually doing that much. We start with a horizontal box for the sheets, first just a text field with “Sheet” in it, followed by our combo box we created earlier and then a button with an icon in it for deleting the selected sheet. Then we do the exact same setup, but for the pages instead. Then we have two buttons, one for uploading and one for downloading. Then we add all these widgets into a vertical box. That’s (finally) it for the slate code. Now it’s time to look at how we actually store the sheet/page data and how we add a new sheet and delete them.

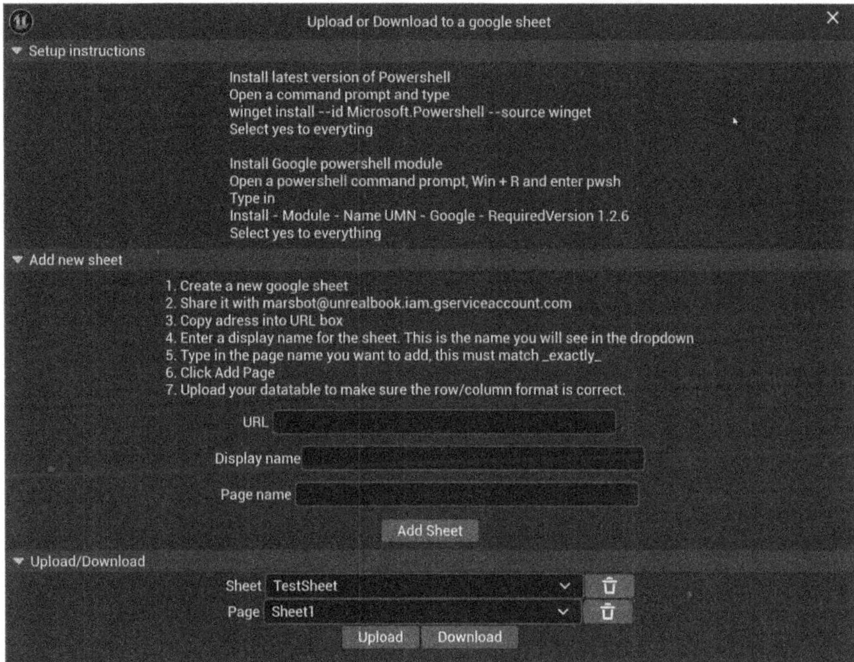

SHEET/PAGE DATA

Now it's time to save the actual sheet/page data, so the first thing we will look at is where we will save this. Before we saved some data in the editor project settings, and we will do that this time also. However, we do not want this setting to be per user but shared between everyone working on the project so in MarsEditorSettings.h add the following code.

```
USTRUCT()
struct FMarsEditorGoogleSheetPageData
{
  GENERATED_BODY()

  UPROPERTY(config, EditAnywhere)
  FString DisplayName;
  UPROPERTY(config, EditAnywhere)
  FString GID;
};

USTRUCT()
struct FMarsEditorGoogleSheetData
```

```
{
  GENERATED_BODY()

  UPROPERTY(config, EditAnywhere)
  FString DisplayName;
  UPROPERTY(config, EditAnywhere)
  FString SheetID;
  UPROPERTY(config, EditAnywhere)
  TArray< FMarsEditorGoogleSheetPageData > Pages;
};

UCLASS(Config = MarsEditorSettings, defaultconfig)
class MARSEDITOR_API UMarsEditorSettings : public UObject
{
 //...

  UPROPERTY(config, EditAnywhere, Category = "Google Sheets")
  TArray< FMarsEditorGoogleSheetData > SheetData;
};
```

We have a struct for every sheet we will save, and every sheet have an array of pages in them. They both have a display name and an ID string. Of note is the `defaultconfig` keyword. This means that changes to this setting should be placed in the default config file and not in the per user save file of the ini file. In other words, this keyword is what makes our settings file be shared between everyone in the project.

Now that we have a settings file to save our data, let's take a look at how we dig out the data itself. We will start with the function we hooked up to the Add sheet button earlier.

```
FReply FMarsEditorDataTableExtension::AddNewSheet()
{
  if (SheetName.IsEmpty())
  {
    FMessageDialog::Open(EAppMsgType::Ok,
FText::FromString("You must enter a valid sheet display
name!"));
    return FReply::Handled();
  }
  if (PageName.IsEmpty())
  {
    FMessageDialog::Open(EAppMsgType::Ok,
FText::FromString("You must enter a valid page name!"));
    return FReply::Handled();
  }
  if (URL.IsEmpty())
  {
```

```
    FMessageDialog::Open(EAppMsgType::Ok,
FText::FromString("You must enter a valid URL!"));
    return FReply::Handled();
  }

  //This pattern is responsible for getting the last number of
the URL, the GID
  const FRegexPattern gidPattern(TEXT("[^gid=]+$"));
  //This pattern is responsible for getting everything before
the GID part start
  const FRegexPattern sheetIDPattern(TEXT("^.*
(?=(\\/edit))"));
  //This pattern is responsible for getting everything after
the last /, this is the sheet id
  const FRegexPattern sheetIDPattern2(TEXT("([^\\/]+$)"));

  FString sheetID, gid;
  FRegexMatcher matcherGID(gidPattern, URL);
  FRegexMatcher matcherSheetID(sheetIDPattern, URL);
  if (matcherGID.FindNext() && matcherSheetID.FindNext())
  {
    gid = matcherGID.GetCaptureGroup(0);
    FString sheetIDURL = matcherSheetID.GetCaptureGroup(0);
    FRegexMatcher matcherSheetID2(sheetIDPattern2,
sheetIDURL);
    if (matcherSheetID2.FindNext())
    {
      sheetID = matcherSheetID2.GetCaptureGroup(0);
    }
  }
  if (sheetID.IsEmpty())
  {
    FMessageDialog::Open(EAppMsgType::Ok,
FText::FromString("URL is incorrect, please copy the entire
URL to the Google Sheet!"));
    return FReply::Handled();
  }

  UMarsEditorSettings* editorSettings = GetMutableDefault<
UMarsEditorSettings >();
  int newSheetIndex = INDEX_NONE;
  for (int i = 0; i < editorSettings->SheetData.Num(); ++i)
  {
    FMarsEditorGoogleSheetData& sheet =
editorSettings->SheetData[i];
    if (sheet.SheetID == sheetID)
    {
      newSheetIndex = i;
      break;
    }
  }
```

```
  if (newSheetIndex == INDEX_NONE)
  {
    FMarsEditorGoogleSheetData newSheet;
    newSheet.DisplayName = SheetName;
    newSheet.SheetID = sheetID;
    newSheetIndex = editorSettings->SheetData.Add(newSheet);
  }
  for (const FMarsEditorGoogleSheetPageData& page :
editorSettings->SheetData[newSheetIndex].Pages)
  {
    if (page.GID == gid)
    {
      FMessageDialog::Open(EAppMsgType::Ok,
FText::FromString("This page is already added!"));
      return FReply::Handled();
    }
  }
  FMarsEditorGoogleSheetPageData newPageData;
  newPageData.DisplayName = PageName;
  newPageData.GID = gid;

  PageIndex = editorSettings->SheetData[newSheetIndex].Pages.
Add(newPageData);
  SheetIndex = newSheetIndex;

  editorSettings->TryUpdateDefaultConfigFile();

  FMessageDialog::Open(EAppMsgType::Ok, FText::FromString("New
sheet added!"));

  LoadDropdownData(true, true);

  return FReply::Handled();
}
```

First, we start off with some easy validation of our data, we require the user to enter a sheet URL, a sheet name and a page name. If any of these are empty, we open a popup with an error message. Then we need to dig out some information from the URL. We need to get the sheet ID and the page ID. For this we will use some regexps. If you don't understand these don't worry, regexp is notoriously cryptic, but with some Google skills you can usually find what you need.

Once we have all the data, we do a check to see if the sheet is already added, if so, we want to add the new page to that existing sheet instead of adding a new sheet. We also verify that the page isn't already added. Finally, we write in our data in the setting file and then we save the file with `TryUpdateDefaultConfigFile()`, this will save the changes to the default ini file, which means once we check in our changes everyone will get them. If we used `SaveConfig()` instead our changes would be changed in a local copy of the ini file under the /Saved/ folder and we would not check it in. So even though we marked the setting file to write all changes in the default ini file, that only applies if we edit the settings file through the editor settings window, when we change the settings from code we have to use the correct save function. After we save the data, we reload it for our dropdowns so the new entry is selectable and open an OK popup to let the user know everything went well. As you can see opening a popup window like this is very easy, this call will pause the code execution here until the user makes a choice, which makes it very easy to use. Next up, deleting a sheet.

```
FReply FMarsEditorDataTableExtension::DeleteSheet()
{
  FText msg = FText::FromString("Are you sure you want to
delete this sheet from this list? (the actual Google Sheet
will still exist)");
  EAppReturnType::Type userResponse = FMessageDialog::Open
(EAppMsgType::YesNo, msg);
  if (userResponse == EAppReturnType::Yes)
  {
    UMarsEditorSettings* editorSettings = GetMutableDefault<
UMarsEditorSettings >();
    if (editorSettings->SheetData.IsValidIndex(SheetIndex))
    {
      editorSettings->SheetData.RemoveAt(SheetIndex);
      SheetIndex = INDEX_NONE;
      editorSettings->TryUpdateDefaultConfigFile();

      LoadDropdownData(true, true);

      FMessageDialog::Open(EAppMsgType::Ok,
FText::FromString("Sheet deleted!"));
    }
    else
    {
      FMessageDialog::Open(EAppMsgType::Ok,
FText::FromString("Invalid sheet selected, cannot delete!"));
    }
  }
  return FReply::Handled();
}
```

We added this function to the delete page button we added earlier. We start with opening a Yes/No dialog box asking if they are sure they want to delete this sheet, always a good idea for destructive actions. We do some error checking and let the user know what went wrong, if we pass all the checks, we delete the sheet, save the file and then reload the data for the dropdown. Next up is the function for deleting a page.

```
FReply FMarsEditorDataTableExtension::DeletePage()
{
```

```
  FText msg = FText::FromString("Are you sure you want to
delete this page from this list? (the actual Google Sheet will
still exist)");
  EAppReturnType::Type userResponse = FMessageDialog::Open
(EAppMsgType::YesNo, msg);
  if (userResponse == EAppReturnType::Yes)
  {
    UMarsEditorSettings* editorSettings = GetMutableDefault<
UMarsEditorSettings >();
    if (editorSettings->SheetData.IsValidIndex(SheetIndex))
    {
      if (editorSettings->SheetData[SheetIndex].Pages.
IsValidIndex(PageIndex))
      {
        editorSettings->SheetData[SheetIndex].Pages.
RemoveAt(PageIndex);
        PageIndex = INDEX_NONE;

        if (editorSettings->SheetData[SheetIndex].Pages.
IsEmpty())
        {
          editorSettings->SheetData.RemoveAt(SheetIndex);
          SheetIndex = INDEX_NONE;
        }

        editorSettings->TryUpdateDefaultConfigFile();

        LoadDropdownData(true, true);

        FMessageDialog::Open(EAppMsgType::Ok,
FText::FromString("Page deleted!"));
      }
      else
      {
        FMessageDialog::Open(EAppMsgType::Ok,
FText::FromString("Invalid page selected, cannot delete!"));
      }
    }
    else
    {
      FMessageDialog::Open(EAppMsgType::Ok,
FText::FromString("Invalid sheet selected, cannot delete!"));
    }
  }
  return FReply::Handled();
}
```

As you might have suspected, it's very similar to how we deleted a sheet. We have a bit more error handling since we verify the sheet data first also and if we deleted the last page we also delete the sheet. With the deletion out of the way it's time to take a look at loading the data.

```
void FMarsEditorDataTableExtension::LoadDropdownData(bool
_sheets, bool _pages)
{
  //Clear and load the sheet/page data
  const UMarsEditorSettings* editorSettings = GetDefault<
UMarsEditorSettings >();
  if (_sheets)
  {
    SheetsDropdownOptions.Reset();
    for (const FMarsEditorGoogleSheetData& sheet :
editorSettings->SheetData)
    {
      SheetsDropdownOptions.Add(MakeShared< FString >(sheet.
DisplayName));
    }
  }
  if (_pages && editorSettings->SheetData.
IsValidIndex(SheetIndex))
  {
    PagesDropdownOptions.Reset();
    for (const FMarsEditorGoogleSheetPageData& page :
editorSettings->SheetData[SheetIndex].Pages)
    {
      PagesDropdownOptions.Add(MakeShared< FString >(page.
DisplayName));
    }
  }

  //Refresh the dropdown wigets
  if (_sheets && SheetComboBox.IsValid())
  {
    if (SheetsDropdownOptions.IsValidIndex(SheetIndex))
    {
      SheetComboBox->SetSelectedItem(SheetsDropdownOptions
[SheetIndex]);
    }
    else
    {
      SheetComboBox->SetSelectedItem(nullptr);
    }
    SheetComboBox->RefreshOptions();
  }
  if (_pages && PageComboBox.IsValid())
  {
    if (PagesDropdownOptions.IsValidIndex(PageIndex))
    {
```

```
            PageComboBox->SetSelectedItem(PagesDropdownOptions
[PageIndex]);
        }
        else
        {
            PageComboBox->SetSelectedItem(nullptr);
        }
        PageComboBox->RefreshOptions();
    }
}
```

Our load function supports only loading the sheets, only the pages or both. The main reason for this is that if we have a sheet selected and add or remove a page, we don't want to reset the sheet dropdown, we want to keep that selection and only refresh the page dropdown data. So first we clear our old options in the data arrays, then we read in the new data from our settings file. After this we reset our selection on the dropdown boxes (since the old one could be invalid by now) and then we force the dropdown boxes to refresh so our change is reflected in the visuals. That's it for how we store, save and load the sheet/page IDs.

LAUNCHING EXTERNAL PROCESS

In order to upload or download to Google Sheet we will be launching an external process that will handle the authorization and the actual upload/download. Launching the external process will be similar to how we did earlier with the commandlets. We will also need to convert our data table to a CSV so that the Google Sheet will understand our data. Let's start with taking a look at the Upload/DownloadSheet functions we still haven't implemented.

```
FReply FMarsEditorDataTableExtension::DownloadSheet()
{
  UploadOrDownloadGoogleDoc(false);
  return FReply::Handled();
}

FReply FMarsEditorDataTableExtension::UploadSheet()
{
  UploadOrDownloadGoogleDoc(true);
  return FReply::Handled();
}
```

Not much to say, we just call the real function with a different parameter value, so let's take a look at that function instead. It's a bit long so I will split it up in segments.

```
void FMarsEditorDataTableExtension::UploadOrDownloadGoogleDoc
(bool _upload)
{
```

```
  const UMarsEditorSettings* editorSettings = GetDefault
< UMarsEditorSettings >();
  if (!editorSettings->SheetData.IsValidIndex(SheetIndex))
  {
    FMessageDialog::Open(EAppMsgType::Ok,
FText::FromString("Not a valid sheet selected!"));
    return;
  }
  if (!editorSettings->SheetData[SheetIndex].Pages
.IsValidIndex(PageIndex))
  {
    FMessageDialog::Open(EAppMsgType::Ok,
FText::FromString("Not a valid sheet page selected!"));
    return;
  }

  FString sheetID = editorSettings->SheetData[SheetIndex]
.SheetID;
  FString pageGID = editorSettings->SheetData[SheetIndex]
.Pages[PageIndex].GID;
  FString pageName = editorSettings->SheetData[SheetIndex]
.Pages[PageIndex].DisplayName;
  FString sheetFile = FString("MarsEditor\\Scripts\\
GoogleSheet.ps1");
  FString tmpCSVFile = FPaths::ConvertRelativePathToFull
(FPaths::ProjectPluginsDir() + FString("MarsEditor\\Scripts\\
tmp.csv"));
  FString projPath = FPaths::ConvertRelativePathToFull
(FPaths::ProjectPluginsDir() + sheetFile);
  FString command = FString("pwsh.exe");
  FString params = FString("-ExecutionPolicy Bypass -File ") +
projPath + FString(" -SpreadsheetID ") + sheetID +
FString(" -CSVFile ") + tmpCSVFile;

  if (_upload)
  {
    FString csvData = SelectedDataTable->
GetTableAsCSV(EDataTableExportFlags::UseSimpleText);
    FFileHelper::SaveStringToFile(csvData, *tmpCSVFile);
    //When uploading we need to use the page name
    params = params + FString(" -Upload true -Page ") +
pageName;
  }
  else
  {
    //When downloading we need to use the page GID
    params = params + FString(" -Upload false -Page ") +
pageGID;
  }
  //TODO - continue with code here
```

We start with some error handling and validation of the data, making sure we have valid sheets and pages selected. Then we start building up our command line with which we will start the external process with. If we are uploading our data table, we first create a CSV string from it and then we write this into a temporary CSV file in our scripts folder and send this file path to our script. Whether we are uploading or downloading we provide the sheet ID, which makes sense. But if we are uploading, we only make use of the page name and when downloading we make use of the page ID. A quirk of the Google API. We will look on the PowerShell file GoogleSheet.ps1 a bit later. Note we use pwsh.exe instead of Powershell.exe, we will use some functionality that requires a later version of PowerShell (Powershell.exe is the old version, pwsh.exe is the newer version). Now we have our command line ready and it's time to launch our new process.

```
  int32 returnCode = -1;
  void* pipeRead = nullptr;
  void* pipeWrite = nullptr;

  if (!FPlatformProcess::CreatePipe(pipeRead, pipeWrite))
  {
    FMessageDialog::Open(EAppMsgType::Ok, FText::FromString("U
ploadDownloadGoogleDoc failed FPlatformProcess::CreatePipe"));
    return;
  }
  bool success = false;
  FProcHandle proc = FPlatformProcess::CreateProc(*command,
*params, false, true, true, nullptr, 0, nullptr, pipeWrite,
pipeRead);
  if (proc.IsValid())
  {
    FString stringOutput;

    FScopedSlowTask slowTask(100.0f, FText::FromString(_upload
? "Uploading to Google Sheet" : "Downloading from Google
Sheet"));
    // Add some progress so we have some progress that
animates nicely so it's clear that the editor hasn't crashed
    slowTask.EnterProgressFrame(0.0f);
    slowTask.MakeDialog(true, true);
    while (FPlatformProcess::IsProcRunning(proc))
    {
      FString thisRead = FPlatformProcess::ReadPipe(pipeRead);
      stringOutput += thisRead;

      if (slowTask.CompletedWork < 95.0f)
      {
        slowTask.EnterProgressFrame(2.0f);
      }

      if (slowTask.ShouldCancel())
```

```
      {
        FPlatformProcess::TerminateProc(proc, true);
      }
      FPlatformProcess::Sleep(0.1f);
    }

    stringOutput += FPlatformProcess::ReadPipe(pipeRead);

    //Check if Google module is installed, it not we need to
display install instructions
    if (stringOutput.Contains("The remote server returned an
error") == false)
    {
      //TODO - Add code here
    }
    else
    {
      FText title = FText::FromString("Install Google
module");
      FMessageDialog::Open(EAppMsgType::Ok,
FText::FromString("Google module is not installed properly,
please follow install instructions"), title);
    }

    FPlatformProcess::GetProcReturnCode(proc, &returnCode);
  }
  else
  {
    FString errorMsg = FString::Printf(TEXT("Process
failed, please make sure you have followed all installation
instructions completly.\n\nFPlatformProcess::CreateProc
Params: %s"), *params);
    FMessageDialog::Open(EAppMsgType::Ok,
FText::FromString(errorMsg), FText::FromString("Failure"));
    return;
  }

  FPlatformProcess::ClosePipe(pipeRead, pipeWrite);
  FPlatformProcess::CloseProc(proc);
}
```

Just like we did in the commandlet chapter, we create some pipes to read the data back and launch the new process. We have no idea how long it will take and no good way of getting progress back from it, so we just create a fake progress bar that we increase the value on until we are close to the end when we stop increasing it. The process of uploading/downloading is usually pretty fast, so this approach is ok. But if you have some really large data tables you might want to improve on this progress bar logic a bit. We also have a bit of error handling if we failed to launch the process completely or if it returned a string indicating that the Google PowerShell module haven't been installed. Now let's take a look at the final piece of code in this function. Replace "`//TODO - Add code here`" with the following code.

```
if (_upload)
{
  success = true;
  FText title = FText::FromString("Upload done");
  FText msg = FText::FromString("Upload is done");
  UE_LOG(LogMarsCommandlet, Display, TEXT("Upload done.\n%s"),
*stringOutput);
  if (stringOutput.Contains("403 (Forbidden)"))
  {
    msg = FText::FromString("Upload failed!\nForbidden
response recieved\nDid you  forget to share you Google Sheet
with unrealbook@unrealbook.iam.gserviceaccount.com?");
  }
  FMessageDialog::Open(EAppMsgType::Ok, msg, title);
}
else
{
  if (stringOutput.Contains("Response status code does not
indicate success") == false)
  {
    TArray< FString > issues = SelectedDataTable
->CreateTableFromCSVString(stringOutput);
    FString errorMsg;
    int numErrors = 0;
    for (const FString& issue : issues)
    {
      errorMsg += issue + "\n";
      ++numErrors;
      if (numErrors > 5)
      {
        break;
      }
    }
    if (!errorMsg.IsEmpty())
    {
      FText title = FText::FromString("CSV to datatable import
failed!");
      FMessageDialog::Open(EAppMsgType::Ok,
FText::FromString(errorMsg), title);
    }
    else
    {
      success = true;
      SelectedDataTable->MarkPackageDirty();
      FText title = FText::FromString("Success!");
      FMessageDialog::Open(EAppMsgType::Ok,
FText::FromString("Download succeeded"), title);
```

```
        }
    }
    else
    {
        FText title = FText::FromString("Download failed!");
        FMessageDialog::Open(EAppMsgType::Ok, FText::
FromString(stringOutput), title);
    }
}
```

First up, the upload case. We check for the 403 (Forbidden) error since that is a quite common to get, it means the user forgot to share the Google Sheet document with our service account, so we have a special popup for that, remember to add the email to the account you created here. If everything went well, we just display a popup for that.

Now onto the download case. We start with checking if the download was successful, if not we display an error message with the full error message. If it succeeded, we send the string (which will be the CSV of the Google Sheet content) into the data table, this will give us a list of all issues back if there are any. If we get any issue, we display them, otherwise we report success. The types of errors we will get here is if a field contains values that cannot be loaded by the data table or if the column IDs no longer match. For example, if a data table was uploaded to a sheet, then we change the format of the table and then download it again then the import will fail.

UPLOAD/DOWNLOAD SCRIPT

Now it's time to take a look at the PowerShell script that does the actual uploading/download. Explaining how PowerShell works is out of scope for this book so I will not go into details of the meaning of everything in this script, just the broad strokes. However, the script is actually quite simple so I think you will be able to follow the general flow of the script without any issues. In /Plugins/MarsEditor/Scripts/ create GoogleSheet.ps1 and add the following code to it.

```
Param(
    [string]$SpreadsheetID = "",
    [string]$CSVFile = "",
    [string]$Page = "",
    [string]$Upload
) #end param

Import-Module UMN-Google

function Authenticate()
{
    # Google API Authozation
    $scope = "https://www.googleapis.com/auth/
spreadsheets https://www.googleapis.com/auth/
```

```
drive https://www.googleapis.com/auth/drive.file"
  $certPath = "$($PSScriptRoot)\unrealbook-d5c43e4feb5d.p12"
  $iss = "marsbot@unrealbook.iam.gserviceaccount.com"
  $certPswd = 'notasecret'
  try
  {
    $accessToken = Get-GOAuthTokenService -scope $scope
-certPath $certPath -certPswd
$certPswd -iss $iss
  }
  catch
  {
    $err = $_.Exception
    $err | Select-Object -Property *
    "Response: "
    $err.Response

    exit 1
  }
  $accessToken
}
```

First, we start with defining our parameters, these parameters are what we added in our command line that launched the process that will be executing this scripts. Then we include our Google module. After that we have our function to set up our access token. Here you will have to enter the path to your P12 file and the email address to the service account you created earlier. We also need to the password, even though it always is "notasecret".

```
function ConvertCSVLineToStringValue($data)
{
  foreach($v in $data.psobject.properties.value)
  {
    $v
  }
}

function GetGoogleSheetColumnLetter($Index)
{
  #This will transform an index to a Google Sheet columns
identifier
  #It handles values all the way up to ZZ (676)
  if($Index -gt 676)
  {
    throw "GetGoogleSheetColumnLetter received an index
$($Index) that is out of range!"
  }
  # 0 -> A, 1 -> B...
  # 27 -> AA, 28 -> AB
  $EndLetter = [char](([int](($Index - 1) % 26) + 65 ) )
```

```
  if($Index -gt 26)
  {
    $EndLetter = [char](([int][Math]::Floor(($Index -1) / 26)
+ 64) ) + $EndLetter
  }
  $EndLetter
}
```

Next up we have two helper functions. The first helps with converting our data we are going to upload to the right format. The second function converts an index to the column letters in the Google Sheet. We will need to this let the sheet knows which area in the sheet we are uploading to. This logic only handles up to ZZ, but that should be more than enough. Next up is our upload function.

```
function Write-GoogleCSV($CSVFile, $SpreadsheetID, $Page)
{
  # Create CSV object
  $import = New-Object System.Collections.ArrayList($null)

  $inputCsv = Import-Csv $CSVFile

  #Add header info first
  $SplitString = ($inputCsv[0].psobject.properties.name).
Split()
  $import.Add(@($SplitString))

  $inputCsv | ForEach-Object{
     $import.Add(@(ConvertCSVLineToStringValue($_))) |
Out-Null
  }

   #Get alphabet position
  $EndLetter = GetGoogleSheetColumnLetter($SplitString.Count)

  # Upload CSV data to Google Sheets with Set-GSheetData
  try
  {
    Set-GSheetData -accessToken $accessToken -rangeA1
"A1:$EndLetter$($import.Count)" -sheetName $Page
-spreadSheetID $SpreadsheetID -values $import -Debug -Verbose
  }
  catch
  {
    $err = $_.Exception
    $err | Select-Object -Property *
    "Response: "
    $err.Response
  }
}
```

The upload is done with the access token we created and by specifying which cells we are uploading our data to, we always start in the upper left corner, or A1 and then we have figured out how many columns and rows we will be uploading and converted them into the sheets letter/number system. We have also done a bit of formatting of the data we upload; we need to write down the column headers first and then we convert all the data in each cell to a string. We have the -Debug flag and -Verbose flag so we get what we need from any error message we might get. This data is what we used to display error messages to the user earlier. Now the download function.

```
function Read-GoogleCSV($SpreadsheetID, $Page)
{
  try
  {
    #In order to get the sheet as a CSV we do a webrequest
with export?format=csv instead of using Get-GSheetData since
that doesn't support CSV
    Invoke-WebRequest -Uri "https://docs.google.com/
spreadsheets/d/$($SpreadsheetID)/export?format=csv&gid=$
($Page)&access_token=$($accessToken)" -UseBasicParsing
  }
  catch
  {
    $err = $_.Exception
    $err | Select-Object -Property *
    "Response: "
    $err.Response
  }
}
```

Since we want to download the data as a CSV we use `Invoke-WebRequest` instead of `Get-GSheetData`, for this we need the page ID (GID) unlike the upload which needed the page name. Finally, we just need to call either upload or download in our script.

```
$accessToken = Authenticate
if( $Upload.Contains("true") )
{
  Write-GoogleCSV -CSVFile $CSVFile -SpreadsheetID
$SpreadsheetID -Page $Page
}
else
{
  $data = Read-GoogleCSV -SpreadsheetID $SpreadsheetID -Page
$Page
  #Write data back to log so we can read it in Unreal Editor
  Write-Host $($data)
}
```

And that's it. You can now upload a data table to a Google Sheet and download it back into the data table from the editor. We could extend on this a bit of we wanted. For example, we could save which data table goes to which sheet/page instead of letting the user choose it. Then we could automate the download every new build if we wanted. We could also add a button that opens the Google Sheet page that we are linking, making it a bit easier for the user. Now obviously not all data will be suitable for being edited in a Google Sheet, asset links for example are a bad choice since typing in the full Unreal path is just cumbersome and error prone. Bool variables by default gets converted to TRUE or FALSE in Google Sheet, while Unreal expects them to be True or False. We could scan for this and fix it before we send the CSV data back into the data table or you can write 'True in the cell instead and Google Sheet will not do its conversion.

Another advantage with uploading data tables to Google Sheets is that is allows designer to make scripts in the sheet that either analyses all the data and presents it in a better way (it's easy to do various diagrams for example) or actually generate the data. For example, the damage value for a weapon could be calculated from the HP from an enemy and the desired time to kill it. It opens up a lot of opportunities for the designers to analyse and manipulate the gameplay data without any need for a programmer to get involved.

8 Blueprint Nodes Customization

In this chapter we will look at Blueprint nodes and how we can control their looks and add more advanced functionality to them. From some basic ways of just tweaking their looks with some flags to how we can create our own wildcard parameters for a node or how we can write a node completely in code.

How we design our Blueprint nodes can have a big impact in the usability and readability of a Blueprint graph. If you don't do a lot of scripting in Blueprints yourself, I strongly recommend you try and do some more or at least look at more Blueprints made by other people in your project. If you see logic that is hard to understand and/or messy take a moment and try and see the problem from the other side. There are several reasons why Blueprint graphs become messy and buggy, one of them is badly designed nodes, which is the problem we will be dealing with in this chapter. Our goal with how we design our nodes is to make them as readable and easy to understand as possible, but also to take as little real estate in the graph as possible. This last point is often missed I think, but the engine has some tools we can use here that we will go through. This does mean that we will be doing more work on the code side for our nodes, adding more complexity there, but the goal with this work is to reduce the complexity of the node the user sees. The nodes will be a bit harder to make, but easier to use. In some cases, the work is quite minimal, but for the more advanced techniques we will cover it can be quite a bit of work. Sometimes it's just not worth it for some nodes, in other cases the work will pay itself of many times over.

META FLAGS

The easiest way to control our Blueprint nodes is through the `UFUNCTION` flags. There are a lot of flags and meta flags you can use to control how Blueprint nodes look and behaves, and I will only go through some off them here, the ones I think are the most useful and/or underused. It's easy to dismiss most of these as not important since they do not make a big difference, and if you just look at one single node it might not seem like it's worth it, but remember, we need to consider how our nodes works and behaves in a bigger more complex graph. Anything that helps that to be more manageable and understandable will be worthwhile. So, for every single function we expose to Blueprint we should always consider if there are any more `UFUNCTION` flags we can apply on the node to make it just a little bit easier to use and understand. The time invest from the programming side is quite low for this after all, there are not that many flags you need to consider.

The first flag to consider is a rather obvious one, the `Category` flag. This is where our function will end up in the Blueprint node list. Using it is very straightforward.

 DOI: 10.1201/9781003511748-9

```
UFUNCTION(BlueprintCallable, Category = "Mars|Util")
void Test();
```

We can use the pipe character "|" to add sub categories.

I think that *all* Blueprint exposed functions should have a category set. In fact, I suggest doing an engine change to make it a compile error if you forget it in one place. Go to /Engine/Source/Programs/Shared/EpicGames.UHT/Types/UhtFunction.cs and find the `Validate` function. In here you will see that the engine already does this check (row 566), but only for engine code and not for game or game plugin code. We can edit this like this.

```
if (HeaderFile.Package.IsPartOfEngine)
{
      this.LogError("An explicit Category specifier is
required for Blueprint accessible functions in an Engine
module.");
}
//#MARS ENGINE MOD START - Require a category to all functions
else
{
      this.LogError("An explicit Category specifier is
required for Blueprint accessible functions.");
}
//#MARS ENGINE MOD END
```

Now all our functions will generate a compile error if we forget a category. What we have done here is tweak UHT, UnrealHeaderTool. This is the tool that runs before the actual compiler starts compiling. This tool scans through all files and generates code from all the Unreal macros we have added, like `UFUNCTION`. This is a good place to start if you want to add you own flags for example. But let's leave UHT behind us and move on.

Except a good name for the nodes and its parameter, a good tooltip description is important, especially for more advanced nodes. There are two ways to create a tooltip, the easiest way is to just write a comment right above the function definition like this.

```
//This comment will automatically become a tooltip
//Multiple lines also work
UFUNCTION(BlueprintCallable, Category = "Mars|Util")
static bool IsAlive(AActor* _actor);
```

Now when you however over the node it will display this comment. The other way to create a tooltip is to enter it in the meta flag field. This can be useful if you want to have a different comment in code versus the tooltip.

```
UFUNCTION(BlueprintCallable, Category = "Mars|Util", meta =
(ToolTip = "This is another\nway of writing tooltips"))
static bool IsAlive(AActor* _actor) { return IsAlive(_actor);
}
```

As you can see, we have to use `\n` to add manual line breaks here.

We can control whether a Blueprint node has execution pints or not with the `BlueprintPure` flag like this.

```
UFUNCTION(BlueprintCallable, Category = "Mars|Util",
BlueprintPure = true)
static bool IsAlive(AActor* _actor);
```

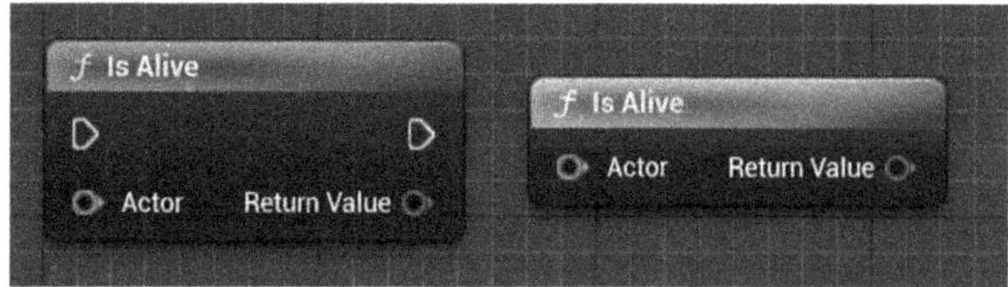

By default, Unreal will make all const function pure, but sometimes we might want to make a non-const function (or a static function) a pure node. Usually, it's the other way around though I find, there's a node I want to make non-pure so that it gets the execution pins. The reason for this is that pure nodes get called once every time *any* value from them is used, instead of once when the node is called. This can waste performance or lead to unintended side effects depending on what the node does. It all depends on the situation, but generally speaking, pure nodes should have no to very little logic inside of them. But they are also very useful in that they make it easier to have a neat and tidy graph. However, if they are misused, they can also make a graph much harder to read and understand since it's very easy to assume that pure nodes don't do much, so you skip over them when trying to understand a graph.

We can also change the look of a node with the `CompactNodeTitle` meta flag.

```
UFUNCTION(BlueprintCallable, Category = "Mars|Util", meta =
(CompactNodeTitle = "Is Alive"))
static bool IsAlive(AActor* _actor);
```

This flag causes the node the change look and makes the title bigger. However, it also removed the parameter names thus it's more useful for small helper functions where the parameter usage is obvious. One advantage that is easy to miss with this node is that since the look of the node is quite different, I find it makes it easier to quickly navigate in a Blueprint you are familiar with since it helps breaking up the pattern a bit.

Next up is one of the more useful meta flags, `ExpandBoolAsExecs` and `ExpandEnumAsExecs`. Just as it sounds, these options expands either a bool or an enum into execution pins. Very useful for nodes that will often be followed by a branch or switch node. Again, saving space is important in the battle against spaghetti Blueprints.

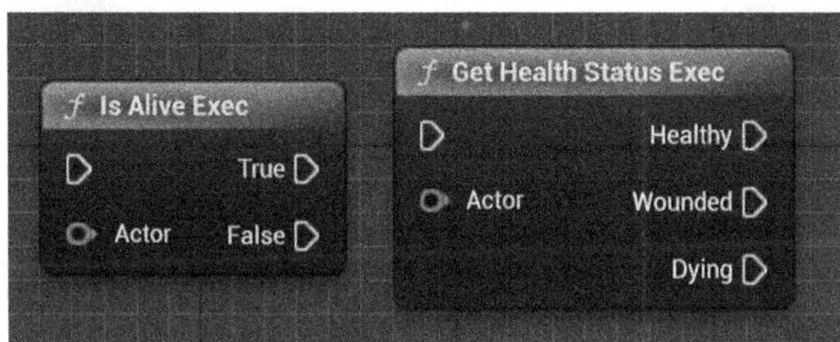


```
UENUM(BlueprintType)
enum class EMarsHealth : uint8
{
  Healthy,
  Wounded,
  Dying,
};

UFUNCTION(BlueprintCallable, Category = "Mars|Util", meta =
(ExpandBoolAsExecs = "ReturnValue"))
static bool IsAliveExec(AActor* _actor);
UFUNCTION(BlueprintCallable, Category = "Mars|Util", meta =
(ExpandEnumAsExecs = " ReturnValue"))
static EMarsHealth GetHealthStatusExec(AActor* _actor);
```

So how do you decide which functions gets an execution expander and which do not? Personally, I think it's best to add them to all functions you are able to. That's why I prefer to add Exec at the end of the function name, so we can easily identify which nodes are execution expanded when selecting a node. So, a function is always doubled up like this

```
  UFUNCTION(BlueprintCallable, Category = "Mars|Util")
  static bool IsAlive(AActor * _actor);
  UFUNCTION(BlueprintCallable, Category = "Mars|Util", meta =
(ExpandBoolAsExecs = "ReturnValue"))
  static bool IsAliveExec(AActor* _actor);
```

Where the IsAliveExec function will just call the IsAlive function. It might sound like a lot of work to double up all functions like this, but in reality, it ends up not being that many functions that you can do an execution expansion on. And by *always* doing it when possible people will get used to them and start using them more, leading to cleaner Blueprints. I find that people often don't bother requesting minor things like this if it's missing, which is a mistake. Because all these small things add up over time and end up doing a difference for how clean a Blueprint is. If people in your project do request small improvements like this, try to add them fast so they don't stop asking for them!

One final note on this is that you can also do this on a parameter, not just the return value.

```
UFUNCTION(BlueprintCallable, Category = "Mars|Util", meta =
(ExpandEnumAsExecs = "_health"))
static void GetHealthStatusExec(AActor* _actor, EMarsHealth&
_health);
```

Instead of specifying "ReturnValue" we just enter the name of the parameter. An important note on this flag is that it can be used on both in and our parameters. While this might not make a lot of sense with the bool version, the enum version can be quite nice to use this way.

The final flag we will take a look at is the AdvancedDisplay flag.

```
UFUNCTION(BlueprintCallable, Category = " Mars|Util ", meta =
(AdvancedDisplay = "_includeDead,_onlyInCombat"))
static void GetAIs(bool _includeDead, bool _onlyInCombat,
TArray<AActor*>& _ais);
```

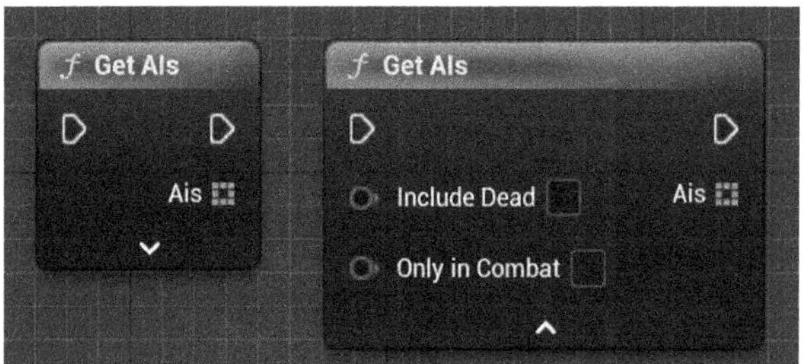

This flag allows us to specify which parameters should start collapsed. By clicking the little arrow, we can expand or collapse the node. Usage of this flag will be very situational. It only makes sense on nodes that have some parameters exposed which are often not used or if the node has a lot of parameters but only a few are always used. This flag then allows us to still preserve space while easily letting the user access everything when needed.

That's it for the UFUNCTION flags, this is not in any way a full walkthrough of all flags and meta flags, but rather the ones I consider to be underused but also helpful to control how the Blueprint nodes look and how we use them. There are plenty of resources online that explain all the flags you can use.

LATENT NODES

Latent nodes are a way for us to easily create nodes that execute over several frames. Examples of latent nodes are `AsyncLoadAsset` or the `Delay` node. Latent nodes are a great way to encapsulate a lot of the boiler plate logic you need to add when waiting on something to finish before you want the execution to progress in the Blueprint graph. You can add everything you need to set up and cleanup inside the node, and you don't need to write a lot of code to create a new latent node. It does come with some drawbacks, however. First, once you start the node it will always tick until you finish it and it does this by registering its own tick function, so it will not run at the same time as the actor's tick. This cost is small so it might not be a problem, but if the node you create is used a lot the cost can add up. Of course, if it's used a lot, it's because it's useful and the work will have to be done even without the node. Secondly the latent action is not an `UObject`, meaning you cannot use `UPROPERTY` flags within it, so you need to be more careful when saving pointers to actors. Usually, you work with the actor you start the node in and then you are safe, if the actor is removed so will the latent node. However external actors need to be handled with a bit more care.

Time to look at an example of this. We will be creating a node that will tick until a condition fails. It will also have a start and finish execution pins. The goal is to get a node that looks like this.

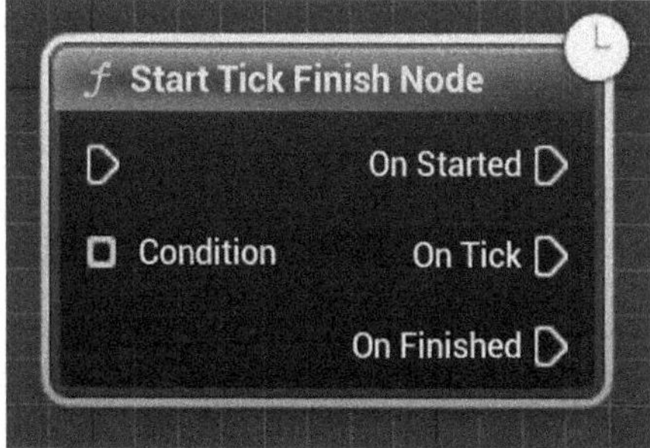

When we start the node, it will execute the `OnStarted` execution pin, then for each frame that the `Condition` delegate returns true, it will execute `OnTick` and once it's done it will execute `OnFinished`.

Since the latent action class itself is not an `UObject`, we will need a helper function in a library that we expose to Blueprint and that handles the creation of the latent action. So, let's start with adding this code to /Plugins/MarsEditor/Source/MarsShared/Public/MarsSharedLibrary.h.

```
UENUM(BlueprintType)
enum class EMarsNodeTickState : uint8
{
```

```
  OnStarted,
  OnTick,
  OnFinished,
};

DECLARE_DYNAMIC_DELEGATE_RetVal(bool, FMarsShouldTick);

UCLASS()
class MARSSHARED_API UMarsSharedLibrary : public
UBlueprintFunctionLibrary
{
  //...
  UFUNCTION(BlueprintCallable, Category = "Mars|Util", meta
= (Latent, LatentInfo = "_latentInfo", WorldContext =
"_worldContextObject", ExpandEnumAsExecs = "_result"))
  static void StartTickFinishNode(const UObject*
_worldContextObject, const FMarsShouldTick& _condition,
EMarsNodeTickState& _result, FLatentActionInfo _latentInfo);
};
```

The enum we are using to create the execution expansion like we saw earlier in this chapter. We are also going to need a world context object, so we capture that with the `WorldContext` flag. When we do it this way the `_worldContextObject` parameter will be hidden if the node is placed in a graph where it can capture it automatically, but if it cannot the parameter will be visible (for example if used in a Blutility graph). Then we must add the `Latent` meta flag to signal that this function call will create a latent object that will keep executing, in the `LatenInfo` meta flag we specify the name of our latent parameter. Now let's take a look at the function definition.

```
void UMarsSharedLibrary::StartTickFinishNode(const UObject*
_worldContextObject, const FMarsShouldTick& _condition,
EMarsNodeTickState& _result, FLatentActionInfo _latentInfo)
{
  if (UWorld* world = GEngine->GetWorldFromContextObject(
_worldContextObject, EGetWorldErrorMode::LogAndReturnNull))
  {
    FLatentActionManager& lam = world->GetLatent
ActionManager();
    if (lam.FindExistingAction<FMarsStartTickEndLatentNode>(
_latentInfo.CallbackTarget, _latentInfo.UUID) == nullptr)
    {
      FMarsStartTickEndLatentNode* action = new
FMarsStartTickEndLatentNode(_latentInfo, _condition, _result);
      lam.AddNewAction(_latentInfo.CallbackTarget,
_latentInfo.UUID, action);
    }
  }
}
```

As you can see, the reason we needed a world context object is so we can get the latent action manager from the world. After checking that we don't have an action already running, which could happen if we call the execution node multiple times without letting the node finish, we register our action class with the manager. We pass in any data we might need to our action class, in this example if we have our condition delegate and the result enum which we expanded to exec pins in the function declaration. Now we should take a look at our action class. In /Plugins/MarsEditor/Source/MarsShared/Public/LatentNodes/ create MarsStartTickFinishLatentNode.h and add the following code.

```
#pragma once

#include "LatentActions.h"

class FMarsStartTickEndLatentNode : public
FPendingLatentAction
{
  //Base functionality variables
  FName ExecutionFunction;
  int32 OutputLink;
  FWeakObjectPtr CallbackTarget;

  //Node specific variables
  FMarsShouldTick Condition;
  EMarsNodeTickState* Result = nullptr;
  bool FirstTick = true;

public:

  FMarsStartTickEndLatentNode(const FLatentActionInfo&
_latentInfo, const FMarsShouldTick& _condition,
EMarsNodeTickState& _result)
      : ExecutionFunction(_latentInfo.ExecutionFunction)
      , OutputLink(_latentInfo.Linkage)
      , CallbackTarget(_latentInfo.CallbackTarget)
      , Condition(_condition)
      , Result(&_result)
  {
  }
  virtual void UpdateOperation(FLatentResponse& _response)
override;
};
```

Our action class needs to inherit from `FPendingLatentAction`, which does not inherit from `UObject`, this is the reason we cannot use `UPROPERTY` macros in here and we need to be careful if we have pointers to external objects, meaning to another object then we start the node in. The base class is also surprisingly sparse and is really more of an interface for us, it doesn't even save the `ExecutionFunction/`

OutputLink/Callbacktarget variables which we will always need. If you will be making a lot of latent nodes, it's definitely worth making your own base class to handle these variables. Since I'm only going to show one example for the latent nodes, I will not be creating that base class here.

After that we have the variables we need for the behaviour of our node. The Condition delegate we will use to check if we should keep ticking, a bool to keep track of it's our first tick or not and a pointer to the result enum so we can write the correct value to it and trigger the execution link. I add a new constructer and pass in all the variables in there, this is mostly to keep it in line with all latent action nodes from the engine. We could just as easily have the constructor just handle the basic variables we need and then set the node specific variables after we have created an instance of our class. You choose whichever pattern you feel comfortable with. Lastly, we override the UpdateOperation function, since this is where all our logic will take place. In /Plugins/MarsEditor/Source/MarsShared/Private/LatentNodes/ create MarsStartTickFinishLatentNode.cpp and add the following code.

```
#include "LatentNodes/MarsStartTickFinishLatentNode.h"

void FMarsStartTickEndLatentNode::UpdateOperation
(FLatentResponse& _response)
{
  if (FirstTick)
  {
    *Result = EMarsNodeTickState::OnStarted;
    _response.TriggerLink(ExecutionFunction, OutputLink,
CallbackTarget);
    FirstTick = false;
  }
  else
  {
    bool conditionPassed = Condition.Execute();
    if (conditionPassed)
    {
      *Result = EMarsNodeTickState::OnTick;
      _response.TriggerLink(ExecutionFunction, OutputLink,
CallbackTarget);
    }
    else
    {
      *Result = EMarsNodeTickState::OnFinished;
      _response.FinishAndTriggerIf(true, ExecutionFunction,
OutputLink, CallbackTarget);
    }
  }
}
```

The important bit here is how we handle the _response parameter. This is how we determine if we want our action to continue running or finish. The usage of it is simple, we can choose to end our action, without triggering any execution pins by calling `DoneIf( true )`. Or we choose to trigger our execution link with `TriggerLink(...)` or to end it and trigger our execution link with `FinishAndTriggerIf(...)`. The last function will only trigger the link if we choose to end the function. In our example we split our enum parameter into multiple execution pins, so we need to set the enum parameter to control what execution pin to execute, this we do by simple setting our `Result` pointer variable to our current state.

In this example we have set up the delegate function so that it must be passed in. However, we can make it optional by adding the `AutoCreateRefTerm` meta flag like this.

```
UFUNCTION(BlueprintCallable, Category = "Utilities",
meta = (Latent, LatentInfo = "_latentInfo", WorldContext
= "_worldContextObject", ExpandEnumAsExecs = "_result",
AutoCreateRefTerm = "_condition"))
```

Just as the `ExpandEnumAsExecs` flag, the `AutoCreateRefTerm` takes the parameter names that we want to automatically create a reference for. This means that we don't have to provide a valid reference to pass in, we can leave it empty. Of course, before we try to use our delegate we must check if it's valid, just calling Execute on it directly will crash since there's no validation within that call. We can do this easily like this.

```
bool conditionPassed = Condition.IsBound() ? Condition.
  Execute() : false;
```

If the condition delegate is bound, we execute it, otherwise we use whatever default value we want. This doesn't make much sense for this specific function, but it's useful in many other cases and if you find that people create empty variables just to pass them into your node, this meta flag will save them the hassle of having to do that.

CustomThunk

So far, we have looked at what we can do to control our nodes without actually understanding anything about the inner workings of a Blueprint node. In this and the next section we will start looking a bit under the surface of the Blueprint nodes. First thing we will look at is the `CustomThunk UPROPERTY` flag. With this we will be able to create functions with parameters or return values that are wildcard, meaning it can take a parameter of any type, and we can still do logic on it. This is how all array functions in Unreal are created for example.

Before we can understand what the `CustomThunk` does, we need to understand what a `thunk` is in Unreal. If we look at the Wikipedia definition we get "a thunk is a subroutine used to inject a calculation into another subroutine.", what this means is in Unreal is that a thunk is a piece of code that tells the Blueprint virtual machine how to call a code function. When the virtual machine does a function call, it will start with creating a memory block and copy all variables into this memory block, so in the thunk the variables will have to be gathered from this memory block and passed to the function. This will involve working with the FProperty system. The fact that the parameters are copied into this memory block for each single call is one reason why Blueprints are slow compared to code. Anyways, whenever we add the BlueprintCallable flag to a UFUNCTION the UnrealHeaderTool, UHT for short, will automatically generate a thunk for us. You can find this generated code in the .gen.cpp of your file (not to be confused with the .generated.h file) and you can take a look at the thunks that are generated. Of course, since this is generated code it's quite cryptic and hard to read. When we add the CustomThunk flag to our function we are telling UHT to not generate a thunk for us, we will be doing it ourselves.

Let's get started with the first example, we will implement a RemoveAtRange function for arrays. This function will take an array of any type and remove _num elements from position _index. In MarsSharedLibrary.h add the following code.

```
class MARSSHARED_API UMarsSharedLibrary : public
{
  //…
  UFUNCTION(BlueprintCallable, CustomThunk, Category =
"Utilities|Array", meta = (DisplayName = "Remove At Range",
ArrayParm = "_array"))
  static void Array_RemoveAtRange(int32 _index, int32 _num,
const TArray<int32>& _array);
  DECLARE_FUNCTION(execArray_RemoveAtRange);
  static void GenericArray_RemoveAtRange(void* _array, const
FArrayProperty* _arrayProp, int32 _index, int32 _num);
};
```

Alright, first new thing in our UFUNCTION list is the CustomThunk flag, which as we just discussed just tells UHT to not generate a thunk for is, we will do that ourselves. The next new thing is the ArrayParm meta flag, this flag takes a comma separated list of all parameters that should be treated as wild card arrays, so we will accept arrays of any types for this function. Then we have the declaration for our function, here we are saying that we will have an int32 array. This will not be true, but the type of this array doesn't really matter since we specify that it is a wildcard array and in our thunk we will have to do some manual memory handling depending on what type the array actually is, more on that sooner. We also specify a DisplayName so we can rid of the Array_ part of the name in the add Blueprint node window.

Next new thing we have is the DECLARE_FUNCTION macro, this is the thunk declaration. It must have the same name as our function, but with the exec prefix. Then we have another function declaration, GenericArray_RemoveAtRange, for a version of our function that takes a void* as the array parameter type, but also take a FArrayProperty parameter, which will have the information from Unreal's reflection system about what kind of data is in our array. This is the function that will be doing the actual work for us. Time to look at the function definitions. In MarsSharedLibrary.cpp start adding the following code.

```
void UMarsSharedLibrary::Array_RemoveAtRange(int32 _index,
int32 _num, const TArray<int32>& _array)
{
  check(0); // should never execute
}
```

This function is empty since we will never call it, we just needed this for all the `UFUNCTION` flags, but we will not ever actually use it. We add a `check(0);` in it in case someone tries to manually call it from code by mistake. Next, we will look at the actual function that will be doing the work.

```
void UMarsSharedLibrary::GenericArray_RemoveAtRange(void*
_array, const FArrayProperty* _arrayProp, int32 _index, int32
_num)
{
  if (_array)
  {
    FScriptArrayHelper arrayHelper(_arrayProp, _array);
    if (arrayHelper.IsValidIndex(_index))
    {
      int num = FMath::Min(arrayHelper.Num() - _index, _num);
      arrayHelper.RemoveValues(_index, num);
    }
  }
}
```

Since we do not know what type of array we have, we are working with a void pointer to our array, but we must know the size of every element in order to do any work on the array. Since Unreal has a reflection system, we do have that information, and we will be passing in the property information about the array in `_arrayProp`. Unreal then has a nice helper class, `FScriptArrayHelper`, we will use to actually modify the array and delete the number of elements from the starting index provided.

The thing missing now is our custom thunk declaration. We know that we must call the `GenericArray_RemoveAtRange` from it and that we must get the `FArrayProperty` parameter also. Let's look at how.

```
#include "Net/Core/PushModel/PushModel.h"
DEFINE_FUNCTION(UMarsSharedLibrary::execArray_RemoveAtRange)
{
  P_GET_PROPERTY(FIntProperty, index);
  P_GET_PROPERTY(FIntProperty, num);
  Stack.MostRecentProperty = nullptr;
  Stack.StepCompiledIn<FArrayProperty>(nullptr);
  void* arrayAddr = Stack.MostRecentPropertyAddress;
  FArrayProperty* arrayProperty = CastField<FArrayProperty>
(Stack.MostRecentProperty);
  if (!arrayProperty)
  {
```

```
    Stack.bArrayContextFailed = true;
    return;
  }
  P_FINISH;

  P_NATIVE_BEGIN;
  MARK_PROPERTY_DIRTY(Stack.Object, arrayProperty);
  GenericArray_RemoveAtRange(arrayAddr, arrayProperty, index,
num);
  P_NATIVE_END;
}
```

To re-iterate, our purpose with this function is to get the variables from the memory block the virtual machine has put them in and then to call our code function. Since we want a wildcard parameter type we must also dig out the `FProperty` type for the parameter and pass it in, in our case it will be a `FArrayProperty` since we have an array. The virtual machine will put all the parameters in the memory block in the order they are declared, so we just need to get them in that order. This memory block is placed in the `Stack` variable, which is of type `FFrame`. This struct has a bunch of helper functions and variables to help us work with it. It has a pointer to all the allocated parameters, called `Locals`. Whenever we get a parameter, it will automatically walk to, or step to, the next parameter. We do not need to handle this stepping bit ourselves.

We use the `P_GET_PROPERTY()` macro for the first two parameters for this. Since we know the data types for these parameters, we can use this macro and just get the values. We provide the macro with the property struct for our data type, in our case `FIntProperty` and then we also give it the name of the local variable it will create for us (`index` and `num`). Sidenote: The P_ in the macro stands for portable, an old term from early interpreters. Anyways, this macro expands into

```
int32 index;
Stack.StepCompiledIn<FIntProperty>(&index);
```

We need to understand what the `Stack.StepCompiledIn` call does, this is the part that will step through the stack for us and give us the correct data pointer and it can also copy the variable data for us directly. In this case it will copy the value since we give it a variable to put the data in. We can do that since we know what data type it is. This call will change several variables in the `Stack` for us. Most importantly these two

```
FProperty* MostRecentProperty;
uint8* MostRecentPropertyAddress;
```

The first of these, `MostRecentProperty`, will contain the data from the reflection system about our data type. In order words this is what we will need to know the size element. We worked a bit with `FProperty` in chapter 4 when we did the custom details for our structs to get a better overview. The second variable,

MostRecectPropertyAddress, points to where the actual data is. Knowing this, we can look at our wildcard array parameter. Since it's wildcard, we do not know what data type it is when we call StepCompiledIn, so we cannot give it a variable to copy the data to. But calling StepCompiledIn will set MostRecentPropertyAdress and MostRecentProperty on our stack variable.

While we don't know what type of data is in our array, we do know that it is in array. This means we can cast MostRecentProperty to a FArrayProperty variable. Now we have the reflection systems data about the array variable, so using this we have the size of the variable. And in MostRecentProperyAddress we have the pointer to the actual data. The praxis in Unreal is to set MostRecentPropertyAddress and sometimes MostRecentPropertyContainer to nullptr before calling StepCompiledIn. I never understood the reason for this since this is never done before any usage of P_GET_PROPERTY, which will expand into the exact same code, proving that it's not needed. I'm breaking against the praxis in Unreal by omitting setting those variables to nullptr, but from what I have seen in the code, all paths seem to always set them correctly, so I'm guessing it's legacy reasons for these lines that isn't needed any more but keeps getting copied over to every new function.

Now that we have all the data we need from the Stack, we call P_FINISH, this lets the system know we are done with getting data from the Stack. Now it's time to call our code function that will do the actual work we need, but before we do that, we should call the P_NATIVE_BEGIN macro. This is for profiling scope so that our code function doesn't end up being included in the Blueprint time scope in Insights. The function will work perfectly without this call, but profiling scopes will be off, so I strongly recommend always marking up your code properly. After this macro we have another macro, MARK_PROPERTY_DIRTY(Stack.Object, arrayProperty), this is to let the network layer know that we have changed this variable and it needs to be replicated if the variable is marked for replication. At last, we have the call to our GenericArray_RemoveAtRange function, then we finish with the P_NATIVE_END macro, which will just insert a "}" to finish the scope started with the begin macro.

That's it! You now have your first Blueprint node that can take a wildcard parameter. The interaction with the virtual machine inside the thunk can be a bit overwhelming and cryptic, don't worry we will look at a couple of more examples to help make it a bit easier to understand. Next thing we will do is add a Push and Pop functions for arrays, let's start with the Push version. This already exists in the engine of course, it's just called Add, so we will not be adding any new functionality here, but it's a useful test case to examine how it's done. In MarsSharedLibrary.h add the following code.

```
class MARSSHARED_API UMarsSharedLibrary : public
UBlueprintFunctionLibrary
{
  //...
  UFUNCTION(BlueprintCallable, CustomThunk, Category
= "Utilities|Array", meta = (DisplayName = "Push",
```

```
CompactNodeTitle = "PUSH", ArrayParm = "_array",
ArrayTypeDependentParams = "_element", AutoCreateRefTerm =
"_element"))
  static void Array_Push(const TArray<int32>& _array, const
int32& _element);
  DECLARE_FUNCTION(execArray_Push);
  static void GenericArray_Push(void* _array, const
FArrayProperty* _arrayProp, const void* _newElement);
};
```

Like last time, we specify we want our own `CustomThunk`, we give ourselves a nicer name for the add Blueprint node window and we specify the array should be wildcard with `ArrayParm`. We also give ourselves a `CompactNodeTitle`, since we don't need to see the variable names for this node, itsusage is obvious. We then use `ArrayTypeDependentParams` to give the parameter name of the element we want to add. This will link the type of this variable to the type of the variable we added to `ArrayParm`. In other words, since we have marked the array as wildcard, this links the `_element` variable to whatever type we actually end up inputting into our array. Finally, we use `AutoCreateRefTerm` to specify that our element should automatically create a reference if the user doesn't specify one. In order words, if we don't add a variable to this parameter the virtual machine will create one automatically and send in. This allows us to inline edit the value directly on the node which is quite nice for nodes like this. After this we have our thunk declaration. Not much more to say here, it needs to have the same name as our function, but with the `exec` prefix. Finally, we have our generic version of the function. Since we know that the element will be of the same type as the array, we do not need a `FProperty*` parameter for the element, we have everything we need in the array property parameter. Time to look at the definitions, in MarsSharedLibrary.cpp add the following code.

```
void UMarsSharedLibrary::Array_Push(const TArray<int32>&
_array, const int32& _element)
{
  check(0); // should never execute
}
```

Same as before, this function should never be called directly, and we add a check in case some programmer calls it directly by mistake. Next up, our custom thunk.

```
DEFINE_FUNCTION(UMarsSharedLibrary::execArray_Push)
{
 Stack.StepCompiledIn<FArrayProperty>(NULL);
 void* arrayAddr = Stack.MostRecentPropertyAddress;
 FArrayProperty* arrayProperty = CastField<FArrayProperty>
(Stack.MostRecentProperty);
 if (!arrayProperty)
 {
   Stack.bArrayContextFailed = true;
```

```
    return;
  }

  //Get the pointer to the element we want to push
  Stack.StepCompiledIn<FProperty>(nullptr);

  P_FINISH;
  P_NATIVE_BEGIN;
  MARK_PROPERTY_DIRTY(Stack.Object, arrayProperty);
  GenericArray_Push(arrayAddr, arrayProperty, Stack.
MostRecentPropertyAddress);
  P_NATIVE_END;
}
```

We get the array property and the array data pointer in the exact same way as before. And we get the pointer to the element we want to add the same way, with another call to `StepCompiledIn`, this will put the pointer in `Stack.MostRecentPropertyAddress` so we can send this into our generic function. Then we mark the array as dirty for network replication and call our functions. Our `Push` function has the exact same behaviour as the normal `Add` function, however our thunk actually looks quite different from the add one. Let's look a bit at the differences. You can find the Unreal array thunks here \Engine\Source\Runtime\Engine\Classes\Kismet\KismetArrayLibrary.h. Let's take a look at the `execArray_Add` thunk. Instead of just getting the pointer to the parameter we want to add like this `Stack.StepCompiledIn<FProperty>(nullptr);`

The Unreal version has this code.

```
    const FProperty* InnerProp = ArrayProperty->Inner;
    const int32 PropertySize = InnerProp->ElementSize *
InnerProp->ArrayDim;
    void* StorageSpace = FMemory_Alloca(PropertySize);
    InnerProp->InitializeValue(StorageSpace);

    Stack.MostRecentPropertyAddress = nullptr;
    Stack.MostRecentPropertyContainer = nullptr;
    Stack.StepCompiledIn<FProperty>(StorageSpace);
```

Quite a bit more code! They start with getting the inner property from the array, in other words the property of the element in the array and then use that to calculate the size. Then they allocate up a new memory buffer of that size and use the inner property to initialize that memory to the correct value. This will either zero it, copy the value from the default object or call the constructor. Then they finally call the `StepCompiledIn` and gives it the address to the new memory buffer, which will copy the actual value into that buffer. Finally, they will use this memory buffer to the call to the generic function and then release the memory. Quite a lot of memory allocations and operations compared to our version which just gets the pointer to the variable and uses it directly. Maybe there's a good reason for this extra code, but I have been unable to find it in my testing and a lot of this code is at least 10+ years old (that's as far back as the history in GitHub goes, it's probably even older). In practice, do these extra operations actually matter for performance? While it's easy to construct a test case to prove that it's faster by just making a long array with big elements, it's harder to be able to prove the improvement in a real project. So, if you are working with really big Blueprint structs or really big arrays, you might be able to do some savings that can be noticed here. But the bigger gain would then be to just move the whole things to code anyways. This pattern is repeated in a lot of the array functions (and the map and set functions). Maybe there used to be a good reason for this, maybe there still are some edge cases that requires this logic. I have been unable to find one. So, if you are desperate for just a little bit more performance in a project, maybe this could be worth your while. Probably not, but none the less I find it interesting. Anyway, this was more of a sidenote so let's return to our code and take a look at the generic function definition.

```
void UMarsSharedLibrary::GenericArray_Push(void* _array, const
FArrayProperty* _arrayProp, const void* _newElement)
{
  if (_array)
  {
    FScriptArrayHelper arrayHelper(_arrayProp, _array);
    int index = arrayHelper.AddValue();

    FProperty* innerProp = _arrayProp->Inner;
    innerProp->CopySingleValueToScriptVM(arrayHelper.
GetRawPtr(index), _newElement);
  }
}
```

Again, we make use of the array helper to increase the size of our array with the `AddValue()` call. And then we use the inner property to copy the data into the array. The `FProperty` class again shows its usefulness and it's a very useful class to be familiar with. Now we only need to take a look at the `Pop` function. Let's start with the function definitions again.

```
  UFUNCTION(BlueprintCallable, CustomThunk, Category
= "Utilities|Array", meta = (DisplayName = "Pop",
CompactNodeTitle = "POP", ArrayParm = "_array",
ArrayTypeDependentParams = "_element"))
  static void Array_Pop(const TArray<int32>& _array, int32&
_element);
  DECLARE_FUNCTION(execArray_Pop);
  static void GenericArray_Pop(void* _array, const
FArrayProperty* _arrayProp, void* _newElement);
```

The only difference from the Push version is that we don't need to auto create a reference this time, since we do not have an input. Let's move on to the declarations.

```
void UMarsSharedLibrary::Array_Pop(const TArray<int32>&
_array, int32& _element)
{
  check(0); // should never execute
}

DEFINE_FUNCTION(UMarsSharedLibrary::execArray_Pop)
{
  Stack.StepCompiledIn<FArrayProperty>(NULL);
  void* arrayAddr = Stack.MostRecentPropertyAddress;
  FArrayProperty* arrayProperty =
CastField<FArrayProperty>(Stack.MostRecentProperty);
  if (!arrayProperty)
  {
    Stack.bArrayContextFailed = true;
    return;
  }

  Stack.StepCompiledIn<FProperty>(nullptr);

  P_FINISH;
  P_NATIVE_BEGIN;
  MARK_PROPERTY_DIRTY(Stack.Object, arrayProperty);
  GenericArray_Pop(arrayAddr, arrayProperty, Stack.
MostRecentPropertyAddress);
  P_NATIVE_END;
}
```

The thunk is almost exactly the same as the Push version for exactly the same reasons. Now Unreal doesn't have a default Pop function, but it's almost the same as the Get function, just with a hardcoded index and a remove. But just like with the Add function, the Get function also does a memory allocation and copies the data into the temporary buffer first. We skip all that and just go directly to the final destination with our data to save on the memory allocation and copy. Same caveat as before, there might be some edge case that the extra memory allocation fixes and I just haven't been able to find it. Now let's take a look at the final function.

```
void UMarsSharedLibrary::GenericArray_Pop(void* _array, const
FArrayProperty* _arrayProp, void* _newElement)
{
  if (_array)
  {
    FScriptArrayHelper arrayHelper(_arrayProp, _array);
    FProperty* innerProp = _arrayProp->Inner;
    if (arrayHelper.Num() > 0)
    {
      int index = arrayHelper.Num() - 1;
      innerProp->CopyCompleteValueFromScriptVM(_newElement,
arrayHelper.GetRawPtr(index) );
      arrayHelper.RemoveValues(index, 1);
```

```
    }
    else
    {
      FFrame::KismetExecutionMessage(*FString::Printf(TEXT("
Attempted to pop from empty array '%s' in '%s'!"),
        *_arrayProp->GetName(),
        *_arrayProp->GetOwnerVariant().GetPathName()),
        ELogVerbosity::Error,
        FName("GetPopEmptyArrayWarning");
      innerProp->InitializeValue(_newElement);
    }
  }
}
```

Again, the `FProperty` class has all the functions we need to work on our raw pointer to our array, we use it to first copy the last element in the array to our destination, then we remove that element from the array. This time we also add some error handling if the array is empty, and someone tries to call `Pop` on it. We display an error message but also initializes the out element. This will either fill in the buffer with zero or run the default constructor on it, it depends on what kind of data it is.

CODING BLUEPRINT NODES

In this chapter we will look at coding our very own Blueprint nodes. This is a fairly big subject, so we will only be scratching the surface of what is possible here. The goal isn't that we should know everything about how to make our own nodes after this chapter, but that you should have enough knowledge to get started and that you can make the most common nodes you will need.

Making our own Blueprint nodes gives us greater control over how they behave and is a great way to pack a lot of complex functionality into one single node. We will be doing this by inheriting from the `UK2Node` class. Every single Blueprint node is of this type in the end. For example, when you create a `BlueprintCallable` function, what is placed in the graph will be a `UK2Node_CallFunction`. These nodes either needs to write the kismet bytecode for the virtual machine or replace themselves with simpler nodes. We will be focusing on the second option, because really all the basic support we need already exists. This means that the nodes we will create, we will replace them with several other nodes when the Blueprint is compiled. So, our new nodes are like a collapsed graph or a function in a Blueprint graph in many ways. There's just no way to "step into" it to see how it looks. Since we do this from code though, we can do some advanced stuff that we cannot do with a Blueprint function. For example, we can have wildcard parameters or change what input/output pins we have depending on other inputs. This is how the `SpawnActor` nodes is able to add pins for variables that should be exposed on spawn. Writing our own `UK2Nodes` gives us the most control over the node, more than the other methods we have covered so far, but it does come with a drawback. The coding for the nodes is very verbose, lot of code required to do a simple node. It can be a bit overwhelming at first, but once you get used to it, it's not very complicated, but it is very error prone coding. Since we will be creating a small Blueprint graph, placing nodes and connecting them, in code where don't see the layout of them it's very easy to make mistakes. We will be creating our own little helper library with some useful helper function to both lessen the amount of code we write, but primarily to make it harder to make mistakes and to make any potential mistakes easier to locate.

We are also going to need a new module for our nodes. We cannot place it in a `Runtime` module, since by then the Blueprint graphs will all be compiled down to kismet bytecode already. We also cannot place it in an `Editor` module because our node needs to work in any uncooked game, not just in the editor. We are going to need to create an `UncookedOnly` module for our nodes. Let's get started with this setup, in MarsEditor.uplugin, update the Modules entry to the following.

```
"Modules": [
  {
    "Name": "MarsEditor",
    "Type": "Editor",
    "LoadingPhase": "PostEngineInit"
  },
  {
    "Name": "MarsShared",
    "Type": "Runtime",
    "LoadingPhase": "Default"
  },
  {
    "Name": "MarsBlueprintNodes",
    "Type": "UncookedOnly",
    "LoadingPhase": "Default"
  }
]
```

The new module is named MarsBlueprintNodes and as mentioned is of the `UncookedOnly` type. We don't have any special requirements about the loading phase, so we leave it as default. Next, we need to create the Build.cs file for our module, so in /Plugins/MarsEditor/Source/MarsBlueprintNodes/ create Mars BlueprintNodes.Build.cs and add the following code.

```
using UnrealBuildTool;
public class MarsBlueprintNodes : ModuleRules
{
  public MarsBlueprintNodes(ReadOnlyTargetRules Target) :
base(Target)
  {
    PCHUsage = ModuleRules.PCHUsageMode.
UseExplicitOrSharedPCHs;

    PublicDependencyModuleNames.AddRange(
      new string[]
      {
        "Core",
```

```
      }
      );

    PrivateDependencyModuleNames.AddRange(
      new string[]
      {
        "ApplicationCore",
        "CoreUObject",
        "Engine",
        "Slate",
        "BlueprintGraph",
        "KismetCompiler",
        "UnrealEd",
        "Mars",
        "GameplayTags",
      }
      );
  }
}
```

Quite standard, we have some includes we need. The Mars include is for the game project, so replace that with whatever your game project is called. We also include the GameplayTags module here since we will be using some gameplay tags in one of the nodes we will create. Since it's a new module we must also add a module class. In /Plugins/MarsEditor/Source/MarsBlueprintNodes/Public/ create Mars BlueprintNodesModule.h and add the following code.

```
#pragma once

#include "CoreMinimal.h"

#include "Modules/ModuleInterface.h"

class FMarsBlueprintNodesModule : public IModuleInterface
{
};
```

Completely empty, we just need this class so that the module loads properly, we don't have need for any code in the module. In /Plugins/MarsEditor/Source/MarsBlueprintNodes/Private/ create MarsBlueprintNodesModule.cpp and add the following code.

```
#include "MarsBlueprintNodesModule.h"

IMPLEMENT_MODULE(FMarsBlueprintNodesModule,
MarsBlueprintNodes)
```

And that is it for the module, we just need the macro that implements it so the module will be created and loaded correctly.

MapForEach Node

Now it's time to discuss the first node we will be creating. We will do a for each node that work on maps and returns both the key and the value every loop. We need to think a bit about how our node will work. First thing we need to consider is what pins we want. Pins are what *all* inputs/outputs on a node are called. It can be a parameter or an execution pin. The parameters can be of any data type, it could be an array of Blueprint structs or just a simple integer. We can look at the `ForEach` node to get a sense of what pins we need to do. We are going to need the following pins.

- In execution pin to start the looping
- In wildcard parameter for the map we will loop on
- Out execution pin we will trigger for every loop
- Out wildcard parameter that will have the key from the map
- Out wildcard parameter that will have the value from the map
- Out execution pin for when the looping is done

Once we are done, this is how our new node will look.

Let's get started on the code for our new node. In /Plugins/MarsEditor/Source/MarsBlueprintNodes/Public/Nodes/ create MarsMapForEach.h and add the following code. We will be adding more code to this file as we go, but for now it should look like this.

```
#pragma once

#include "K2Node.h"
#include "BlueprintActionDatabaseRegistrar.h"

#include "MarsMapForEach.generated.h"

UCLASS()
```

```
class MARSBLUEPRINTNODES_API UMarsK2Node_MapForEach : public
UK2Node
{
  GENERATED_BODY()
public:
  virtual bool IsNodeSafeToIgnore() const override { return
true; }
  virtual void GetMenuActions(FBlueprintActionDatabase
Registrar& _actionRegistrar) const override;

  virtual FText GetMenuCategory() const override;
  virtual FText GetNodeTitle(ENodeTitleType::Type _titleType)
const override;
  virtual FText GetTooltipText() const override;

  UEdGraphPin* GetOutLoopExecPin() const;
  UEdGraphPin* GetOutLoopCompletedExecPin() const;
  UEdGraphPin* GetInMapPin() const;
  UEdGraphPin* GetOutValuePin() const;
  UEdGraphPin* GetOutKeyPin() const;

private:
  static const FName OutLoopExecPinName;
  static const FName OutLoopCompletedExecPinName;
  static const FName InMapPinName;
  static const FName OutValuePinName;
  static const FName OutKeyPinName;
};
```

First off, we inherit from UK2Node, as I mentioned before this is the base class of all Blueprint nodes. Since the pins on nodes are identified by names, we have a name variable and getter function for each of the pins we need, except the in execution pin since the base class has this already. I'm very explicit in my naming of these variables, clearly defining if it's an in or out pin. I find that this helps, and I recommend this naming convention.

Then we have some functions for getting the node name/tooltip/category. The category is where our function will be in the add node window you get by right clicking in the Blueprint editor. Then we have `GetMenuActions()`, this is the function that actually registers our node to the add node window. Finally, we have `IsNodeSafeToIgnore()`. This one can be a bit cryptic just from looking at the name. But as I mentioned earlier there are two types of nodes, the ones that compile into kismet bytecode and the ones that replaces themselves with a bunch of simpler nodes. Returning true here means that we are safe to ignore, because when the Blueprint is compiled, we will have replaced ourselves with simpler nodes. Let's start looking at the implementation of this. In /Plugins/MarsEditor/Source/MarsBlueprintNodes/Private/Nodes/ create MarsMapForEach.cpp and start adding the following code.

```
#include "Nodes/MarsMapForEach.h"

#include "Kismet/BlueprintMapLibrary.h"
#include "Kismet/KismetArrayLibrary.h"
#include "Kismet/KismetSystemLibrary.h"
#include "Kismet/KismetMathLibrary.h"
#include "KismetCompiler.h"
#include "K2Node_TemporaryVariable.h"
#include "K2Node_AssignmentStatement.h"
#include "K2Node_CallFunction.h"
#include "K2Node_ExecutionSequence.h"
#include "K2Node_IfThenElse.h"

#include "MarsBlueprintNodesLibrary.h"

const FName UMarsK2Node_MapForEach::OutLoopExecPinName(TEXT
("OutLoopExec"));
const FName UMarsK2Node_MapForEach::OutLoopCompletedExecPin
Name(TEXT("OutLoopCompletedExec"));
const FName UMarsK2Node_MapForEach::InMapPinName(TEXT
("InMap"));
const FName UMarsK2Node_MapForEach::OutValuePinName(TEXT
("OutValue"));
const FName UMarsK2Node_MapForEach::OutKeyPinName(TEXT("OutKey
PinName"));

FText UMarsK2Node_MapForEach::GetMenuCategory() const
{
  return FText::FromString("Mars - Blueprint Nodes");
}

FText UMarsK2Node_MapForEach::GetNodeTitle(ENodeTitleType::
Type _titleType) const
{
  return FText::FromString("MapForEach");
}

FText UMarsK2Node_MapForEach::GetTooltipText() const
{
  return FText::FromString("Node that iterates over map,
returning both key and value");
}

UEdGraphPin* UMarsK2Node_MapForEach::GetOutLoopExecPin() const
{
  return FindPinChecked(OutLoopExecPinName);
}

UEdGraphPin* UMarsK2Node_MapForEach::GetOutLoopCompletedExec
Pin() const
{
  return FindPinChecked(OutLoopCompletedExecPinName);
```

```
}

UEdGraphPin* UMarsK2Node_MapForEach::GetInMapPin() const
{
  return FindPinChecked(InMapPinName);
}

UEdGraphPin* UMarsK2Node_MapForEach::GetOutValuePin() const
{
  return FindPinChecked(OutValuePinName);
}

UEdGraphPin* UMarsK2Node_MapForEach::GetOutKeyPin() const
{
  return FindPinChecked(OutKeyPinName);
}
```

First off, we just fill in the names for our static variables. Then the menu category name we want our node in, again this is the category in the add nodes window. After this we have the actual display name of the node in `GetNodeTitle` and after that a tooltip text if the user hovers over our node. Then we have a bunch of helper functions to get our pins we will have on our node. While we technically don't need them, it's a common pattern in Unreal to provide them and it makes life a little bit easier so I will be using them. Then comes the `GetMenuAction()` where we register ourselves.

```
void UMarsK2Node_MapForEach::GetMenuActions(FBlueprintAction
DatabaseRegistrar& _actionRegistrar) const
{
  MarsBlueprintNodesLibrary::RegisterBlueprintNode(GetClass(),
_actionRegistrar);
}
```

This is the function that register us to the add node window. In my experience this implementation will always be like this, so we will place this function in a helper library. In /Plugins/MarsEditor/Source/MarsBlueprintNodes/Public/ create Mars BlueprintNodesLibrary.h and add the following code.

```
#pragma once

namespace MarsBlueprintNodesLibrary{
  static void RegisterBlueprintNode(UClass* _nodeClass,
FBlueprintActionDatabaseRegistrar& _actionRegistrar);
};
```

And then in /Plugins/MarsEditor/Source/MarsBlueprintNodes/Private/ add MarsBlueprintNodesLibrary.cpp and add the following code.

```
#include "MarsBlueprintNodesLibrary.h"
#include "BlueprintNodeSpawner.h"
```

```
void MarsBlueprintNodesLibrary::RegisterBlueprintNode
(UClass* _nodeClass, FBlueprintActionDatabaseRegistrar&
_actionRegistrar)
{
  if (_actionRegistrar.IsOpenForRegistration(_nodeClass))
  {
    UBlueprintNodeSpawner* nodeSpawner =
UBlueprintNodeSpawner::Create(_nodeClass);
    check(nodeSpawner != nullptr);

    _actionRegistrar.AddBlueprintAction(_nodeClass,
nodeSpawner);
  }
}
```

That is all that is needed to register our node. Now we have a node that is registered but it's not quite ready to be added yet. Our next step is to set up all the pins our node will have; we will also add some variables for our wildcard pins. In MarsMapForEachNode.h add the following code.

```
class MARSBLUEPRINTNODES_API UMarsK2Node_MapForEach : public
UK2Node
{
  //...
  virtual void AllocateDefaultPins() override;
private:
  void RestoreAllPinsToWildcard();

  UPROPERTY()
  FEdGraphPinType CurrentMapType;

  UPROPERTY()
  FEdGraphPinType KeyCurrentType;

  UPROPERTY()
  FEdGraphPinType ValueCurrentType;

  UPROPERTY()
  bool FirstInit = true;
};
```

The first function, `AllocateDefaultPins`, is the function responsible for actually creating all the pins we are going to need in our node. Every node must have this function. Since we will be having some of our pins be wildcards so we can plug in any data, we must keep track of what we have plugged into those pins. For example, if we plug in a map in the in map pin, we want to change the out key and out value pins to the correct values. We make them `UPROPERTY` just so they are serialized. Finally, we also declare `RestoreAllPinsToWildcard`, this helper function will be used to restore the node pins to being wildcard again and will for example be used if we disconnect a connection to a pin. Let's look at the function definitions in MarsMapForEach.cpp next.

```
void UMarsK2Node_MapForEach::AllocateDefaultPins()
{
  UEdGraphPin* inExecPin = CreatePin(EGPD_Input,
UEdGraphSchema_K2::PC_Exec, UEdGraphSchema_K2::PN_Execute);
  inExecPin->PinFriendlyName = FText::FromString("Exec");

  UEdGraphPin* outLoopExecPin = CreatePin(EGPD_Output,
UEdGraphSchema_K2::PC_Exec, UMarsK2Node_MapForEach::
OutLoopExecPinName);
  outLoopExecPin->PinFriendlyName = FText::FromString("Loop");

  UEdGraphPin* inMapPin = CreatePin(EGPD_Input,
UEdGraphSchema_K2::PC_Wildcard, InMapPinName);
  inMapPin->PinFriendlyName = FText::FromString("Map");

  UEdGraphPin* outKeyPin = CreatePin(EGPD_Output,
UEdGraphSchema_K2::PC_Wildcard, OutKeyPinName);
  outKeyPin->PinFriendlyName = FText::FromString("Key");

  UEdGraphPin* outValuePin = CreatePin(EGPD_Output,
UEdGraphSchema_K2::PC_Wildcard, OutValuePinName);
  outValuePin->PinFriendlyName = FText::FromString("Value");

  UEdGraphPin* outLoopCompletedPin = CreatePin(EGPD_Output,
UEdGraphSchema_K2::PC_Exec, UMarsK2Node_MapForEach::
OutLoopCompletedExecPinName);
  outLoopCompletedPin->PinFriendlyName = FText::FromString
("Completed");

  if ( FirstInit )
  {
    RestoreAllPinsToWildcard();
    FirstInit = false;
  }
  else
  {
    inMapPin->PinType = CurrentMapType;
    outKeyPin->PinType = KeyCurrentType;
    outValuePin->PinType = ValueCurrentType;
  }
}
```

We create all the pins we need with the `CreatePin` function. The order we create our pins in is the order they will be displayed on the node, so keep that in mind when setting up pins. The `CreatePin` function first takes what direction the pins should be in, in or out, as a parameter, then we have the type of pin. We are using execution pins and wildcard pins in this example, but there are of course a lot more types. You find the full list of them in \Engine\Source\Editor\BlueprintGraph\Classes\

EdGraphSchema_K2.h. Next up we need to specify the pin identifier name. For the in execution pin there's already a name defined we make use of, for the rest of the pins we have defined our own names. Then we set some nice display names for our pins. When coding names like `OutLoopCompletedExec` are nice since they give us good information about what this pin is, but on the actual Blueprint node a lot of that information is redundant since we see that just from the placement on the node and the look of the pin. A clear, short name makes for more readable Blueprint nodes, longer more verbose names make for clearer more readable code. At least for me, your coding habits might be different so use whatever naming method you prefer of course.

Next, we have some code to handle the data on our pin types. Whenever we open a Blueprint graph `AllocateDefaultPins` is called for each node. That's why we need to save the data types of our pins once they are set (we will do this soon) so that when we re-init the node, we can set them to the correct values. If it's our first time allocating, we call our helper function that resets the pins back to their original state. Otherwise, we apply our save data types on the pins. Let's take a look at `RestoreAllPinsToWildcard` next.

```
void UMarsK2Node_MapForEach::RestoreAllPinsToWildcard()
{
  CurrentMapType.PinCategory = UEdGraphSchema_K2::PC_Wildcard;
  CurrentMapType.PinValueType.TerminalCategory =
UEdGraphSchema_K2::PC_Wildcard;
  CurrentMapType.ContainerType = EPinContainerType::Map;
  CurrentMapType.bIsConst = true;
  CurrentMapType.bIsReference = true;
  KeyCurrentType.PinCategory = UEdGraphSchema_K2::PC_Wildcard;
  ValueCurrentType.PinCategory = UEdGraphSchema_K2
::PC_Wildcard;

  UEdGraphPin* ourMapInPin = GetInMapPin();
  UEdGraphPin* ourValueOutPin = GetOutValuePin();
  UEdGraphPin* ourKeyOutPin = GetOutKeyPin();
  ourMapInPin->PinType = CurrentMapType;
  ourKeyOutPin->PinType = KeyCurrentType;
  ourValueOutPin->PinType = ValueCurrentType;
  ourValueOutPin->BreakAllPinLinks(true);
  ourKeyOutPin->BreakAllPinLinks(true);
}
```

We start with setting the data types on our saved variables. The key and value pins are straightforward, we just set the `PinCategory` to be wildcard. But the map pin has a bit more going on. We set both `PinCategory` and `PinValueType.TerminalCategory` to wildcard. Since this is a map container, `PinCategory` is the key part of the map, `PinValueType.TerminalCategory` is the value part of the map. We want both parts to be a wildcards so we need to specify that. Then we also specify that we want our parameter to be const and a reference. Then we dig out our pins with the helper function we used and apply the data types to each pin. We also disconnect the key and value pin. This is not needed when initializing, but we will need this if the user disconnects the map pin and also if we copy paste the node without the map pin. Let's take a look at this next, add the following function declarations in MarsMapForEach.h.

```
class MARSBLUEPRINTNODES_API UMarsK2Node_MapForEach : public
UK2Node
{
  //...
  virtual void PinConnectionListChanged(UEdGraphPin* _pin)
override;
  virtual void PostPasteNode() override;
  //...
};
```

The functions names are pretty clear, the first function gets called whenever a pin changes connection status on our node, meaning it gets a new connection or it gets disconnected. The second is called after we pasted this node in. Let's look at the function for the pin connection change first.

```
void UMarsK2Node_MapForEach::PinConnectionListChanged
(UEdGraphPin* _pin)
{
  Super::PinConnectionListChanged(_pin);

  if (_pin->PinName == InMapPinName)
  {
    if (_pin->LinkedTo.Num() > 0)
    {
      CurrentMapType = _pin->LinkedTo[0]->PinType;
      KeyCurrentType = FEdGraphPinType::GetTerminalTypeFor
Container(CurrentMapType);
      ValueCurrentType = FEdGraphPinType::GetPinTypeForTerminal
Type(CurrentMapType.PinValueType);
      _pin->PinType = CurrentMapType;

      UEdGraphPin* ourValueOutPin = GetOutValuePin();
      UEdGraphPin* ourKeyOutPin = GetOutKeyPin();
      ourKeyOutPin->PinType = KeyCurrentType;
      ourValueOutPin->PinType = ValueCurrentType;
    }
    else
    {
      RestoreAllPinsToWildcard();
    }
  }
}
```

Normally pins handle resetting themselves back to the default value, this is what happens inside the super call. But in our case, we want to change the key and value pins depending on what happens with our map pin. First, we check that it's our map key that has changed status, if not we just ignore it and do nothing. If it is our map pin, we check how many connections is has by checking the size of `LinkedTo`. Of course, our map pin can only ever have one connection, but some pin types can have multiple connections. If it's empty, that means we just got disconnected so we call our `RestoreAllPinsToWildcard` function that will reset the map pin, but also reset and disconnect the key and value pins. Since we do not know the data type of them any longer, it doesn't make sense to keep any connections we might have had. It's not going to work so we disconnect it automatically, so the user doesn't have to do it manually.

If we have a link to our map pin however, we start with saving the data type of the pin we are connected to, we also dig out the key and value data types from the pin with `GetTerminalTypeForContainer` and `GetPinTypeForTerminalType`. These names can be a bit cryptic, but since we are working with a map pin, we have two data types in one pin, usually you only ever have one type, so the pin handling is a bit easier then. Lastly, we apply the new pin data types we have dug out from the connection and saved in our variables to the actual pins themselves. Again, we save them in our variables so that we can restore this node properly next time `AllocateDefaultPins` gets called.

Time for the paste function.

```
void UMarsK2Node_MapForEach::PostPasteNode()
{
  Super::PostPasteNode();

  UEdGraphPin* ourMapInPin = GetInMapPin();
  if (ourMapInPin->LinkedTo.IsEmpty())
  {
    RestoreAllPinsToWildcard();
  }
}
```

This one if easy, after we have pasted in our node and if we have no connections to our map pin, we reset the pins on the nodes with our helper function `RestoreAllPinsToWildcard`.

Now it's time for the final function we need to make our node work. Let's add the following function declaration to MarsMapForEach.h.

```
class MARSBLUEPRINTNODES_API UMarsK2Node_MapForEach : public
UK2Node
{
  //...
  virtual void ExpandNode(FKismetCompilerContext&
_compilerContext, UEdGraph* _sourceGraph) override;
  //...
};
```

Earlier I said that our node will need to replace itself with simpler nodes (and those nodes will also replace themselves with simpler nodes until it's only kismet bytecode remaining). This is the function that does it. This function will expand our nodes into new, simpler nodes and move all pin connections to those new nodes, leaving our node completely disconnected. In other words, we are going to set up a Blueprint graph in it, but in code. While a simple loop node might sound trivial, we are going to need quite a few nodes, and we are going to need to do a lot of connections between them. In fact, it can be quite helpful to draw up this graph on paper first to figure out the nodes you need and how they are going to be connected. It can be error prone to code a 2D node layout. This is also why we will be creating some helper functions in this next part that will help us catch mistakes we do. We are going to need to create the following nodes and connect them:

- An integer variable node for our loop counter
- An assignment node to initialize the counter to zero
- An assignment node to set a new value of our counter variable
- A node to add an integer to another integer. This is for adding the value 1 to our counter variable
- A branch node that will check if we should loop one more time or not
- An execution sequence node. Every loop we will increase our counter and set our out pins and call the loop execution pin, this will make that setup a bit easier
- A call function node to compare if an integer is smaller than another integer. This will be used by the branch node
- A call function node to get the length of the map
- A call function node to get the key array from the map
- A call function node to get the value array from the map
- A call function to get an element from the key array
- A call function to get an element from the value array

Quite a list! We are going to have to create all these nodes, then get several pins from each node and connect those nodes together so we end up with a Blueprint graph. When ExpandNode is called, all we have is our node with its connections. We will create these new nodes, move our connections from our node to where they belong on the new nodes, and we will need to create a lot of new connections between the nodes we created. Right about now you might be wondering if all this is really worth it? If you look at the array ForEach node, it's not done in code, it's actually just a Blueprint macro. So could this node also be, except that currently doing macros with maps and wildcards doesn't work properly and the bug for this is currently marked as won't fix in Epic's official bug tracker. So, we need to program this node ourselves, plus this is a good node to show how programming nodes work, the how and the why of it. The helper library we will be making will be designed to deal with the common errors we can make here. You might think that since we are doing it in code our node will be faster. But this is not correct, our code will only run during the compilation of the Blueprint, not when the game is actually running. By then all the Blueprint graphs are compiled down to kismet bytecode that is executing. Looking at the implementation of the array ForEach node helps with visualizing the node graph we need to build (just double click on any ForEach node in a Blueprint graph). When programming nodes like this, it can be helpful to draw the graph you need. Here's an image of the node graph we will need to build.

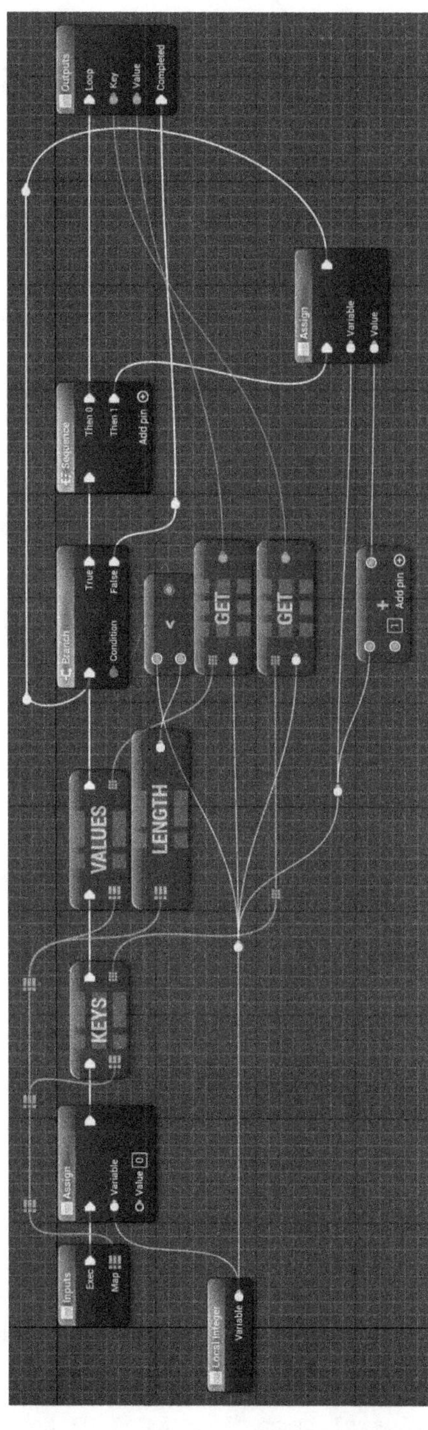
Outputs
Loop
Key
Value
Completed
Assign
Variable
Value
Sequence
Then 0
Then 1
Add pin
Branch
Condition
True
False
GET
GET
+
Add pin
VALUES
LENGTH
KEYS
Assign
Variable
Value
Inputs
Exec
Map
Local Integer
Variable

If you compare this to the node list above, you will see we have every node, except the `Inputs` and `Outputs` node. I made this image as a macro (which as I mentioned currently doesn't work since Unreal gets the wildcards wrong on our out parameters) which is why there are Inputs/Outputs nodes here. These two nodes we will not be creating in code, but this is where the connections to the rest of the graph is coming in/going out. Every other node and link you see in this image we will have to create in code.

Ok time to start looking at the implementation of the `ExpandNode` function in MarsMapForEach.cpp.

```
void UMarsK2Node_MapForEach::ExpandNode(FKismetCompiler
Context& _compilerContext, UEdGraph* _sourceGraph)
{
  Super::ExpandNode(_compilerContext, _sourceGraph);

  //Our pins
  UEdGraphPin* ourExecInPin = GetExecPin();
  UEdGraphPin* ourLoopExecOutPin = GetOutLoopExecPin();
  UEdGraphPin* ourLoopCompletedExecOutPin =
GetOutLoopCompletedExecPin();
  UEdGraphPin* ourMapInPin = GetInMapPin();
  UEdGraphPin* ourValueOutPin = GetOutValuePin();
  UEdGraphPin* ourKeyOutPin = GetOutKeyPin();

  //...
};
```

We start simple enough with just digging out our pins. When doing nodes like this that require a lot of Blueprint nodes to replace, it's important to have a naming system that helps us. As you can see, I'm going with NodeName_PinName_Direction as I find that to be the most helpful. Next up we need to create all the Blueprint nodes. We do this by spawning new nodes through the compiler context parameter. Once we have spawned the nodes, and if needed done any setup on them, we then create the pins on them with a call to `AllocateDefaultPins`. It's important we do all the setup we need first because on some nodes the number of pins might depend on the setup we do.

```
UK2Node_TemporaryVariable* loopCounterVarNode =
_compilerContext.SpawnIntermediateNode< UK2Node
_TemporaryVariable >(this, _sourceGraph);
loopCounterVarNode->VariableType.PinCategory =
UEdGraphSchema_K2::PC_Int;
loopCounterVarNode->AllocateDefaultPins();
```

Here we created an integer variable. This is going to be our loop counter.

```
UK2Node_AssignmentStatement* initLoopCounterVarNode=
_compilerContext.SpawnIntermediateNode< UK2Node
_AssignmentStatement >(this, _sourceGraph);
initLoopCounterVarNode->AllocateDefaultPins();
```

```
UK2Node_AssignmentStatement* incrementLoopCounterVarNode =
_compilerContext.SpawnIntermediateNode< UK2Node
_AssignmentStatement >(this, _sourceGraph);
incrementLoopCounterVarNode->AllocateDefaultPins();
```

These are the two assignment nodes we are going to need. The first will be to initialize our counter variable to 0, the second one will be to assign the increase value of the counter after every loop.

```
  UK2Node_IfThenElse* ifElseNode = _compilerContext.
SpawnIntermediateNode< UK2Node_IfThenElse >(this,
_sourceGraph);
  ifElseNode->AllocateDefaultPins();
```

This is the branch node we will use after every loop to see if we have reached the end of our map.

```
  UK2Node_ExecutionSequence* executionSequenceNode
= _compilerContext.SpawnIntermediateNode< UK2Node
_ExecutionSequence >(this, _sourceGraph);
  executionSequenceNode->AllocateDefaultPins();
```

The execution sequence node is needed since every loop we first want to trigger the user's execution path, then once that path is done, we will add our loop counter increase and branch check as the second pin in the sequence node.

```
  UK2Node_CallFunction* callFunctionCompareLessThenNode =
_compilerContext.SpawnIntermediateNode< UK2Node_CallFunction
>(this, _sourceGraph);
  callFunctionCompareLessThenNode->FunctionReference.
SetExternalMember(GET_FUNCTION_NAME
_CHECKED(UKismetMathLibrary, Less_IntInt), UKismetMathLibrary::
StaticClass());
  callFunctionCompareLessThenNode->AllocateDefaultPins();
```

This is the first of our call function nodes. These nodes are used to call any `BlueprintCallable` function. Once the node is created, we need to link it to the function we want. We do this with the call to `SetExternalMember` and use the `GET_FUNCTION_NAME_CHECKED` macro which will verify that the function exists during compile.

```
  UK2Node_CallFunction* callFunctionMapGetLengthNode =
_compilerContext.SpawnIntermediateNode< UK2Node_CallFunction
>(this, _sourceGraph);
  callFunctionMapGetLengthNode->FunctionReference.
SetExternalMember(GET_FUNCTION_NAME
_CHECKED(UBlueprintMapLibrary, Map_Length), UBlueprintMap
Library::StaticClass());
  callFunctionMapGetLengthNode->AllocateDefaultPins();
```

This length node is what we are going to use for the compare node, we are going to compare our loop counter against the length of the map.

```
  UK2Node_CallFunction* callFunctionMapKeysNode =
_compilerContext.SpawnIntermediateNode< UK2Node_CallFunction
>(this, _sourceGraph);
  callFunctionMapKeysNode->FunctionReference.
SetExternalMember(GET_FUNCTION_NAME_CHECKED
(UBlueprintMapLibrary, Map_Keys), UBlueprintMapLibrary
::StaticClass());
  callFunctionMapKeysNode->AllocateDefaultPins();

  UK2Node_CallFunction* callFunctionMapValuesNode =
_compilerContext.SpawnIntermediateNode< UK2Node_CallFunction
>(this, _sourceGraph);
  callFunctionMapValuesNode->FunctionReference.
SetExternalMember(GET_FUNCTION_NAME_CHECKED
(UBlueprintMapLibrary, Map_Values), UBlueprintMapLibrary::
StaticClass());
  callFunctionMapValuesNode->AllocateDefaultPins();
```

These nodes will give us the two arrays we need, one for the keys and one for the values in the map.

```
  UK2Node_CallFunction* callFunctionArrayGetKeyNode =
_compilerContext.SpawnIntermediateNode< UK2Node_CallFunction
>(this, _sourceGraph);
  callFunctionArrayGetKeyNode->FunctionReference.
SetExternalMember(GET_FUNCTION_NAME_CHECKED
(UKismetArrayLibrary, Array_Get), UKismetArrayLibrary::Static
Class());
  callFunctionArrayGetKeyNode->AllocateDefaultPins();

  UK2Node_CallFunction* callFunctionArrayGetValueNode =
_compilerContext.SpawnIntermediateNode< UK2Node_CallFunction
>(this, _sourceGraph);
  callFunctionArrayGetValueNode->FunctionReference.
SetExternalMember(GET_FUNCTION_NAME_CHECKED
(UKismetArrayLibrary, Array_Get), UKismetArrayLibrary::
StaticClass());
  callFunctionArrayGetValueNode->AllocateDefaultPins();
```

We are going to need on get node for each of the arrays. We will send this value out each loop.

```
  UK2Node_CallFunction* callFunctionAddIntNode =
_compilerContext.SpawnIntermediateNode< UK2Node_CallFunction
>(this, _sourceGraph);
  callFunctionAddIntNode->FunctionReference.
SetExternalMember(GET_FUNCTION_NAME_CHECKED
```

```
(UKismetMathLibrary, Add_IntInt), UKismetMathLibrary::
StaticClass());
  callFunctionAddIntNode->AllocateDefaultPins();
```

Finally, we need the node to increase the value of the loop counter.

Now we have all the nodes we need; next step is going to get all the pins from the nodes before we can finally start connecting them. Now you will see why we created those helper functions for getting pins on our nodes, it's expected that every node has these helper functions so we can use the node easily in other nodes like this.

```
  UEdGraphPin* loopCounterVarOutPin =
loopCounterVarNode->GetVariablePin();
```

Our loop counter variable node is quite simple, it just has one pin for the variable.

```
  UEdGraphPin* initLoopCounterVarExecInPin =
initLoopCounterVarNode->GetExecPin();
  UEdGraphPin* initLoopCounterVarVariableInPin =
initLoopCounterVarNode->GetVariablePin();
  UEdGraphPin* initLoopCounterVarValueInPin =
initLoopCounterVarNode->GetValuePin();
  UEdGraphPin* initLoopCounterVarThenOutPin =
initLoopCounterVarNode->GetThenPin();

  UEdGraphPin* incrementLoopCounterVarExecInPin =
incrementLoopCounterVarNode->GetExecPin();
  UEdGraphPin* incrementLoopCounterVarThenOutPin =
incrementLoopCounterVarNode->GetThenPin();
  UEdGraphPin* incrementLoopCounterVarVariableInPin =
incrementLoopCounterVarNode->GetVariablePin();
  UEdGraphPin* incrementLoopCounterVarValueInPin =
incrementLoopCounterVarNode->GetValuePin();
```

Our assignment nodes have a few more pins (like most nodes do). They both have an execution in/out pin, these are the `*ExecInPin` and `*ThenOutPin`. `Exec` is the Unreal name for the in execution pin, `then` is the name for the out execution pin.

```
  UEdGraphPin* ifElseExecInPin = ifElseNode->GetExecPin();
  UEdGraphPin* ifElseConditionInPin =
ifElseNode->GetConditionPin();
  UEdGraphPin* ifElseThenOutPin = ifElseNode->GetThenPin();
  UEdGraphPin* ifElseElseOutPin = ifElseNode->GetElsePin();
```

The branch node has two out execution pins, the then pin is the true branch, the else pin is (obviously) the false path.

```
  UEdGraphPin* compareAInPin =  callFunctionCompareLessThenNode
->FindPinChecked(TEXT("A"));
```

```
  UEdGraphPin* compareBInPin =  callFunctionCompareLessThenNode
->FindPinChecked(TEXT("B"));
  UEdGraphPin* compareResultOutPin =
callFunctionCompareLessThenNode->GetReturnValuePin();
```

From the call function nodes, we need to get the parameter pins a bit different. Since there's a pin for each parameter in the function and it has the name of the parameter, there's no helper function for us. We have to use the `FindPinChecked` function and type in the name of the parameter we want to find the pin for. If you check the `UKismetMathLibrary::Less_IntInt` function you will see that the two parameters are named `A` and `B`. Also since this is a pure node, it doesn't have any execution pins.

```
  UEdGraphPin* getMapLengthTargetMapInPin =
callFunctionMapGetLengthNode->FindPinChecked
(TEXT("TargetMap"));
  UEdGraphPin* getMapLengthResultOutPin =
callFunctionMapGetLengthNode->GetReturnValuePin();
```

Another pure call function node we are getting the pins for, just one pin to send in the map and one pin to get the length result back out.

```
  UEdGraphPin* getMapKeysExecInPin =
callFunctionMapKeysNode->GetExecPin();
  UEdGraphPin* getMapKeysThenOutPin =
callFunctionMapKeysNode->GetThenPin();
  UEdGraphPin* getMapKeysTargetMapInPin =
callFunctionMapKeysNode->FindPinChecked(TEXT("TargetMap"));
  UEdGraphPin* getMapKeysResultOutPin =
callFunctionMapKeysNode->FindPinChecked(TEXT("Keys"));

  UEdGraphPin* getMapValuesExecInPin =
callFunctionMapValuesNode->GetExecPin();
  UEdGraphPin* getMapValuesThenOutPin =
callFunctionMapValuesNode->GetThenPin();
  UEdGraphPin* getMapValuesTargetMapInPin =
callFunctionMapValuesNode->FindPinChecked(TEXT("TargetMap"));
  UEdGraphPin* getMapValuesResultOutPin =
callFunctionMapValuesNode->FindPinChecked(TEXT("Values"));
```

The two nodes for getting the key and value arrays from our map are not pure, so these do have execution pins.

```
  UEdGraphPin* getArrayKeyArrayInPin = callFunctionArray
GetKeyNode->FindPinChecked(TEXT("TargetArray"));
  UEdGraphPin* getArrayKeyIndexInPin =
callFunctionArrayGetKeyNode->FindPinChecked(TEXT("Index"));
  UEdGraphPin* getArrayKeyItemOutPin =
callFunctionArrayGetKeyNode->FindPinChecked(TEXT("Item"));
```

```
  UEdGraphPin* getArrayValueArrayInPin = callFunctionArray
GetValueNode->FindPinChecked(TEXT("TargetArray"));
  UEdGraphPin* getArrayValueIndexInPin =
callFunctionArrayGetValueNode->FindPinChecked(TEXT("Index"));
  UEdGraphPin* getArrayValueItemOutPin =
callFunctionArrayGetValueNode->FindPinChecked(TEXT("Item"));
```

The get nodes for the arrays are also pure, so no execution pins needed for them either.

```
  UEdGraphPin* sequenceExecInPin =
executionSequenceNode->GetExecPin();
  UEdGraphPin* sequenceThen1OutPin =
executionSequenceNode->GetThenPinGivenIndex(0);
  UEdGraphPin* sequenceThen2OutPin =
executionSequenceNode->GetThenPinGivenIndex(1);
```

The sequence node is a bit different; we can get as many pins as we want from this one. We only need two however.

```
  UEdGraphPin* addIntAInPin =
callFunctionAddIntNode->FindPinChecked(TEXT("A"));
  UEdGraphPin* addIntBInPin =
callFunctionAddIntNode->FindPinChecked(TEXT("B"));
  UEdGraphPin* addIntResultOutPin =
callFunctionAddIntNode->GetReturnValuePin();
```

Finally, the pins for our node that will increase the loop counter value. Now before we start connecting all these pins, we still have a bit of setup that we need to do on some of the pins. Just like our node has wildcard pins, so do some of the pins to these nodes. Thus, we need to set the correct pin type on these pins. We know what type we need from our own pins, since they are already connected and we have converted them to the correct types, this is what we did in `PinConnectionListChanged`.

```
  //Setup pin types to all wildcard nodes
  getMapLengthTargetMapInPin->PinType = ourMapInPin->PinType;
  getMapKeysTargetMapInPin->PinType = ourMapInPin->PinType;
  getMapValuesTargetMapInPin->PinType = ourMapInPin->PinType;

  getArrayKeyItemOutPin->PinType = ourKeyOutPin->PinType;
  getArrayKeyArrayInPin->PinType = KeyCurrentType;
  getArrayKeyArrayInPin->PinType.ContainerType =
EPinContainerType::Array;

  getArrayValueItemOutPin->PinType = ourValueOutPin->PinType;
  getArrayValueArrayInPin->PinType = ValueCurrentType;
  getArrayValueArrayInPin->PinType.ContainerType =
EPinContainerType::Array;
```

We set the pintype on all of the map and array nodes we have created. When we set the key/value in pin for the arrays we set it to the pin type we got from our in map pin (`KeyCurrentType` and `ValueCurrentType`), these two are not arrays (since our map doesn't have an array in each key/value slot), so we need to set this pin back to being an array container type.

Now, finally, it's time to start connecting all these pins. Our node, which will be removed after this, currently has all the connections. Once we are done it shouldn't have any connections left. We will want to move these connections into the new graph we are building. We will also need to create completely new connections between a lot of these new pins. Refer to the image of the graph we are building. Our map pin is going to be needed in several places, so this connection we are going to have to create copies of. We will start with creating some helper functions for these 3 cases, move, copy and make. We are also going to add a function for setting the default value on a pin. Add the following function declarations in MarsBlueprintNodesLibrary.h.

```
class FKismetCompilerContext;
class UEdGraphPin;

namespace MarsBlueprintNodesLibrary
{
  //...
  static void MovePinLinkTo(FKismetCompilerContext&
_compilerContext, UEdGraphPin* _sourcePin, UEdGraphPin*
_destPin);
  static void CopyPinLinkTo(FKismetCompilerContext&
_compilerContext, UEdGraphPin* _sourcePin, UEdGraphPin*
_destPin);
  static void MakePinLinkTo(FKismetCompilerContext&
_compilerContext, UEdGraphPin* _sourcePin, UEdGraphPin*
_destPin);
  static void SetDefaultValue(UEdGraphPin* _pin, FString
_value, FName _category);
};
```

We will need to compiler context to do the actual work, and of course we need a source pin and a destination pin. Onto the function definitions.

```
#include "KismetCompiler.h"

void MarsBlueprintNodesLibrary::MovePinLinkTo(FKismetCom
pilerContext& _compilerContext, UEdGraphPin* _sourcePin,
UEdGraphPin* _destPin)
{
```

```
  FPinConnectionResponse result = _compilerContext.
MovePinLinksToIntermediate(*_sourcePin, *_destPin);
  ensureAlwaysMsgf(result.CanSafeConnect(), TEXT("Failed to
connect pins - %s!"), *result.Message.ToString());
}
```

Our helper function just calls a function in the compiler context that does all the work, we could just as easily have called this function directly. However, if we have made a mistake with our connection, we will get an error message when we compile the Blueprint graph, but it can be hard to figure out what connection is actually causing the error. That's why we check if we succeeded inside an ensure, so that the debugger will break for us on the line that caused the error if there is one. As I said earlier, this helper library is designed to help us develop these nodes, not to lessen the code we need to write.

```
void MarsBlueprintNodesLibrary::CopyPinLinkTo(FKismet
CompilerContext& _compilerContext, UEdGraphPin* _sourcePin,
UEdGraphPin* _destPin)
{
  FPinConnectionResponse result = _compilerContext.
CopyPinLinksToIntermediate(*_sourcePin, *_destPin);
  ensureAlwaysMsgf(result.CanSafeConnect(), TEXT("Failed to
copy pins! - %s"), *result.Message.ToString());
}
```

The copy node is almost exactly the same, we just do the copy and ensure on the result, same as the move function.

```
void MarsBlueprintNodesLibrary::MakePinLinkTo(FKismetCompiler
Context& _compilerContext, UEdGraphPin* _sourcePin,
UEdGraphPin* _destPin)
{
  const UEdGraphSchema_K2* schema = _compilerContext.
GetSchema();
  const FPinConnectionResponse result = schema->CanCreate
Connection(_sourcePin, _destPin);
  //If the directions are the same, did you mean to use
MovePinLink instead?
  ensureAlwaysMsgf(result.CanSafeConnect(),
TEXT("MakePinLinkTo failed - %s"), *result.Message.
ToString());
  //Trigger callbacks that changes wildcard type on some
nodes, other nodes (like CallFunction) cannot convert so we
need to set it up on our own
  schema->TryCreateConnection(_sourcePin, _destPin);
```

```
  ensureAlwaysMsgf(_sourcePin->PinType.PinCategory !=
UEdGraphSchema_K2::PC_Wildcard, TEXT("MakePinLinkTo failed,
pin is still wildcard!"));
  ensureAlwaysMsgf(_destPin->PinType.PinCategory !=
UEdGraphSchema_K2::PC_Wildcard, TEXT("MakePinLinkTo failed,
pin is still wildcard!"));
}
```

The make function is the same idea, but it has even more checks to see that we have done everything correct. Then we have the function for setting a value directly on a pin.

```
void MarsBlueprintNodesLibrary::SetDefaultValue(UEdGraphPin*
_pin, FString _value, FName _category)
{
  _pin->DefaultValue = _value;
  _pin->PinType.PinCategory = _category;
}
```

Again, this function doesn't do anything that we couldn't do without our helper library. But this function forces you to also set the pin data type, sometimes this is not needed, but sometimes it is because it is still a wildcard pin. By forcing ourselves to specify the data, we lessen the possibility of mistakes.

Personally, I prefer that this helper library do as much error checking as possible for me, because I find keeping a graph like this with several nodes and even more pins in my head and doing the connections to these to be quite error prone. Anything I can do to catch errors earlier and point out exactly where the error is, is worth it to me. Now we are finally ready to start connecting the pins so let's go back to MarsMapForEach.cpp and continue adding code in `ExpandNode()`,

```
  //Init counter
  MarsBlueprintNodesLibrary::MovePinLinkTo(_compilerContext,
ourExecInPin, initLoopCounterVarExecInPin);
  MarsBlueprintNodesLibrary::SetDefaultValue(initLoopCounter
VarValueInPin, TEXT("0"), UEdGraphSchema_K2::PC_Int);
  MarsBlueprintNodesLibrary::MakePinLinkTo(_compilerContext,
loopCounterVarOutPin, initLoopCounterVarVariableInPin);
  MarsBlueprintNodesLibrary::MakePinLinkTo(_compilerContext,
initLoopCounterVarThenOutPin, getMapKeysExecInPin);
```

The first node we will connect is the assignment node to set our loop counter to 0. We move the execution connection from our execution pin to the assignment's nodes execution pin. We set the value to be 0 and integer type, then we make a connection to the loop counter variable pin, since that's the variable we want to assign 0 to. Then we make a new connection from our then (out) execution pin to the next node, which will be getting the keys array from the map.

```
  //Get Keys array
```

```
  MarsBlueprintNodesLibrary::CopyPinLinkTo(_compilerContext,
ourMapInPin, getMapKeysTargetMapInPin);
  MarsBlueprintNodesLibrary::MakePinLinkTo(_compilerContext,
getMapKeysThenOutPin, getMapValuesExecInPin);
```

We copy the map connection, since we will be using this in more places after this, we cannot move it (or we could move it, but then we have to copy it from this pin, which is less readable). Then we make a link to the next node, getting the value array.

```
  //Get Values array
  MarsBlueprintNodesLibrary::CopyPinLinkTo(_compilerContext,
ourMapInPin, getMapValuesTargetMapInPin);
  MarsBlueprintNodesLibrary::MakePinLinkTo(_compilerContext,
getMapValuesThenOutPin, ifElseExecInPin);
```

Same thing really, we still need the map after this, so we copy that connection. Then we make a connection to the next node, which will be our branch node. The branch node will have the less than node connected to it, and one of the variables to this will be the map length. The map length node is also a wildcard node. We didn't manually set the map type on this, since all we need to do is connect it and the node handles it. But that does mean we need to connect it before we start using it. In order words, the order we do our connections in also matters.

```
  //GetMapLength node
  MarsBlueprintNodesLibrary::MovePinLinkTo(_compilerContext,
ourMapInPin, getMapLengthTargetMapInPin);
```

This time we move our map connection here; we will not need any more map connections after this.

```
  //Less than node
  MarsBlueprintNodesLibrary::MakePinLinkTo(_compilerContext,
loopCounterVarOutPin, compareAInPin);
  MarsBlueprintNodesLibrary::MakePinLinkTo(_compilerContext,
getMapLengthResultOutPin, compareBInPin);
```

We plug in our loop counter variable and our map length to this less than node.

```
  //Branch node
  MarsBlueprintNodesLibrary::MakePinLinkTo(_compilerContext,
compareResultOutPin, ifElseConditionInPin);
  MarsBlueprintNodesLibrary::MakePinLinkTo(_compilerContext,
ifElseThenOutPin, sequenceExecInPin);
  MarsBlueprintNodesLibrary::MovePinLinkTo(_compilerContext,
ourLoopCompletedExecOutPin, ifElseElseOutPin );
```

The result pin of the less than node goes into our branch node, then we link the true path to our sequence node and on the false path, we move our loop done connection.

```
//Sequence node
MarsBlueprintNodesLibrary::MovePinLinkTo(_compilerContext,
ourLoopExecOutPin, sequenceThen1OutPin);
MarsBlueprintNodesLibrary::MakePinLinkTo(_compilerContext,
incrementLoopCounterVarExecInPin, sequenceThen2OutPin );
```

On the first pin in our sequence node, we move the loop connection from our node, this will now trigger any logic the user has connected to it. We have no way of connecting our loop counter increment after this, that's why we need the sequence node, so in the second pin we connect our increment loop counter node.

```
  //Add 1 to loop counter
  MarsBlueprintNodesLibrary::MakePinLinkTo(_compilerContext,
loopCounterVarOutPin, addIntAInPin);
  MarsBlueprintNodesLibrary::SetDefaultValue(addIntBInPin,
TEXT("1"), UEdGraphSchema_K2::PC_Int);
```

We need to increase our loop counter, so we add 1 to our current loop counter value, this will give us a result we can then use to assign to the loop counter variable.

```
  //Assign new loop counter value
  MarsBlueprintNodesLibrary::MakePinLinkTo(_compilerContext,
loopCounterVarOutPin, incrementLoopCounterVarVariableInPin);
  MarsBlueprintNodesLibrary::MakePinLinkTo(_compilerContext,
addIntResultOutPin, incrementLoopCounterVarValueInPin);
  MarsBlueprintNodesLibrary::MakePinLinkTo(_compilerContext,
incrementLoopCounterVarThenOutPin, ifElseExecInPin);
```

And here we assign our new value to the loop counter. Then we make a connection to our first branch node again, the node that will check if we should do another loop or finish looping. Now the only thing missing is that we haven't assigned any values to the key and value output pins yet.

```
  //Send out Key value
  MarsBlueprintNodesLibrary::MakePinLinkTo(_compilerContext,
loopCounterVarOutPin, getArrayKeyIndexInPin);
  MarsBlueprintNodesLibrary::MakePinLinkTo(_compilerContext,
getMapKeysResultOutPin, getArrayKeyArrayInPin);
  MarsBlueprintNodesLibrary::MovePinLinkTo(_compilerContext,
ourKeyOutPin, getArrayKeyItemOutPin);

  //Send out Value value
```

```
  MarsBlueprintNodesLibrary::MakePinLinkTo(_compilerContext,
loopCounterVarOutPin, getArrayValueIndexInPin);
  MarsBlueprintNodesLibrary::MakePinLinkTo(_compilerContext,
getMapValuesResultOutPin, getArrayValueArrayInPin);
  MarsBlueprintNodesLibrary::MovePinLinkTo(_compilerContext,
ourValueOutPin, getArrayValueItemOutPin);
```

We connect the get node to the arrays with the loop counter variable and the corresponding arrays. Then we move the key/value links from our node to these two get nodes. Since these are all pure, they will execute whenever someone uses the value, which should be in the user code after the first pin on the sequence node. Now we are done and have a functional node, but there's one last safety helper function I want to add. Add the following function declaration to MarsBlueprintNodesLibrary.h.

```
namespace MarsBlueprintNodesLibrary
{
  //...
  static void CheckAllPinsDisconnected(UEdGraphNode* _node);
};
```

And then the following code in MarsBlueprintNodesLibrary.cpp.

```
void MarsBlueprintNodesLibrary::CheckAllPinsDisconnected
(UEdGraphNode* _node)
{
  for (UEdGraphPin* pin : _node->Pins)
  {
    ensureAlwaysMsgf(pin->LinkedTo.IsEmpty(), TEXT("Pin %s
hasn't been properly disconnected!"), *pin->GetName());
  }
}
```

This simple goes through all the pins on our node and checks that they are disconnected. It's a common pattern to just disconnect all pins once you are done expanding your node with `BreakAllNodeLinks()`, but I don't like that pattern since if you have a connection left, something has gone wrong in the logic and we should fix it, not silently ignore it and hope it's not critical. That's why this helper function just asserts if any connection is still left. Now we just need to add a call to this function, and we are done.

```
MarsBlueprintNodesLibrary::CheckAllPinsDisconnected(this);
```

Now you have your very own `ForEach` node that works on maps. The purpose with this example was to get you to understand how programming your own Blueprint nodes works, the how and the why of it. The next node we will look at is going to be a more practical and useful example now that we have a solid basic understanding of this system.

ALARM NODE

The second node we will create is an alarm node. Our node will allow us to register and unregister to an alarm actor and receive callbacks when the alarm is started, stopped and every tick the alarm is active.

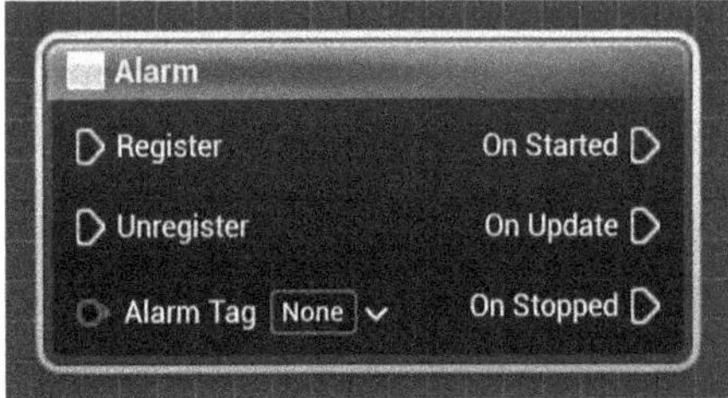

We could of course implement all this with delegates, but then we have to sign up to each delegate manually instead of getting everything encapsulated in one nice node. By doing nodes like this, we have good control of the pattern people will use when implementing our node. Since we will have an OnStarted, OnUpdate and OnStopped execution pin for the alarm, it will be very easy for people to place their logic in the correct place instead of implementing their own solution. It also increases the chances they will remember to do any cleanup that is needed. This is the real strength with writing your own Blueprint nodes in my opinion. It's not about creating new functionality that is impossible to do without your node (although this is certainly possible also), rather it's about creating custom nodes that help people make better Blueprint graphs that have less bugs and are easier to maintain. In small examples like this, it might not seem worth the effort and it's true that for some cases it's not worth the effort to make your own node. But by identifying which problems in your games deserve a custom node and taking the time to write it you can save a lot of development time and increase the quality of the Blueprint graphs people create.

Some things to consider when deciding if it's worth the time the write a custom node is in how many places will the node be used in? If the usage is widespread throughout the project, it will probably be worth it. This doesn't only go for how many Blueprints the node is used in, but by how many different people will use it. The more different people that will use, tweak and change the logic our node is used in the more important it is that our node helps with a good, common pattern that people can get used to.

The node we will create will have two in execution pins, one for starting to listen to an alarm actor and one for stopping. We will have an in-parameter for choosing which alarm we want to listen to. I will use a gameplay tag for this, but in your game it might be an actor pointer or an enum. Any data type to identify the alarm is possible, it will just change the data we send in. Personally, I think gameplay tags are great for things like this so we will go with that in this example. We will also have a setting on the node for choosing team (this is just to show how to make a setting on a node). As output pins we will have three execution pins, one for when an alarm is started and one for when it's stopped. And one that will trigger each frame the alarm is active. For the user these will look like normal execution pins but on the gameplay side of the code, these will be delegates. Our node will convert these delegate calls to triggering the execution pins. This is a really useful pattern, and it will allow us to execute several pins on the node in the same frame if we want to. But most importantly it gives us very good control over the pattern people will script with these nodes.

Before we start with the node itself, we need to create a basic alarm actor and some utility functionality around it. I'm going to keep it very basic, just what I need to show how the Blueprint node will interact with it. We are going to create an alarm actor, let the game mode work as a manager for all alarms and one utility function in a Blueprint function library. Let's start with the alarm actor, in /Source/Mars/Alarm/ (change Mars to your project name of course) create MarsAlarm.h and add the following code.

```
#pragma once

#include "Mars/MarsGameLibrary.h"

#include "MarsAlarm.generated.h"

USTRUCT()
struct FAlarmNode
{
  GENERATED_BODY()

  UPROPERTY()
  FMarsDelegateExecPin OnStartDelegate;
  UPROPERTY()
  FMarsDelegateExecPin OnUpdateDelegate;
  UPROPERTY()
  FMarsDelegateExecPin OnStopDelegate;
};

UCLASS()
class MARS_API AMarsAlarm : public AActor
{
  GENERATED_BODY()
public:
  AMarsAlarm(const FObjectInitializer& _objectInitializer);
  virtual void BeginPlay() override;
  virtual void EndPlay(EEndPlayReason::Type _endPlayReason)
override;

  virtual void Tick(float _deltaTime) override;

  void RegisterNode(UObject* _owner, ETeams _team, const
FMarsDelegateExecPin& _onStart, const FMarsDelegateExecPin&
_onUpdate, const FMarsDelegateExecPin& _onStop);
```

```
  void UnregisterNode(UObject* _owner);

  UFUNCTION(BlueprintCallable, Category = "Alarm")
  void StartAlarm();

  UFUNCTION(BlueprintCallable, Category = "Alarm")
  void StopAlarm();

  UPROPERTY()
  bool IsAlarmActive = false;

  UPROPERTY(EditInstanceOnly)
  FGameplayTag AlarmTag;

  UPROPERTY()
  TMap<UObject*,FAlarmNode> AlarmListeners;
};
```

We have a `Begin/EndPlay` where we will register/unregister the alarm to our manager we will add later. The `RegisterNode/UnregisterNode` functions which is going to be used by the Blueprint node we will create. Then we have a `Start/StopAlarm` function which can be called from Blueprints to actually start and stop the alarm. `AlarmTag` is used to tell which alarm this it, then finally the `AlarmListeners` which keeps track of all nodes that have registered to this alarm and their delegates. In /Source/Mars/Alarm/ add MarsAlarm.cpp and add the following code.

```
#include "MarsAlarm.h"

#include "Kismet/GameplayStatics.h"
#include "Mars/MarsGameMode.h"

AMarsAlarm::AMarsAlarm(const FObjectInitializer&
_objectInitializer)
{
  PrimaryActorTick.bCanEverTick = true;
}

void AMarsAlarm::BeginPlay()
{
  Super::BeginPlay();

  AMarsGameModeBase* gameMode = Cast< AMarsGameModeBase
>(UGameplayStatics::GetGameMode(GetWorld()));
  if (gameMode != nullptr)
  {
    gameMode->RegisterAlarm(this);
  }
}
```

```
void AMarsAlarm::EndPlay(EEndPlayReason::Type _endPlayReason)
{
  AMarsGameModeBase* gameMode = Cast< AMarsGameModeBase
>(UGameplayStatics::GetGameMode(GetWorld()));
  if (gameMode != nullptr)
  {
    gameMode->UnregisterAlarm(this);
  }
  Super::EndPlay(_endPlayReason);
}
```

We just register ourselves in the game mode class, but really you can place the manager for this wherever you want. We will cover the changes in the game mode soon.

```
void AMarsAlarm::StartAlarm()
{
  if (IsAlarmActive == false)
  {
    IsAlarmActive = true;
    for (TPair<UObject*, FAlarmNode> alarm : AlarmListeners)
    {
      if (alarm.Key != nullptr)
      {
        alarm.Value.OnStartDelegate.Execute();
      }
    }
    SetActorTickEnabled(true);
  }
}
```

When the alarm is started, we go through all our listeners and execute the delegate. This is going to trigger the execution pin on our node, we will go through exactly how this works when we set up the node later. Next, we need to do the same thing with the `StopAlarm` and `OnUpdate`.

```
void AMarsAlarm::StopAlarm()
{
  if (IsAlarmActive)
  {
    IsAlarmActive = false;
    for (TPair<UObject*, FAlarmNode> alarm : AlarmListeners)
    {
      if (alarm.Key != nullptr)
      {
        alarm.Value.OnStopDelegate.Execute();
      }
    }
    SetActorTickEnabled(false);
  }
```

```
}

void AMarsAlarm::Tick(float _deltaTime)
{
  if (IsAlarmActive)
  {
    for (TPair<UObject*, FAlarmNode> alarm : AlarmListeners)
    {
      if (alarm.Key != nullptr)
      {
        alarm.Value.OnUpdateDelegate.Execute();
      }
    }
  }
}
```

And finally, we have the functions for registering and unregistering our nodes.

```
void AMarsAlarm::RegisterNode(UObject* _owner, ETeams
_team, const FMarsDelegateExecPin& _onStart, const
FMarsDelegateExecPin& _onUpdate, const FMarsDelegateExecPin&
_onStop)
{
  FAlarmNode node;
  node.OnStartDelegate = _onStart;
  node.OnUpdateDelegate = _onUpdate;
  node.OnStopDelegate = _onStop;
  AlarmListeners.Add(_owner,node);
}

void AMarsAlarm::UnregisterNode(UObject* _owner)
{
  AlarmListeners.Remove(_owner);
}
```

In the register node we simple save away the delegates we want to execute in our listener array. We will go through how these delegates are set up soon. Let's quickly look at the changes we need to do to our game mode (or your own manager class if you prefer to make one). In /Source/Mars/ add MarsGameMode.h and add the following code.

```
#pragma once


#include "CoreMinimal.h"
#include "GameFramework/GameModeBase.h"

#include "MarsGameMode.generated.h"

struct FGameplayTag;
```

```
class AMarsAlarm;

UCLASS()
class MARS_API AMarsGameModeBase : public AGameModeBase
{
  GENERATED_BODY()
public:
  void RegisterAlarm(AMarsAlarm* _alarm);
  void UnregisterAlarm(AMarsAlarm* _alarm);
  AMarsAlarm* GetAlarm(FGameplayTag _tag);

private:
  UPROPERTY()
  TArray<AMarsAlarm*> Alarms;
};
```

We have functions for register and unregistering an alarm and also a function for finding an alarm from a gameplay tag. Of course, we also have an array of all registered alarms as well. Next up, in /Source/Mars/ add MarsGameMode.cpp and the following code.

```
#include "MarsGameMode.h"

#include "GameplayTagContainer.h"

#include "Mars/Alarm/MarsAlarm.h"

void AMarsGameModeBase::RegisterAlarm(AMarsAlarm* _alarm)
{
  Alarms.Add(_alarm);
}

void AMarsGameModeBase::UnregisterAlarm(AMarsAlarm* _alarm)
{
  Alarms.RemoveSingleSwap(_alarm);
}

AMarsAlarm* AMarsGameModeBase::GetAlarm(FGameplayTag _tag)
{
  for (AMarsAlarm* alarm : Alarms)
  {
    if (alarm->AlarmTag.MatchesTagExact(_tag))
    {
      return alarm;
    }
  }
  return nullptr;
}
```

Nothing surprising here, with that out of the way we can start with the more interesting bits (do remember to switch to your new game mode class in your project also). We will need a Blueprint callable function that handles the register/unregistering and hooks up our delegates. This is the function that our node will call. In /Source/Mars/ create MarsGameLibrary.h and add the following code.

```
#pragma once

#include "Kismet/BlueprintFunctionLibrary.h"
#include "GameplayTagContainer.h"

#include "MarsGameLibrary.generated.h"

DECLARE_DYNAMIC_DELEGATE(FMarsDelegateExecPin);

UENUM()
enum class EMarsAlarmStateEntry : uint8
{
  Start,
  Stop,
};

UCLASS()
class MARS_API UMarsGameLibrary : public
UBlueprintFunctionLibrary
{
  GENERATED_BODY()

public:
  UFUNCTION(BlueprintCallable, BlueprintInternalUseOnly,
Category = "Mars|Alarm", meta = (ExpandEnumAsExecs =
"_inExec", AutoCreateRefTerm = "_onStart, _onUpdate,
_onStopped"))
  static void RegisterAlarmInternal(EMarsAlarmStateEntry
_inExec, UObject* _object, UPARAM(meta = (Categories = "Mars.
Alarm")) FGameplayTag _alarmTag, ETeams _team,
    const FMarsDelegateExecPin& _onStart, const
FMarsDelegateExecPin& _onUpdate, const FMarsDelegateExecPin&
_onStopped);
};
```

First, we declare our delegate, it doesn't have any parameters. This delegate is what we will convert to an execution pin on our node. Then we have an enum to choose if we should start or stop listening to the alarm from our node, this we will also convert to exec pins.

Then we have our actual function that our Blueprint node will use. There's quite a bit going on here, so let us go through it piece by piece. First, we need the function to be `BlueprintCallable` so that we can call it from our node. Nothing to strange about that. However making it `BlueprintCallable` also means we can call it from any Blueprint, which we do not want, we want people to use our custom node instead. This is where BlueprintInternalUseOnly comes in. This hides the function so it cannot be placed in a Blueprint manually, only through code.

After this we use ExpandEnumAsExecs on our enum that will control if we start or stop listening to the alarm. We will create and connect one link for each of these exec pins in our node. Another way of doing this would be to create two of these functions instead, one for registering and one for unregistering and then when we replace our node with calls to this, we would need two call function nodes instead of one. So, by using an enum which we expand as an exec, we save ourselves quite a bit of work in our node code. Also, we get the register/unregister calls in the same function which I think is nice and we have the possibility to expand this in the future if we want, maybe with a pause input for example.

After this we have the AutoCreateRefTerm meta flag which we give the names of our delegate parameters. Since we are passing these delegates as references, we must have one for the Blueprint to compile. This is fine if we require the user to hook up execution pin on the node. But if we want the execution pins on the node to be optional, this flag auto creates an empty reference and passes it along. This way we can control if an execution pin in our node is optional or not. If we want to enforce the user to hook in an _onStopped execution link to do cleanup for example, we could just remove it from AutoCreateRefTerm.

The function itself makes use of the UPARAM() macro to set a filter on the gameplay tag, so it doesn't show all the tags in the game but only the tags we want to show. Really, whenever you have gameplay tag as a parameter you should add a filter like this. Now let's look at the .cpp file, in /Source/Mars/ create MarsGameLibrary.cpp and add the following code.

```
#include "MarsGameLibrary.h"

#include "CoreMinimal.h"
#include "Kismet/GameplayStatics.h"
#include "Mars/MarsGameMode.h"
#include "Mars/Alarm/MarsAlarm.h"

void UMarsGameLibrary::RegisterAlarmInternal(EMarsAlarmState
Entry _inExec, UObject* _object, FGameplayTag _alarmTag,
ETeams _team, const FMarsDelegateExecPin& _onStart,
  const FMarsDelegateExecPin& _onUpdate, const
FMarsDelegateExecPin& _onStopped)
{
  UWorld* world = GEngine->GetWorldFromContextObject(_object,
EGetWorldErrorMode::ReturnNull);
  AMarsGameModeBase* gameMode = Cast< AMarsGameModeBase >
(UGameplayStatics::GetGameMode(world));
  if (gameMode != nullptr)
  {
    AMarsAlarm* alarm = gameMode->GetAlarm(_alarmTag);
    if (alarm != nullptr)
    {
```

```
      if (_inExec == EMarsAlarmStateEntry::Start)
      {
        alarm->RegisterNode(_object, _team, _onStart,
_onUpdate, _onStopped);
      }
      else
      {
        alarm->UnregisterNode(_object);
      }
    }
  }
}
```

We dig out our game mode (or whatever manager you put the alarms in) and find our alarm, then register or unregister to it. Now we are finally ready to start looking at the node code itself! In /Plugins/MarsEditor/Source/MarsBlueprintNodes/Public/Nodes/ create MarsAlarmNode.h and add the following code.

```
#pragma once

#include "K2Node.h"
#include "BlueprintActionDatabaseRegistrar.h"

#include "Mars/MarsStructs.h"

#include "MarsAlarmNode.generated.h"

UCLASS()
class MARSBLUEPRINTNODES_API UMarsK2Node_Alarm : public
UK2Node
{
  GENERATED_BODY()
public:
  virtual bool IsNodeSafeToIgnore() const override { return
true; }
  virtual void GetMenuActions(FBlueprintActionDatabaseRegist
rar& _actionRegistrar) const override;

  virtual FText GetMenuCategory() const override;
  virtual FText GetNodeTitle(ENodeTitleType::Type _titleType)
const override;
  virtual FText GetTooltipText() const override;

  virtual void AllocateDefaultPins() override;
  virtual void ExpandNode(FKismetCompilerContext&
_compilerContext, UEdGraph* _sourceGraph) override;

  UEdGraphPin* GetInStartPin() const;
  UEdGraphPin* GetInStopPin() const;
  UEdGraphPin* GetInAlarmTagPin() const;
```

```
  UEdGraphPin* GetOutOnStartedPin() const;
  UEdGraphPin* GetOutOnUpdatePin() const;
  UEdGraphPin* GetOutOnStoppedPin() const;

  //TODO property code here

private:
  static const FName InStartPinName;
  static const FName InStopPinName;
  static const FName InAlarmTagPinName;
  static const FName OutOnStartedPinName;
  static const FName OutOnUpdatePinName;
  static const FName OutOnStoppedPinName;
};
```

This should be familiar from the MapForeEach node, we have the same functions (for the same reason). The only difference is that we have different pins on our node, so we need the names and helper functions for getting those pins. We will add some code later to expose settings on this node, but more on that later. Let's look at the .cpp file, in /Plugins/MarsEditor/Source/MarsBlueprintNodes/Private/Nodes/ create MarsAlarmNode.cpp and start adding the following code.

```
#include "Nodes/MarsAlarmNode.h"

#include "BlueprintNodeSpawner.h"
#include "KismetCompiler.h"
#include "K2Node_CallFunction.h"
#include "GameplayTagContainer.h"
#include "K2Node_Self.h"

#include "MarsBlueprintNodesLibrary.h"

#include "Mars/MarsGameLibrary.h"

const FName UMarsK2Node_Alarm::InStartPinName(TEXT
("Register"));
const FName UMarsK2Node_Alarm::InStopPinName(TEXT
("Unregister"));
const FName UMarsK2Node_Alarm::InAlarmTagPinName
(TEXT("AlarmTag"));
const FName UMarsK2Node_Alarm::OutOnStartedPinName
(TEXT("OnStarted"));
const FName UMarsK2Node_Alarm::OutOnUpdatePinName
(TEXT("OnUpdate"));
const FName UMarsK2Node_Alarm::OutOnStoppedPinName
(TEXT("OnStopped"));

void UMarsK2Node_Alarm::GetMenuActions(FBlueprintActionDatabas
eRegistrar& _actionRegistrar) const
{
```

```
  MarsBlueprintNodesLibrary::RegisterBlueprintNode(GetClass(),
_actionRegistrar);
}

FText UMarsK2Node_Alarm::GetMenuCategory() const
{
  return FText::FromString("Mars - Blueprint Nodes");
}

FText UMarsK2Node_Alarm::GetNodeTitle(ENodeTitleType::Type
_titleType) const
{
  return FText::FromString("Alarm");
}

FText UMarsK2Node_Alarm::GetTooltipText() const
{
  return FText::FromString("Node for handling alarms");
}

void UMarsK2Node_Alarm::AllocateDefaultPins()
{
  Super::AllocateDefaultPins();

  CreatePin(EGPD_Input, UEdGraphSchema_K2::PC_Exec,
InStartPinName);
  CreatePin(EGPD_Input, UEdGraphSchema_K2::PC_Exec,
InStopPinName);
  CreatePin(EGPD_Input, UEdGraphSchema_K2::PC_Struct,
FGameplayTag::StaticStruct(), InAlarmTagPinName);

  CreatePin(EGPD_Output, UEdGraphSchema_K2::PC_Exec,
OutOnStartedPinName);
  CreatePin(EGPD_Output, UEdGraphSchema_K2::PC_Exec,
OutOnUpdatePinName);
  CreatePin(EGPD_Output, UEdGraphSchema_K2::PC_Exec,
OutOnStoppedPinName);
}

UEdGraphPin* UMarsK2Node_Alarm::GetInStartPin() const
{
  return FindPinChecked(InStartPinName);
}

UEdGraphPin* UMarsK2Node_Alarm::GetInStopPin() const
{
  return FindPinChecked(InStopPinName);
}

UEdGraphPin* UMarsK2Node_Alarm::GetInAlarmTagPin() const
{
```

```
  return FindPinChecked(InAlarmTagPinName);
}

UEdGraphPin* UMarsK2Node_Alarm::GetOutOnStartedPin() const
{
  return FindPinChecked(OutOnStartedPinName);
}

UEdGraphPin* UMarsK2Node_Alarm::GetOutOnUpdatePin() const
{
  return FindPinChecked(OutOnUpdatePinName);
}

UEdGraphPin* UMarsK2Node_Alarm::GetOutOnStoppedPin() const
{
  return FindPinChecked(OutOnStoppedPinName);
}
```

We set up all the names and helper functions that we need for our pins. We create three execution output pins for the different alarm triggers OnStarted/OnUpdate/OnStopped. We will connect a delegate to these execution pins soon. We also set up an input pin for a gameplay tag struct, this is what we will use to determine which alarm we are going to connect to. Now it's time to take a look at the `ExpandNode` function.

```
void UMarsK2Node_Alarm::ExpandNode(FKismetCompilerContext&
_compilerContext, UEdGraph* _sourceGraph)
{
  Super::ExpandNode(_compilerContext, _sourceGraph);

  UEdGraphPin* ourStartInExec = GetInStartPin();
  UEdGraphPin* ourStopInExec = GetInStopPin();
  UEdGraphPin* ourAlarmTagInExec = GetInAlarmTagPin();
  UEdGraphPin* ourOnStartedOutExec = GetOutOnStartedPin();
  UEdGraphPin* ourOnUpdateOutExec = GetOutOnUpdatePin();
  UEdGraphPin* ourOnStoppedOutExec = GetOutOnStoppedPin();

  //The nodes we will need
  UK2Node_CallFunction* callFunctionAlarm = _compilerContext.
SpawnIntermediateNode< UK2Node_CallFunction >(this,
_sourceGraph);
  callFunctionAlarm->FunctionReference.SetExternalMember
(GET_FUNCTION_NAME_CHECKED(UMarsGameLibrary,
RegisterAlarmInternal),
UMarsGameLibrary::StaticClass());
  callFunctionAlarm->AllocateDefaultPins();

  UK2Node_Self* selfNode = _compilerContext.
SpawnIntermediateNode<UK2Node_Self>(this, _sourceGraph);
  selfNode->AllocateDefaultPins();
```

```
  //Pins to our new nodes
  UEdGraphPin* startAlarmStartInPin =
callFunctionAlarm->FindPin(TEXT("Start"));
  UEdGraphPin* startAlarmStopInPin =
callFunctionAlarm->FindPin(TEXT("Stop"));
  UEdGraphPin* startAlarmSelfInPin =
callFunctionAlarm->FindPin(TEXT("_object"));
  UEdGraphPin* startAlarmAlarmTagInPin =
callFunctionAlarm->FindPin(TEXT("_alarmTag"));
  UEdGraphPin* startAlarmOnStartOutPin =
callFunctionAlarm->FindPin(TEXT("_onStart"));
  UEdGraphPin* startAlarmOnUpdateOutPin =
callFunctionAlarm->FindPin(TEXT("_onUpdate"));
  UEdGraphPin* startAlarmOnStoppedOutPin =
callFunctionAlarm->FindPin(TEXT("_onStopped"));

  UEdGraphPin* selfOutPin =
selfNode->FindPin(UEdGraphSchema_K2::PN_Self);

  //TODO Add property code later

  MarsBlueprintNodesLibrary::MovePinLinkTo(_compilerContext,
ourStartInExec, startAlarmStartInPin);
  MarsBlueprintNodesLibrary::MovePinLinkTo(_compilerContext,
ourStopInExec, startAlarmStopInPin);
  MarsBlueprintNodesLibrary::MovePinLinkTo(_compilerContext,
ourAlarmTagInExec, startAlarmAlarmTagInPin);

  MarsBlueprintNodesLibrary::MakePinLinkTo(_compilerContext,
selfOutPin, startAlarmSelfInPin);

  MarsBlueprintNodesLibrary::TransformExecPinToEventDelegate
Node(_compilerContext, _sourceGraph, this,
ourOnStartedOutExec, startAlarmOnStartOutPin);
  MarsBlueprintNodesLibrary::TransformExecPinToEventDelegate
Node(_compilerContext, _sourceGraph, this, ourOnUpdateOutExec,
startAlarmOnUpdateOutPin);
  MarsBlueprintNodesLibrary::TransformExecPinToEventDelegate
Node(_compilerContext, _sourceGraph, this,
ourOnStoppedOutExec, startAlarmOnStoppedOutPin);

  MarsBlueprintNodesLibrary::CheckAllPinsDisconnected(this);
}
```

As with our `ForEachMap` node, we start with getting all pins to our node, then we create the new nodes we will replace this node with. All we will need is one call function node and one self node. After this we get all the pins to these nodes, one pin for each parameter in the `RegisterAlarmInternal` function we created. We then move the start/stop execution pins from our node to the start/stop pin on the call function node. These pins are the enum expanded variable in the RegisterAlarmInternal function, we also make a link to our self node. Now the only thing left is to move our out-execution links (`_onStart`, `_onUpdate` and `_onStopped`). However, we have three delegates in our function. This means we need to create three delegate nodes and then connect those nodes. This is what we are going to do in a new helper function since this operation is very useful in many different nodes. Add the following code in MarsBlueprintNodeLibrary.h.

```
namespace MarsBlueprintNodesLibrary
{
  //...
  static void TransformExecPinToEventDelegateNode(FKismet
CompilerContext& _compilerContext, UEdGraph* _sourceGraph,
UK2Node* _sourceNode, UEdGraphPin* _execPin, UEdGraphPin*
_delegatePin);
};
```

And then the following code in MarsBlueprintNodeLibrary.cpp

```
void MarsBlueprintNodesLibrary::TransformExecPinToEventDele
gateNode(FKismetCompilerContext& _compilerContext, UEdGraph*
_sourceGraph, UK2Node* _sourceNode, UEdGraphPin* _execPin,
UEdGraphPin* _delegatePin)
{
  if (_execPin->HasAnyConnections())
  {
    UK2Node_Event* eventNode = _compilerContext.
SpawnIntermediateNode< UK2Node_Event >(_sourceNode,
_sourceGraph);
    eventNode->EventReference.SetExternalDelegateMember(FName
("DelegateExecPin__DelegateSignature"));
    eventNode->CustomFunctionName = FName(FString::
Printf(TEXT("MarsEditor_%s_%s"), *GetNameSafe(_sourceNode),
*_execPin->GetName()));
    eventNode->bInternalEvent = false;
    eventNode->AllocateDefaultPins();

    UEdGraphPin* thenPin = eventNode->GetThenPin();
    UEdGraphPin* delegatePin = eventNode->FindPin
(UK2Node_Event::DelegateOutputName);

    MarsBlueprintNodesLibrary::MovePinLinkTo(_compilerContext,
_execPin, thenPin);
    MarsBlueprintNodesLibrary::MakePinLinkTo(_compilerContext,
delegatePin, _delegatePin);
  }
}
```

Alright let's go through what is happening in this function. First off, if the execution pin we want to transform into a delegate node has no connection we simple do nothing, we will just leave this pin empty. But if it has a connection, we start with spawning an event node. If you take a look at the `ExpandNode` function on the `UK2Node_Event` node you will see that this node will in turn create a create delegate node and handle the connections. We don't have to worry about the internal details of this function, just about how we use it. The first thing we need to set on the event node is the delegate. We do this by giving it the name of the delegate and removing the first F and adding "__DelegateSignature" to it. If you remember we created our delegate like this.

```
DECLARE_DYNAMIC_DELEGATE(FMarsDelegateExecPin);
```

This gives it a name of

```
FName("DelegateExecPin__DelegateSignature")
```

So, if we had another delegate we want to use, we need to replace this name. Easiest is to just use the same delegate for all execution pins we want to convert in our project.

Next thing we need to do is give our spawned event node a unique function name, it doesn't have to match anything, but it needs to be unique. We generate the name from the node name combined with the pin name and also our plugin name. If we have multiple nodes in the same graph they will get unique names. We set this name to the `CustomFunctionName` variable like this.

```
eventNode->CustomFunctionName = FName(FString::Printf
(TEXT("MarsEditor_%s_%s"), *GetNameSafe(_sourceNode),
*_execPin->GetName()));
```

We need to do one final things on the event node before we allocate the pins and connect it, we set the `InternalEvent` to be false.

```
eventNode->bInternalEvent = false;
```

This is needed so the event node will mark itself as `BlueprintCallable`, as we are calling it from a Blueprint. That's it for the helper function and now we have a functional node! This node is now very easy to use. For example, if we want to make a light turn on and spin around while the alarm is on, we only need to add this node into a Blueprint and we can hook up the logic we need directly. We don't need to find the alarm and bind delegates to it; the node handles all this internally for us, making the node very easy to use. The start and stop are right next to each other, making it easier to keep them in sync. We trigger the update node, so the user doesn't have to worry about handling ticking for their Blueprint. This approach to making nodes have many advantages. But there's more we can do, let's look at how we can add settings to the node. Let's say we want to have a setting on the node to control which team we want to listen on the alarm for and for some reason we do not want it as an input parameter on the node. In this example we will add a team setting, so let's start with adding the following to MarsAlarmNode.h, as you will see this is quite simple.

```
class MARSBLUEPRINTNODES_API UMarsK2Node_Alarm : public
UK2Node
{
  //...
public:
  virtual bool ShouldShowNodeProperties() const override
{ return true; }

  UPROPERTY(EditDefaultsOnly)
  ETeams Team = ETeams::Red;
};
```

First, we just need to return true in `ShouldShowNodeProperties` to let the Blueprint editor know that we want to show properties for our node. After this we just mark all our variables with `UPROPERTY(EditDefaultsOnly)` and they will show up automatically. Setting it up is quite simple, using the data is also not very hard. In the `RegisterAlarmInternal` function we created we have a parameter for the team already, so we just need to fill it on in our `ExpandNode` function like this. Find and replace "`//TODO Add property code later`" with the following code.

```
UEdGraphPin* startAlarmTeamInPin = callFunctionAlarm
->FindPin(TEXT("_team"));
FName name = UEnum::GetValueAsName(Team);
MarsBlueprintNodesLibrary::SetDefaultValue(startAlarmTeamIn
Pin, name.ToString(), UEdGraphSchema_K2::PC_Byte);
```

Like always, we first need to get the pin. However, this pin we will not connect any node, we just want to send in data on it. We will just set the default value on it instead. The default values on pins are stored in strings, so first we need to convert our data to a string and then set it. Since we created a helper function for setting the default value we will use it here also, the reason we created this was to help with wildcard pins and making sure the data is correct on them, this is not a wildcard pin so it's not really necessary. We will just end up setting the `PinCategory` (which is what data the pin has) to what it already is. Which is a byte.

Now if you click on our node in the Blueprint editor, you can see our variable on the details panel and change it and it will get passed into our function. Sometimes it makes sense to have things as settings, sometimes as parameters. It all depends on your Blueprint node and the design you want for it.

That is it for this chapter. We covered several ways of controlling and creating Blueprint nodes. There's plenty more that is possible with these methods, especially for the K2Nodes but this is hopefully enough to give you a solid foundation to start from.

Index

I

K

L

M

N

O

P

R

S

T

U

V

W

For Product Safety Concerns and Information please contact our EU representative GPSR@taylorandfrancis.com
Taylor & Francis Verlag GmbH, Kaufingerstraße 24, 80331 München, Germany

www.ingramcontent.com/pod-product-compliance
Lightning Source LLC
Chambersburg PA
CBHW060345220326
41598CB00023B/2816

* 9 7 8 1 0 3 2 8 4 0 4 0 6 *